TOUCHING A NERVE

A curly collection of churchy cartoons by Jim.

Brendan Boughen

Philip Garside Publishing Ltd.

© 2019 Brendan Boughen.

All rights reserved. No part of this publication may be reproduced, stored in a retrieval system or transmitted, in any form or by any means electronic, mechanical, photocopied, recording or otherwise, without written permission.

Cartoons by Jim
PO Box 11615
Ellerslie
Auckland 1542
NEW ZEALAND

Email Brendan: **cartoonsbyjim.com**

• • •

For Kiersten

My constant companion through life and cartooning.

Thank you. I love you.

• • •

International print edition (2020)
ISBN 978-1-98-857252-9

Philip Garside Publishing Ltd
PO Box 17160
Wellington 6147
New Zealand

bookspgpl@gmail.com — www.pgpl.co.nz

PDF, ePub and Kindle editions also available

Contents

foreword 4

introduction 5

Cartoons 7

Acknowledgements 128

More Cartoon Books By Jim! 130

foreword

The Methodist Church of New Zealand is to be commended for giving outsiders a go. After all, it took a bit of a risk when it appointed me, an American who left the church in his teens, the responsibility to edit its national newspaper, *Touchstone*.

As editor, with light oversight from the Methodist Publishing Board, I had the freedom to carry out the newspaper's mandate – to explore today's faith issues – as I thought best.

The Publishing Board was also willing to look outside the square when it accepted my recommendation to publish a monthly cartoon by Jim/Brendan. It did take a wee bit of convincing given the good-natured but irreverent tone of some of the toons in his first book Gone Astray, but it was a happy match.

Brendan was ideally positioned to offer humorous insights that appeal to Touchstone readers. As the son of a minister he has deep insights into the church community, with all of its virtues and foibles. And with his employment in the tech sector in Auckland, he was well placed to offer observations on the trends and events shaping the world we live in today.

So, for more than a decade, one of my monthly pleasures was the little buzz I got when Jim's cartoon arrived in my email inbox. What had he decided to poke fun at this time?

I have always thought the work of a cartoonist is much more difficult than that of a writer (and certainly that of a journalist). When faced with that blank slate, they must not only come up with a witty idea, they must express it with a concise phrase or two and a clever drawing.

So we should honour Jim/Brendan's gifts and thank him for compiling this collection. It touches on theological and ecclesiastical themes and provides a glimpse back at some of the major cultural and political issues of the day – from same-sex marriage to the Occupy Wall Street movement to planking and the Rugby World Cup. Indeed, some of his billboard cartoons were themselves cultural milestones as they attracted the attention of the wider media.

As they would say in church, 'Well done, good and faithful servant.'

Paul Titus

Editor, *Touchstone* magazine (2003 – 2018)

introduction

I have a confession to make. I have not actually 'gone to church', in the traditional sense, for a very long time – about 15 years now, to be exact. I have entered church buildings, sure ... but proactively deciding to attend a church service for the purposes of spiritual enlightenment or sustenance is just not something I do anymore.

Contrast this to the first 30 years of my life, where every day was incredibly churchy, and steeped in religious Christianity in some way, either through my education, workplace or family life as the son of a Lutheran minister. It was the family business, so to speak, and I was a firm believer.

Slowly however, from my late teen years until the year I entered my fourth decade of life, those beliefs crumbled away, and I discovered a hunger for meaning underneath which 'going to church' could no longer satisfy. So, I left. (My previous book of so-called '(sac)religious' cartoons, *Gone Astray*, chronicles something of that journey of moving beyond the traditional faith of my younger years.)

A few years later, I received a phone call from Paul Titus, the editor of *Touchstone* magazine, the official publication of the Methodist Church of New Zealand / Te Haahi Weteriana O Aotearoa. I had sent him a copy of Gone Astray to review, which he did, and he followed this with an invitation to submit some cartoons for consideration for a monthly slot in the magazine. That invitation turned into a cartooning gig that has since lasted 12 years (so far) and the inky products of which form the majority of the book you now hold in your hands.

While cartooning for *Touchstone* has been a decidedly enjoyable monthly challenge, it's also been my main ongoing connection with any kind of church since I officially parted ways with the one of my upbringing, and one to which I've been proud to contribute.

What I have found most admirable about the MCNZ is that it does not shy away from discussing difficult topics or facing challenging issues that may have profound impacts on traditional faith. I was always hugely grateful to Paul for his encouragement to be provocative with my cartoons, which appeared on page four of every edition during his tenure there, and continue to be so encouraged as the MCNZ continues to deal with issues that many churches don't even go near.

Of course, not all readers have been so enthusiastic about cartoons that push the boundaries of traditional theologies and understandings of what church can be. Quite a few of these cartoons touched raw nerves that prompted stridently worded letters back to the editor. Some have been called "blasphemous", "offensive" and "shocking", while others have won awards, but all aim to provoke those inside churches to think about how what happens to them within those walls affects what they do outside of them.

While most of the cartoons in this book have appeared in Touchstone, a few have appeared on public billboards for St Matthew-in-the-City Anglican Church in Auckland city (where I also worked for a time) and the Community of St Luke's Presbyterian Church in Remuera; two New Zealand church communities that are also enthusiastically grappling with the challenges of being the Church in the modern world. Notably, two of these cartoons went global, hitting world news cycles as they highlighted the progressive Christian points of view that these churches were sharing, and touching millions more nerves as a result.

Several other cartoons are first published in this edition, having not seen the light of day due to either being deemed too controversial (yes, it does happen!) or simply sitting in my folio like lost souls waiting for a publication to give them proper context. They are also organised in rough calendar order of publication, so as well as being a record of my own spiritual journey, they chronicle key world events from the last decade and my perspective on those events as they happened. For those cartoons which may benefit from a quick reminder of their context, a web link to the original news story that inspired them is included.

...

The phrase "going to church" is an interesting one. It suggests that 'church' – a place where one presumably encounters God and receives spiritual sustenance – is located somewhere physically separate from ourselves where we must 'go' to have that encounter, be it a fancy stone building or similar establishment made from wood, bricks and mortar.

What I've grown to realise as I've reached the stereotypical mid-life years is that cartoons are my church. In the process of creating them (writing, drawing, publishing) and setting them loose to interact with humanity, ideally resulting in laughter, thought provocation or impassioned letters, I encounter life's meaning, and hopefully bring a little of that meaning to others. So, every time I draw a cartoon, I'm going to church.

These cartoons reflect on some tumultuous times for humanity from the past decade, which seem to have only

increased in recent years. In a time when much of the evangelical Christian church (in the US at least) has lost the final shreds of its credibility by supporting a political leader who embodies the opposite of everything their founder stood for, the need for cartoons that reveal truth, expose hypocrisy and make us laugh is as vital as it's ever been, if not more so.

So, I hope you enjoy this new collection of Jim's churchy cartoons, and as you read them may you encounter a small piece of that same life-giving energy that I found in creating them.

Jim.

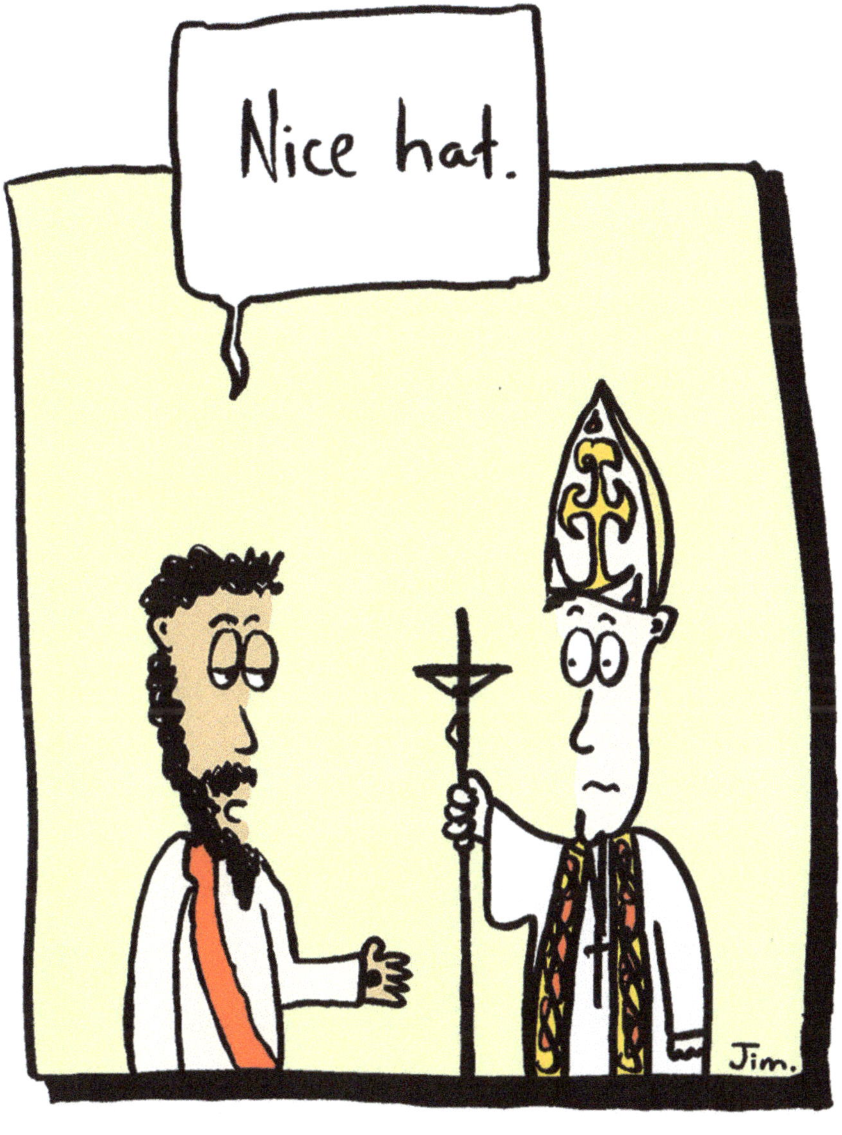
Nice hat.
Jim.

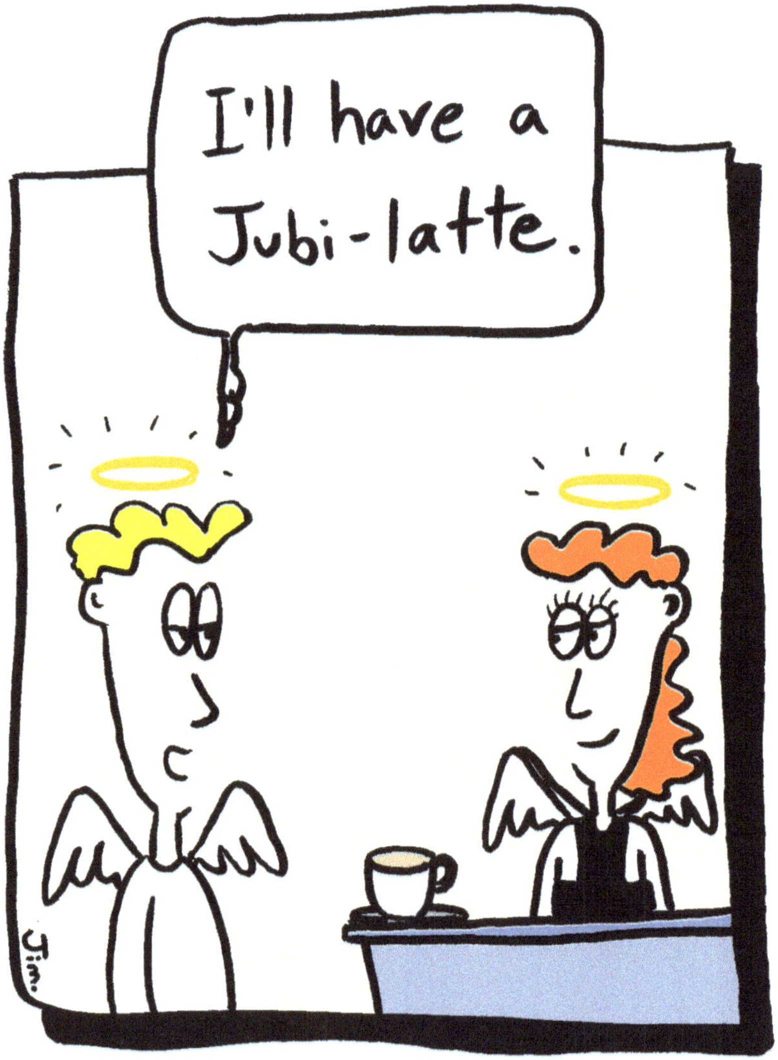
I'll have a Jubi-latte.
Jim.

Heaven's coffee shop.

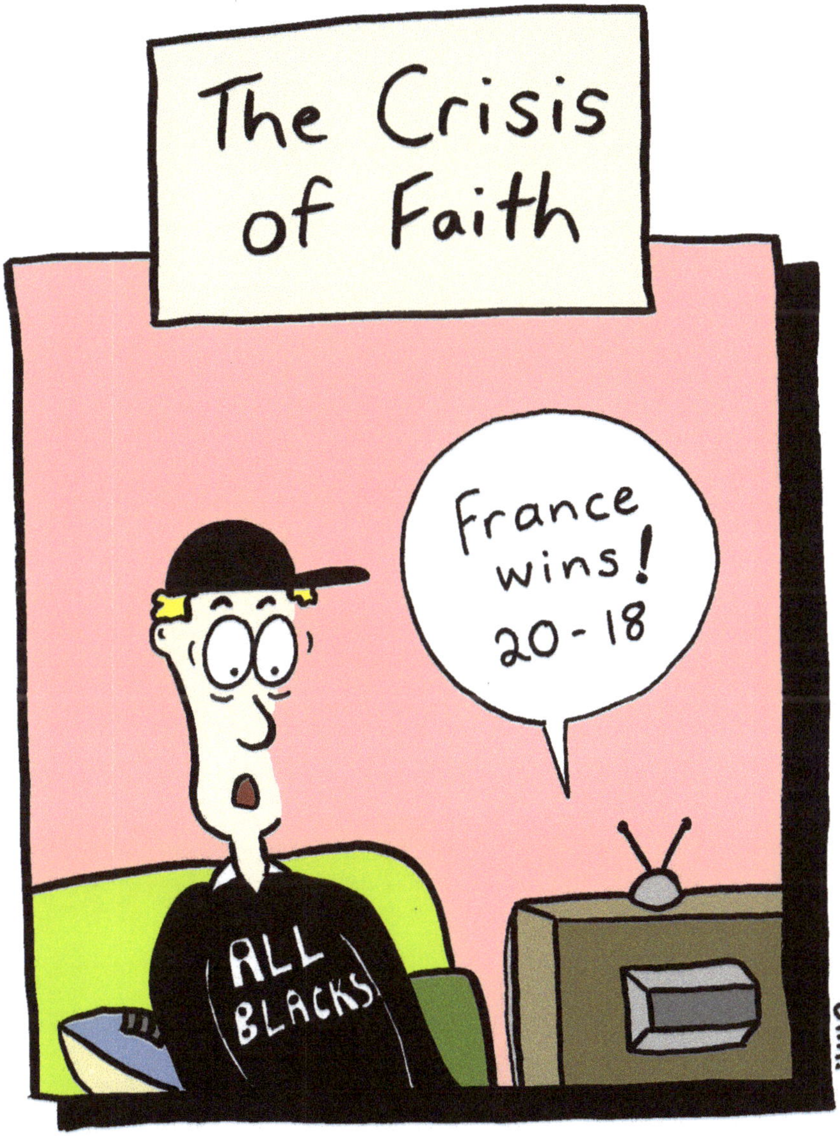
The Crisis of Faith
France wins! 20-18
ALL BLACKS
Jim.

French stun All Blacks to book semi-final spot – 6 October 2007.
http://en.espn.co.uk/scrum/rugby/story/81008.html

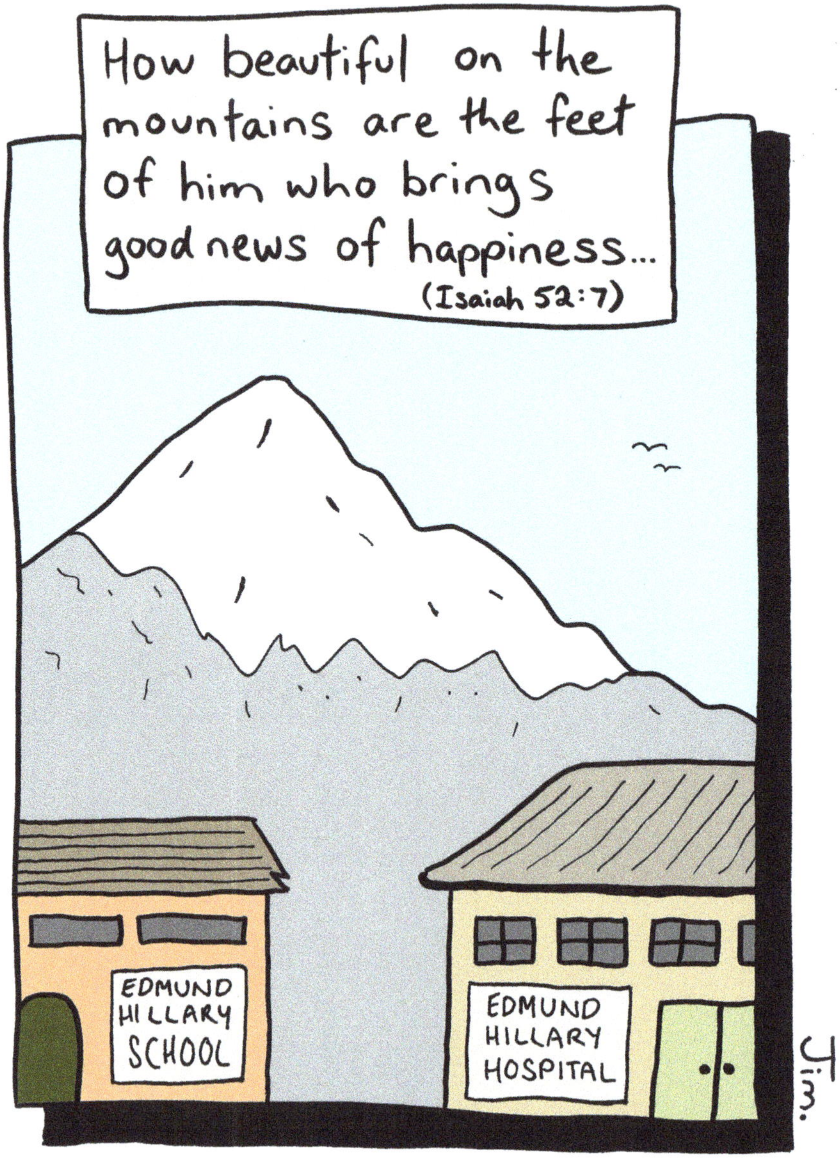
How beautiful on the mountains are the feet of him who brings good news of happiness...
(Isaiah 52:7)
EDMUND HILLARY SCHOOL
EDMUND HILLARY HOSPITAL
Jim.

Sir Edmund Hillary Obituary – 11 January 2008.
http://www.radionz.co.nz/collections/siredmundhillary/sir-edmund-hillary-obituary

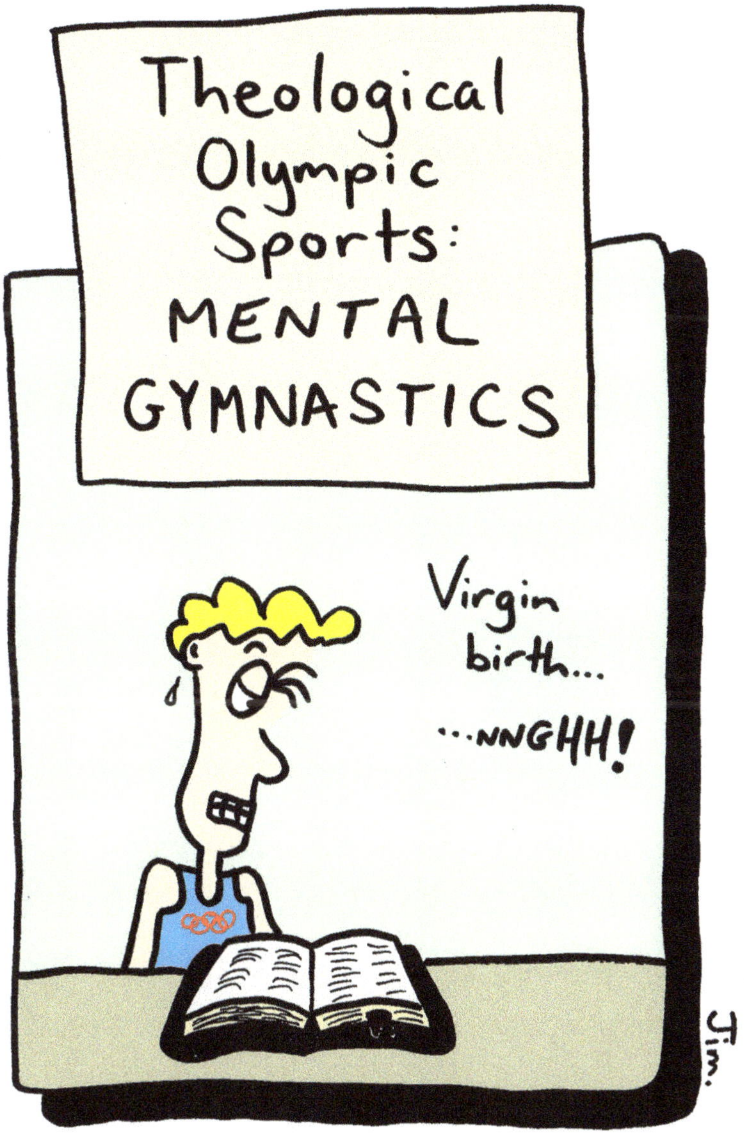
Theological Olympic Sports: MENTAL GYMNASTICS
Virgin birth...
...NNGHH!
Jim.

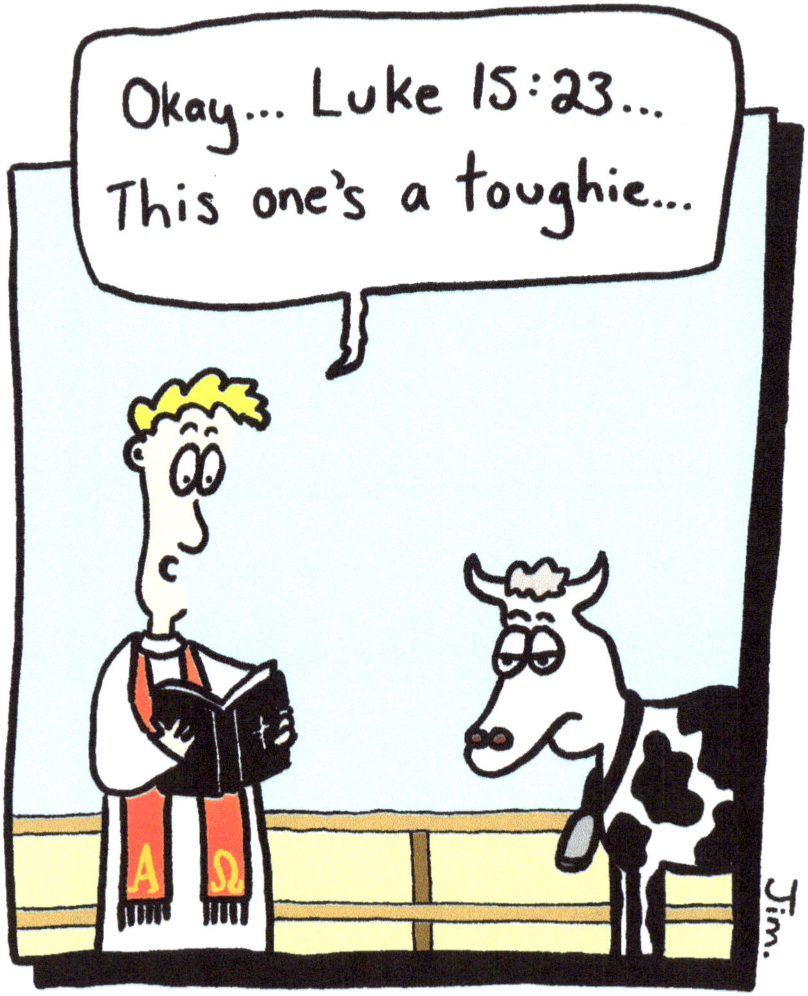
Okay... Luke 15:23...
This one's a toughie...
Jim.

Roger found rural ministry to be a unique challenge.

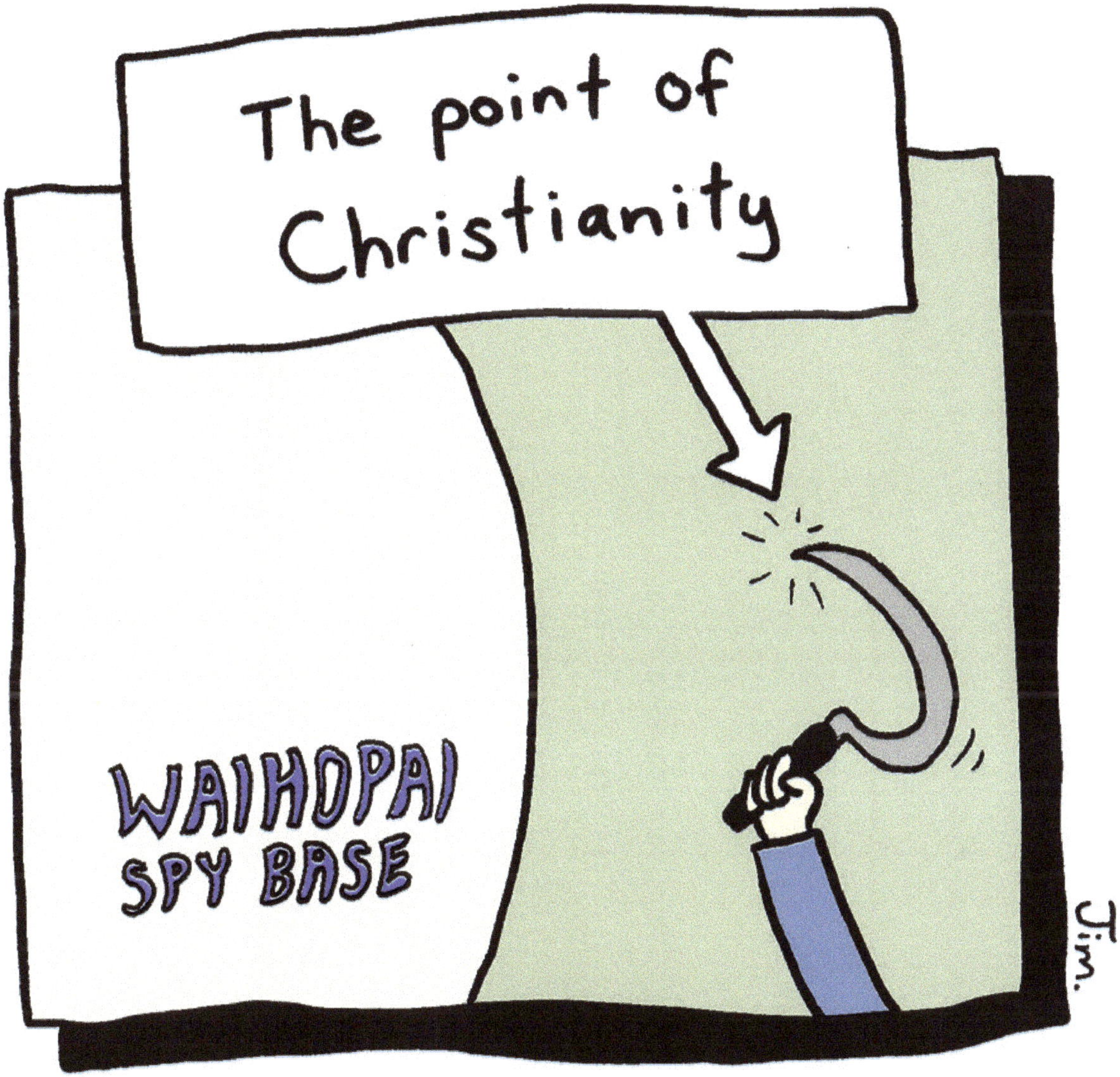
The point of Christianity
WAIHOPAI SPY BASE
Jim.

Interview with Waihopai protester Peter Murnane – 31 January 2009.
http://www.stuff.co.nz/national/415756/Interview-with-Waihopai-protester-Peter-Murnane

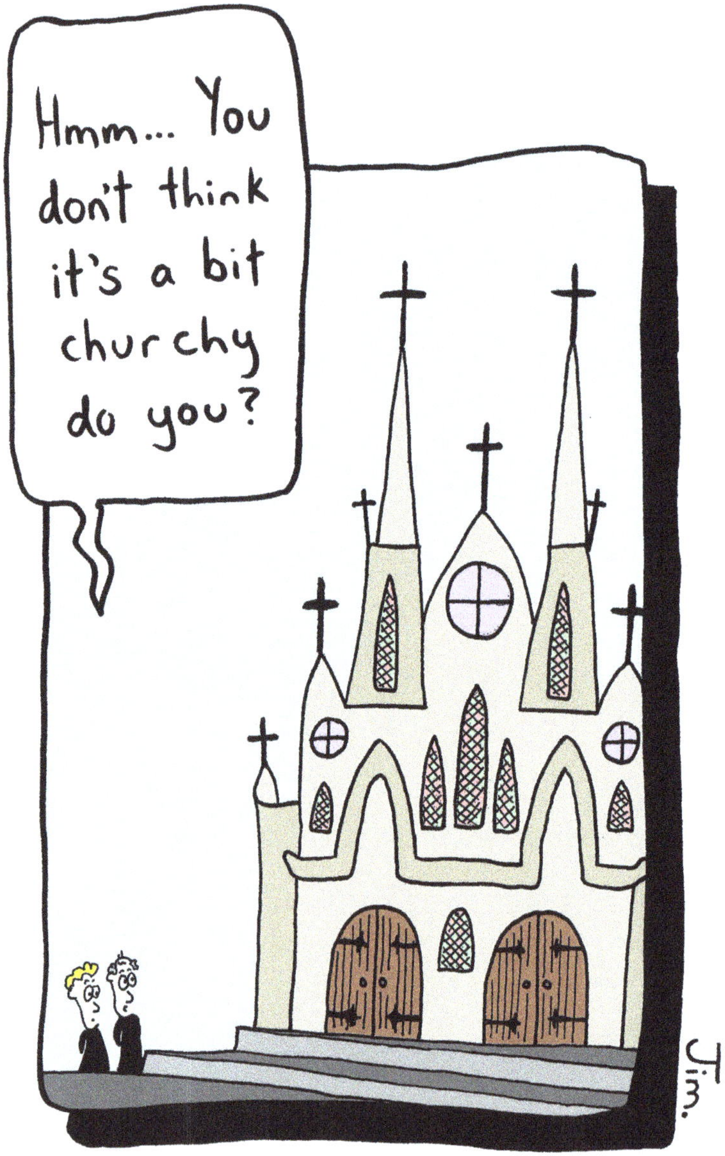
Hmm... You don't think it's a bit churchy do you?
Jim.

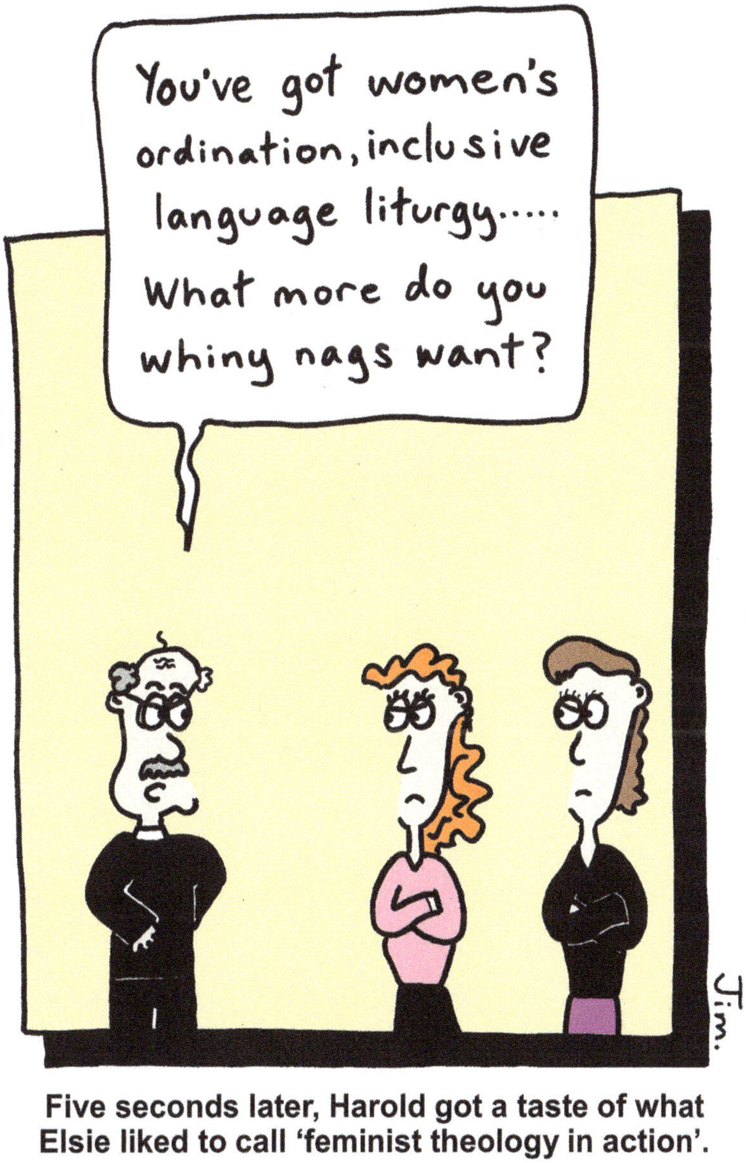
You've got women's ordination, inclusive language liturgy..... What more do you whiny nags want?
Jim.

Five seconds later, Harold got a taste of what Elsie liked to call 'feminist theology in action'.

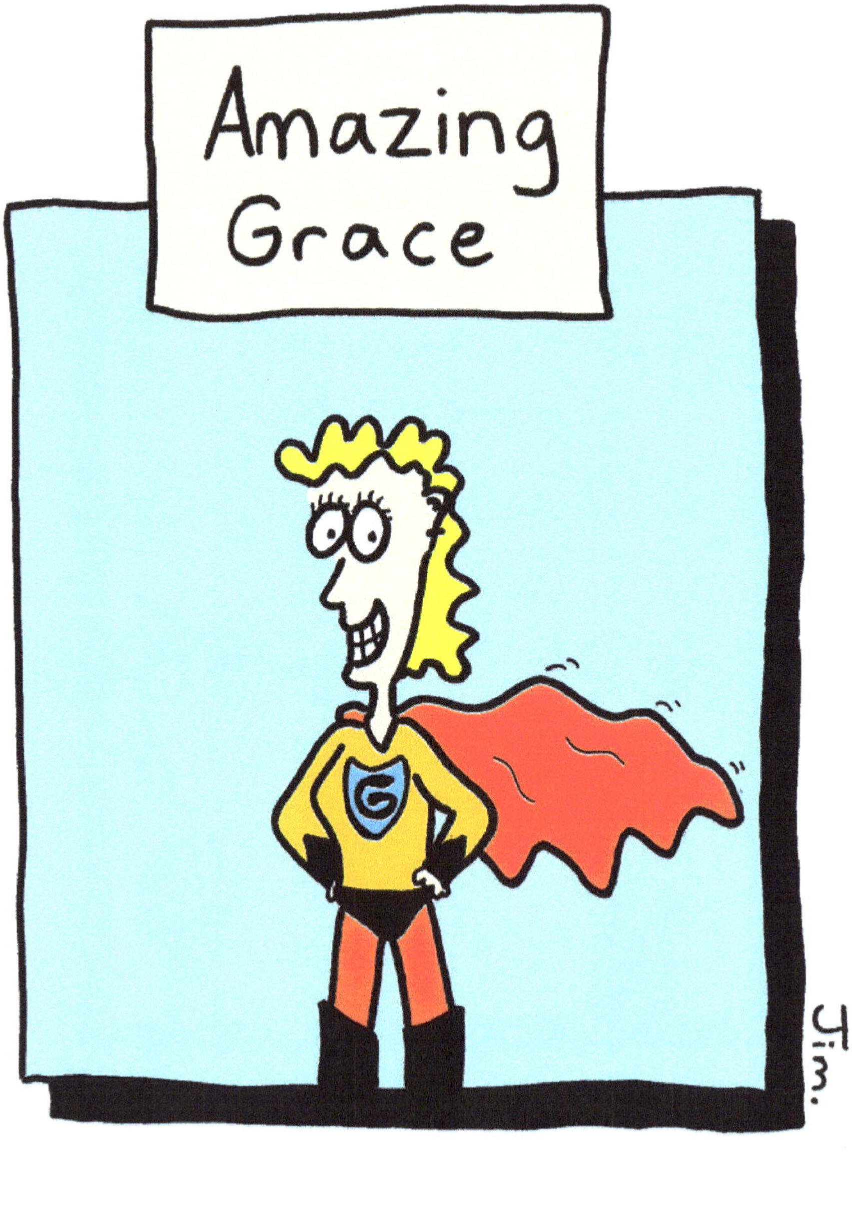
Amazing Grace
Jim.

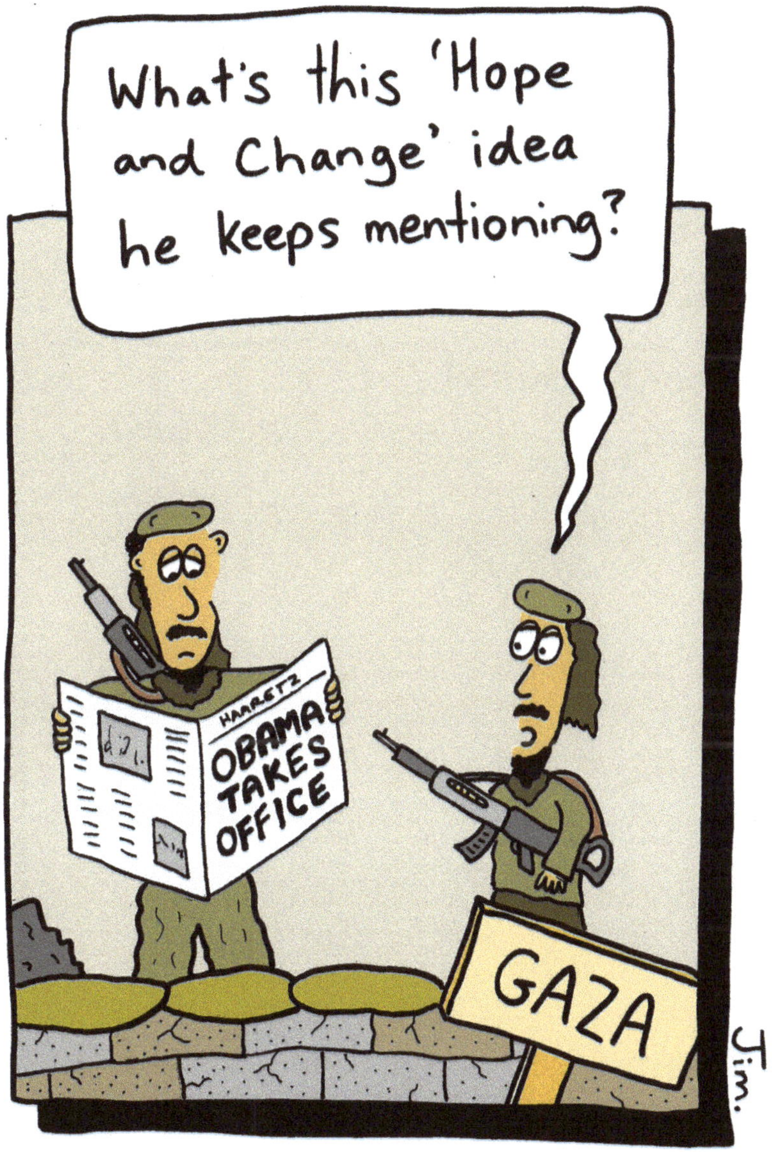
What's this 'Hope and Change' idea he keeps mentioning?
HAARETZ
OBAMA TAKES OFFICE
GAZA
Jim.

Obama defers to Bush, for now, on Gaza crisis – 28 December 2009.
http://www.nytimes.com/2008/12/29/washington/29diplo.html

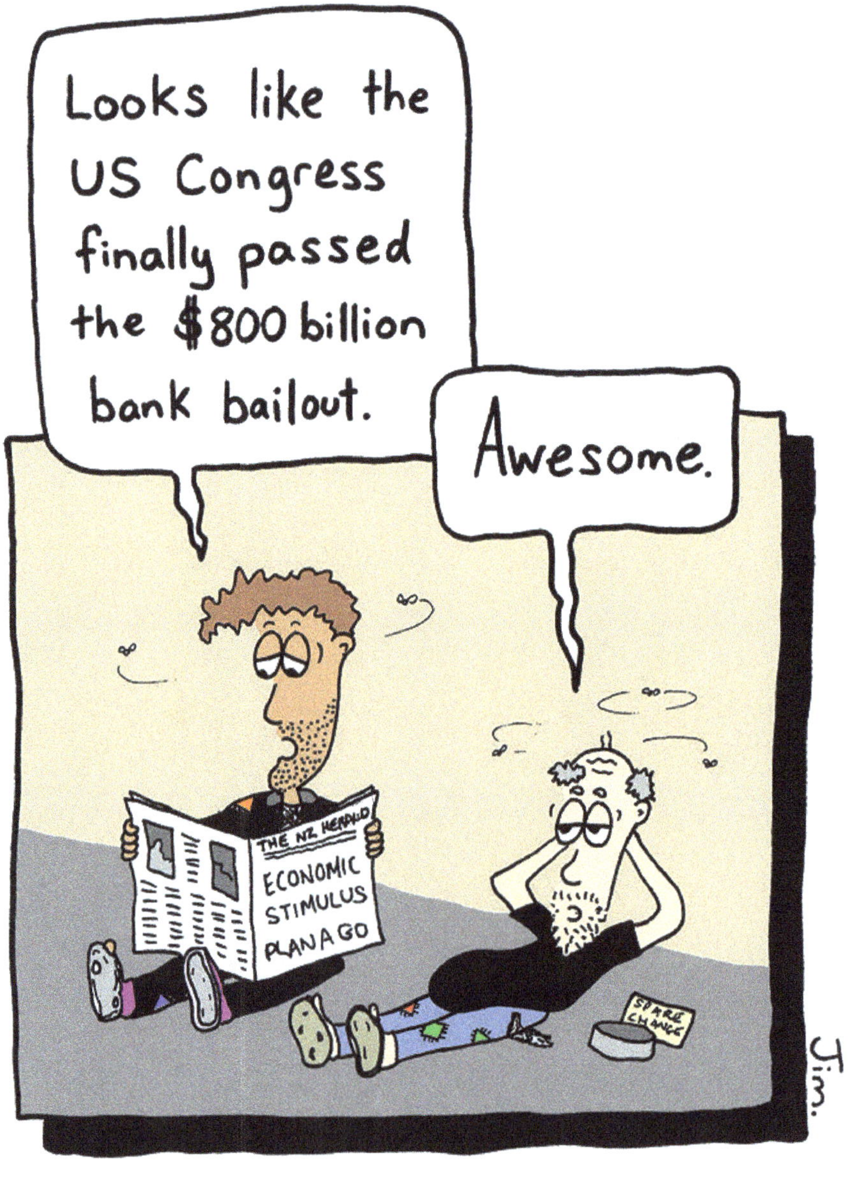
Looks like the US Congress finally passed the $800 billion bank bailout.
Awesome.
THE NZ HERALD
ECONOMIC STIMULUS PLAN A GO
SPARE CHANGE
Jim.

Bailout increases by $800 billion – 26 November 2008.
https://www.washingtontimes.com/news/2008/nov/26/bailout-increases-by-800-billion

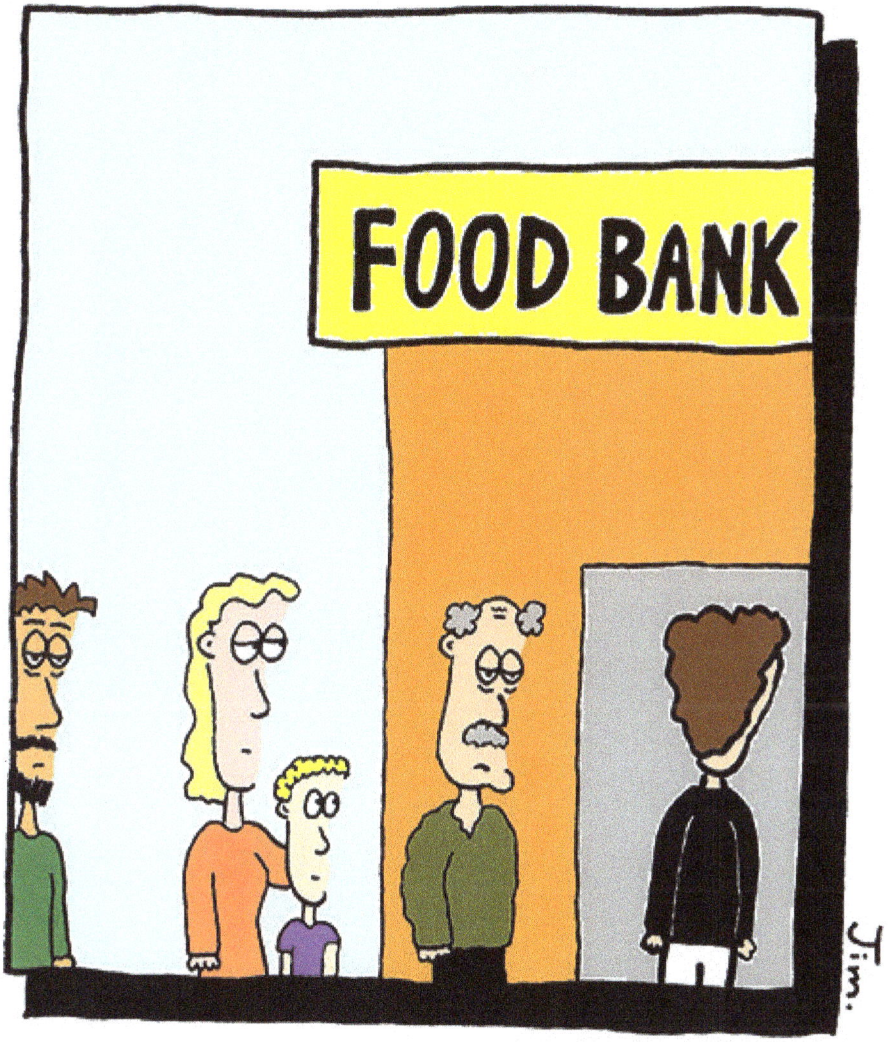
FOOD BANK
Jim.

The bank that really deserves a bailout.

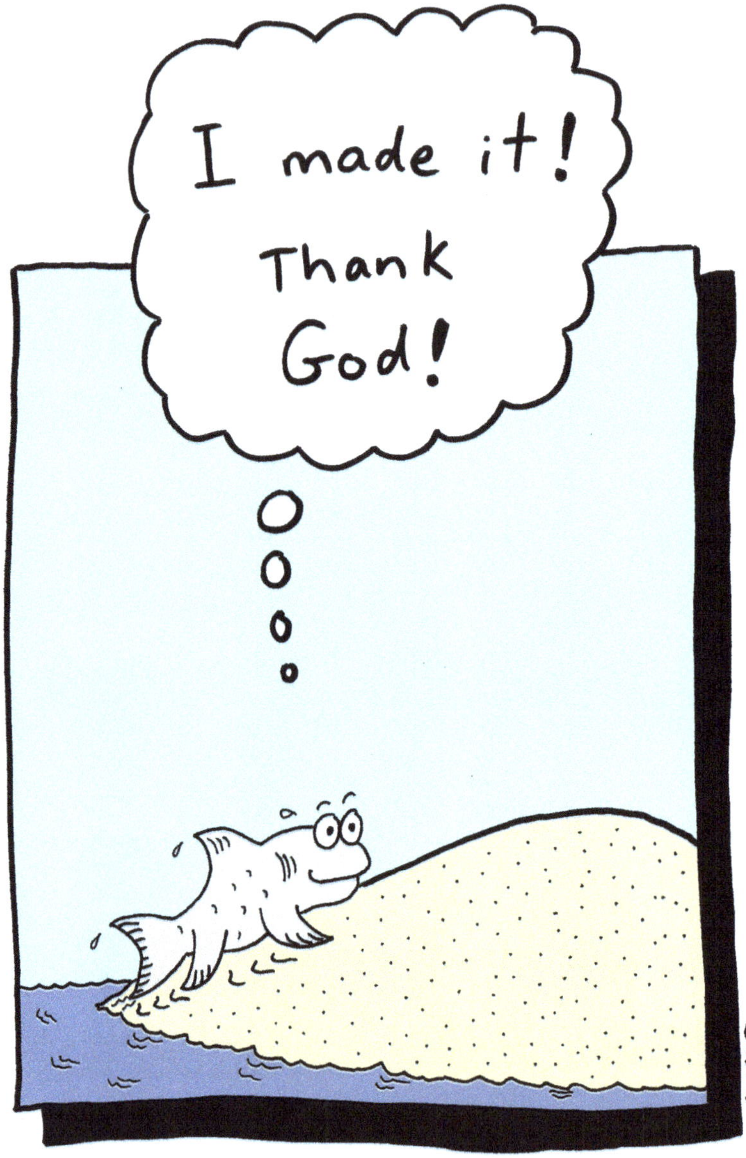
I made it! Thank God!
Jim.

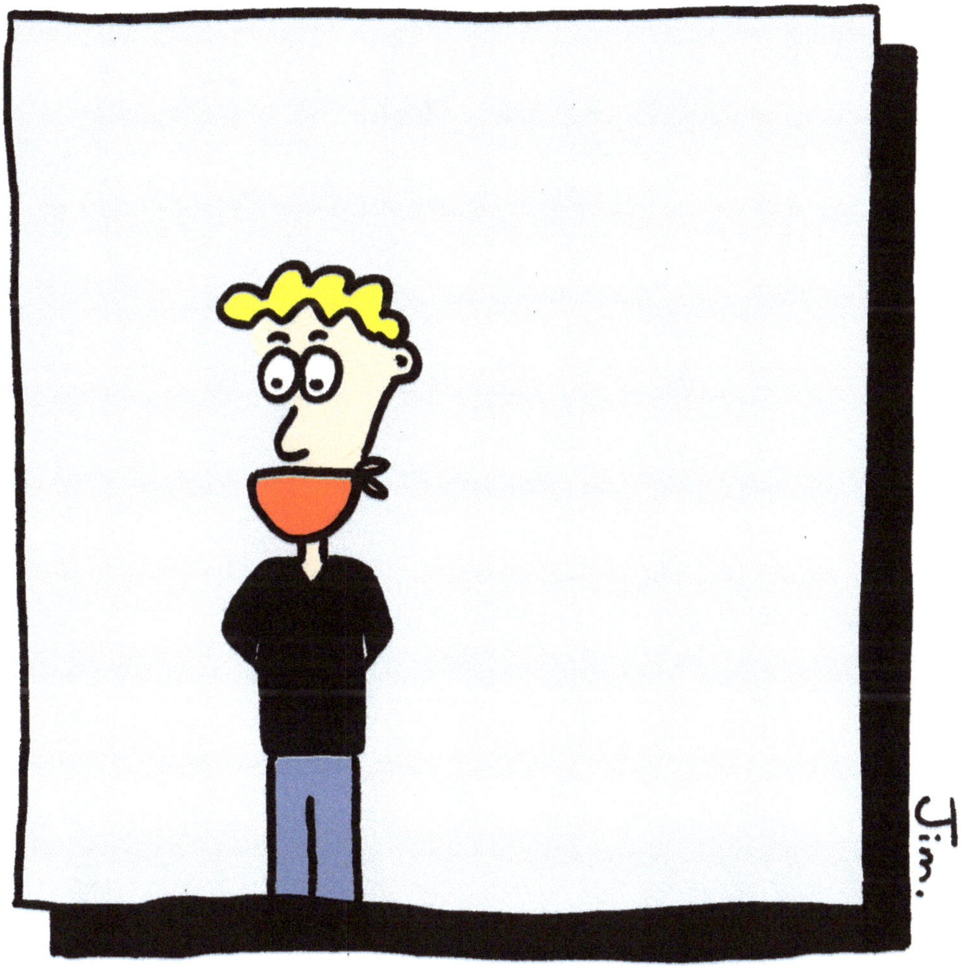
Jim.

Roger was trying a radical new form of ministry - shutting the hell up.

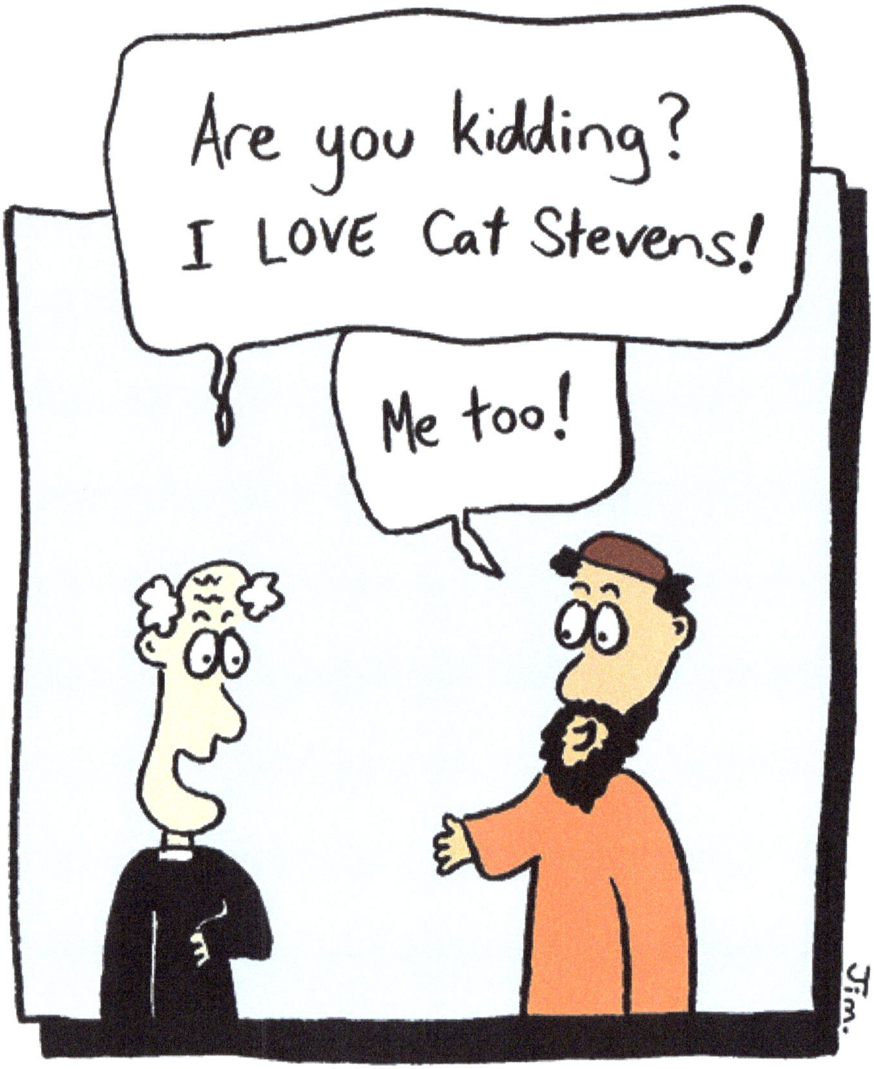
Are you kidding? I LOVE Cat Stevens!
Me too!
Jim.

A great day for Christian-Muslim relations.

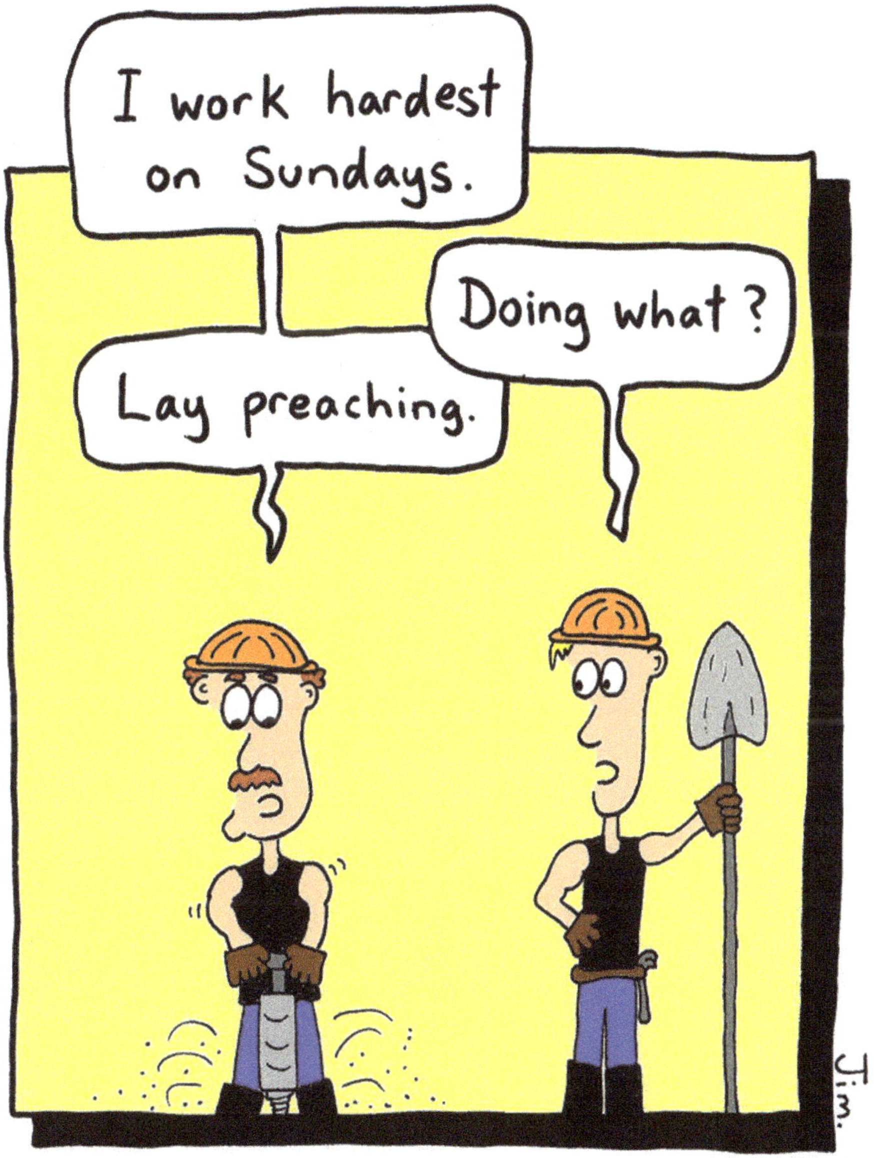
I work hardest on Sundays.
Doing what?
Lay preaching.
Jim.

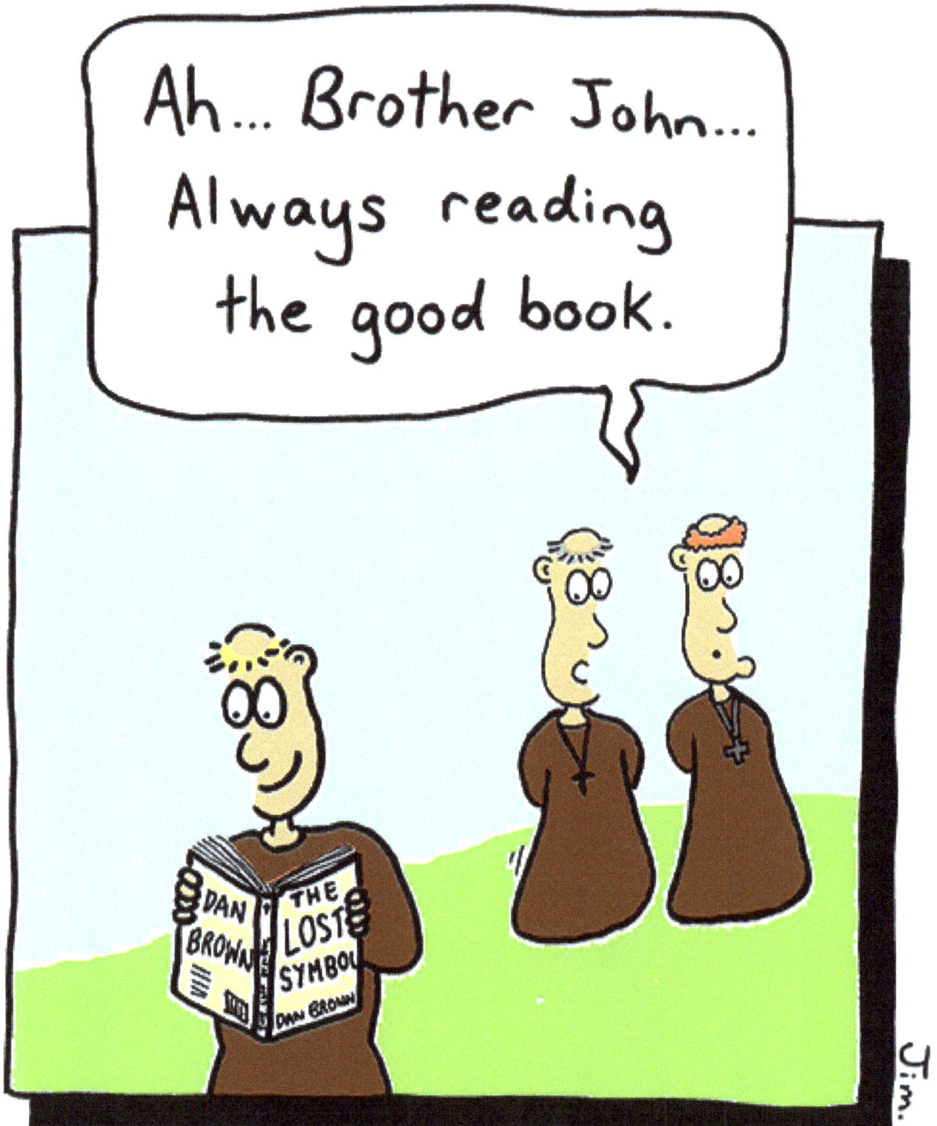
Ah... Brother John... Always reading the good book.
DAN BROWN
THE LOST SYMBOL
DAN BROWN
Jim.

'The Lost Symbol' book review – 30 September 2009.
http://www.nytimes.com/2009/10/11/books/review/Dowd-t.html

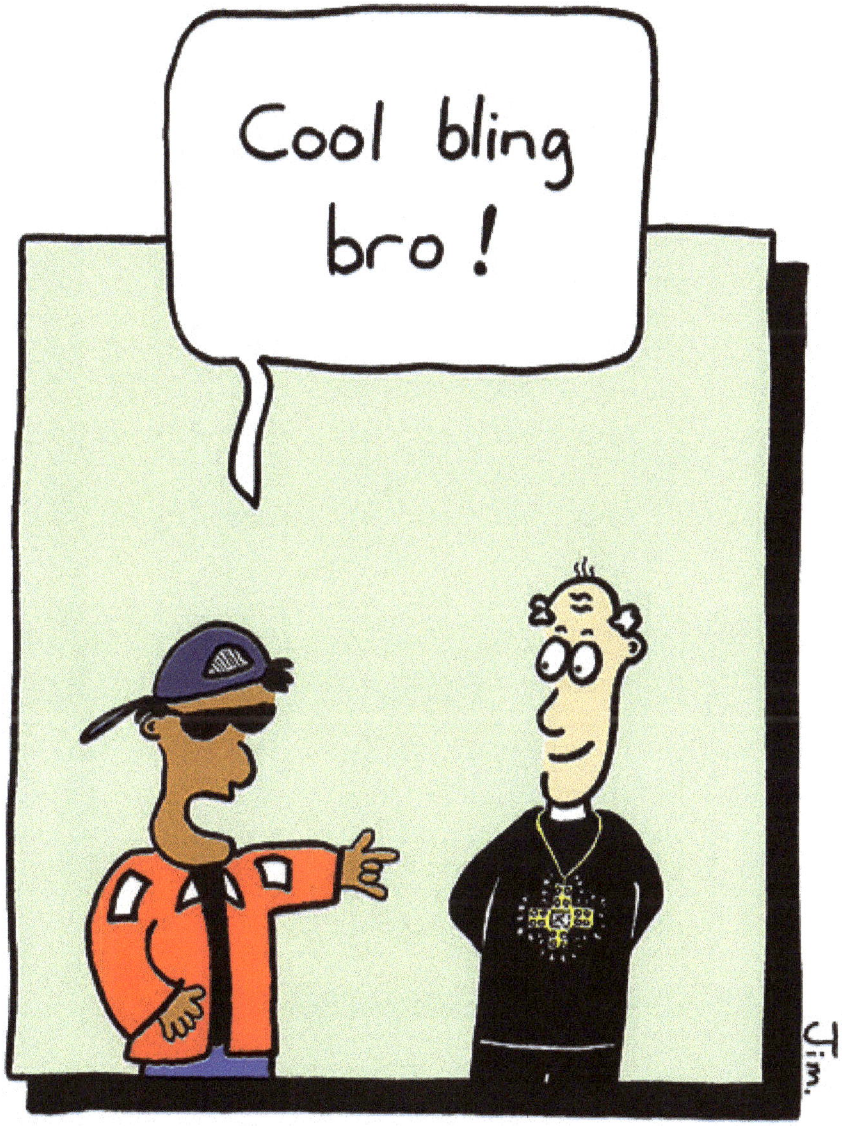
Cool bling bro!
Jim.

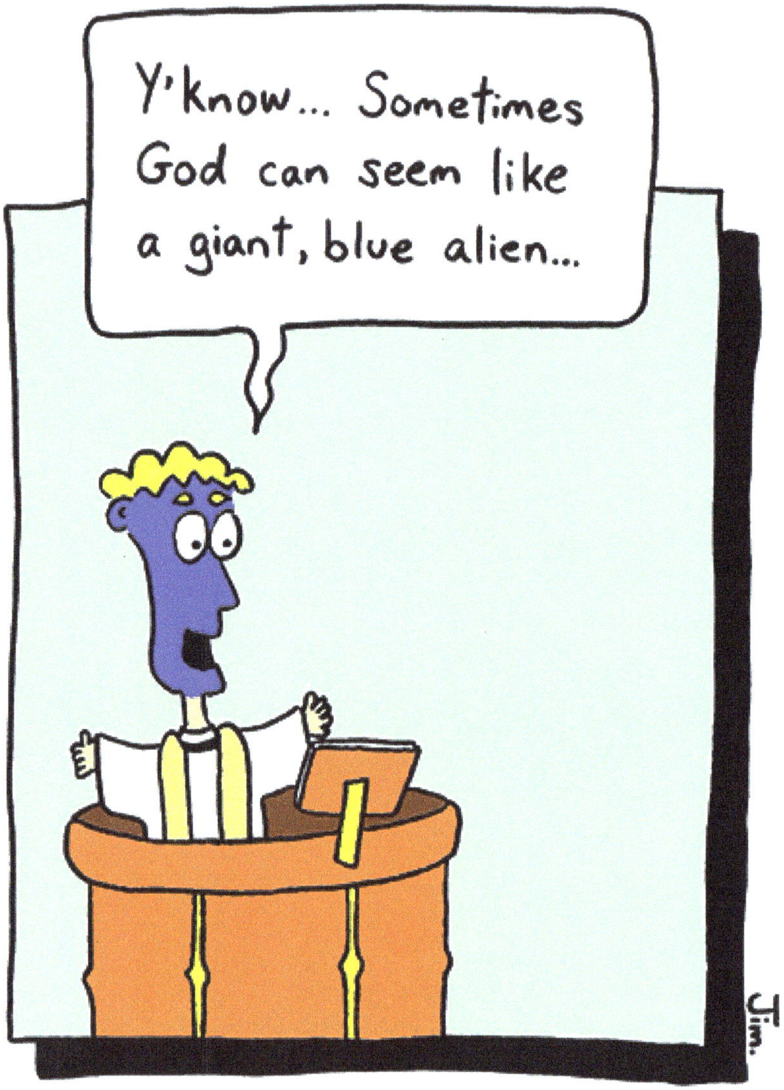
Y'know... Sometimes God can seem like a giant, blue alien...
Jim.

Nigel was a minister first and a movie-buff second ... but it was a pretty close second.

'Avatar'
https://en.wikipedia.org/wiki/Avatar_(2009_film)

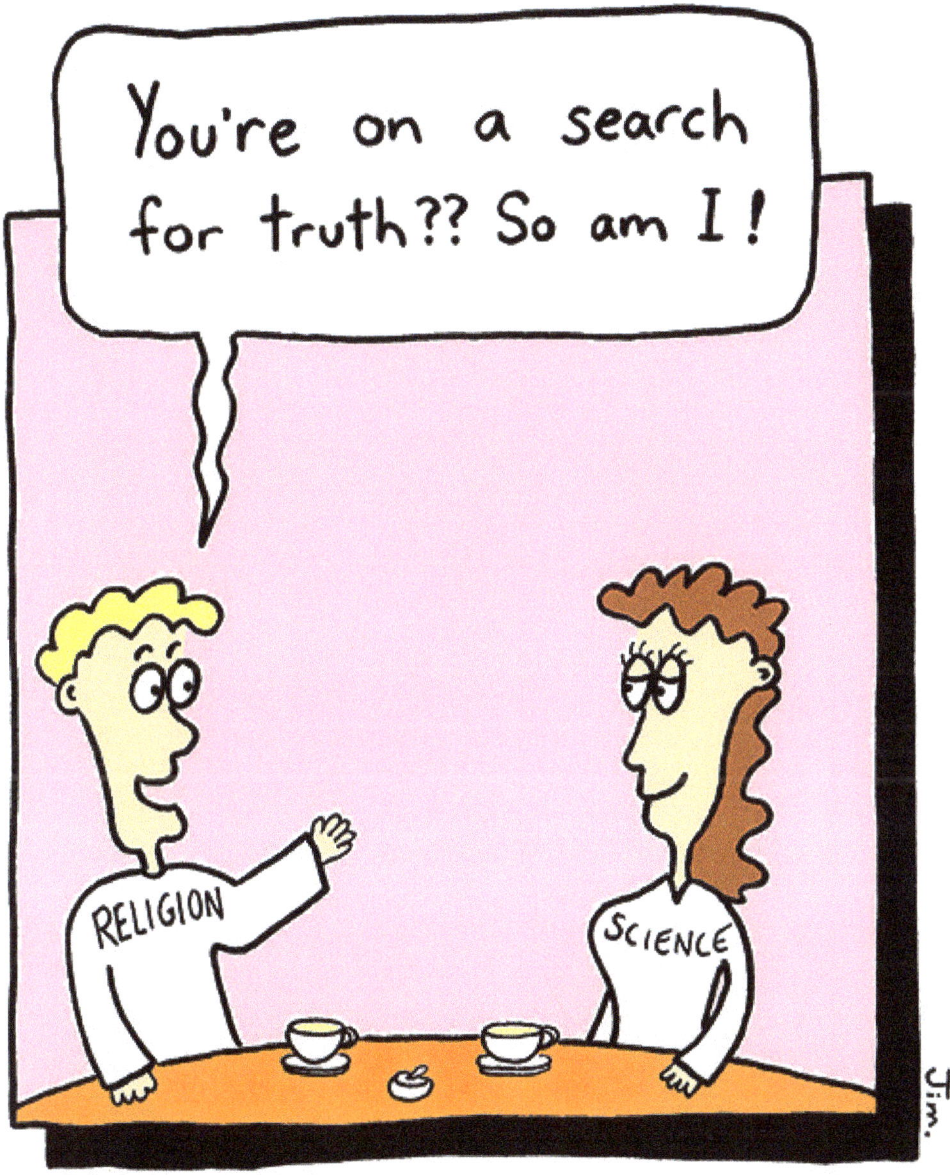
You're on a search for truth?? So am I!
RELIGION
SCIENCE
Jim.

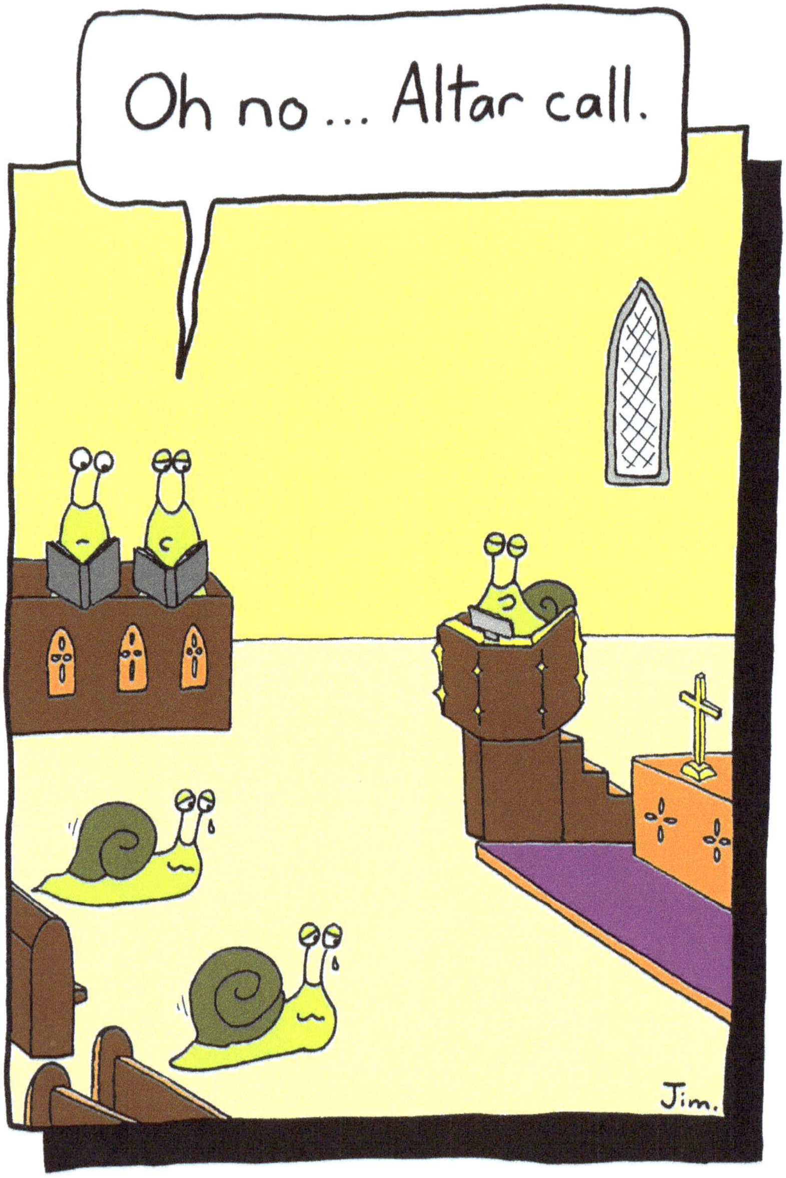
Oh no... Altar call.
Jim.

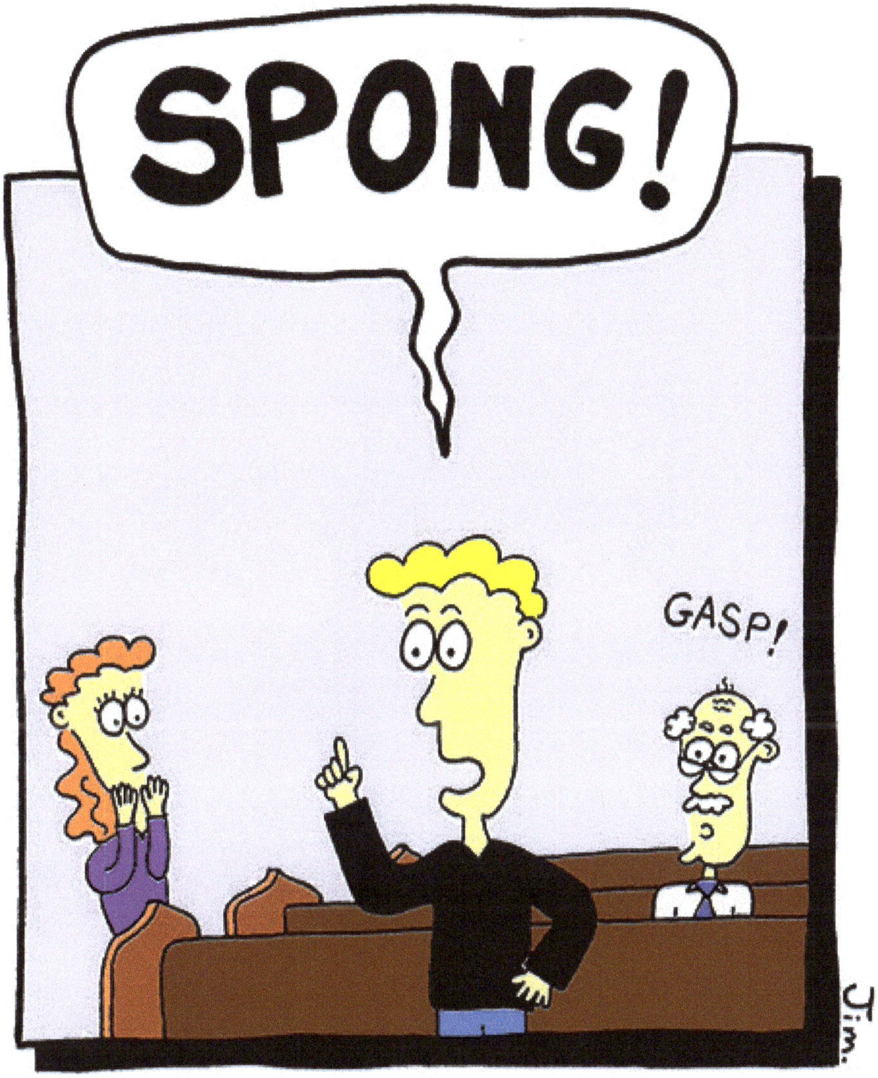
SPONG!
GASP!
Jim.

Jeff says the 'S' word' in church.

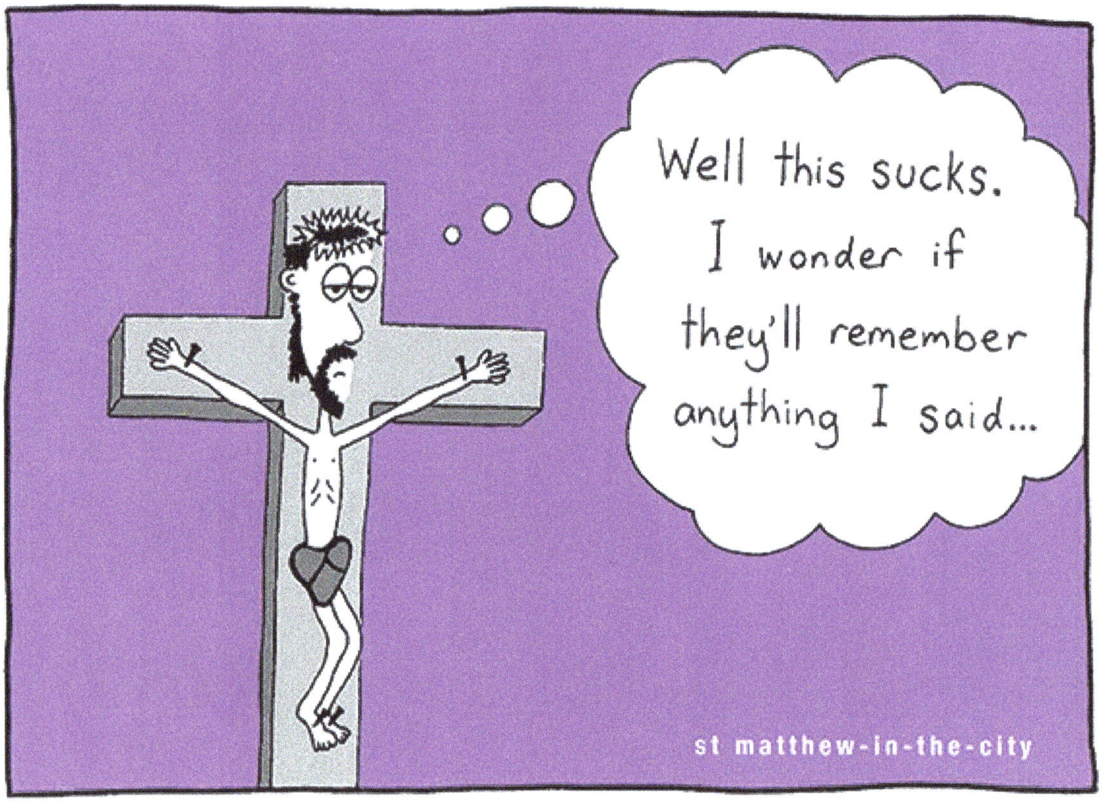
Well this sucks. I wonder if they'll remember anything I said...
st matthew-in-the-city

Church's Easter billboard has Christ using youthful slang

1 April 2010

http://www.nzherald.co.nz/nz/news/article.cfm?c_id=1&objectid=10635774

Vandals deface Easter billboard in New Zealand

5 April 2010

http://religiondispatches.org/vandals-deface-easter-billboard-in-new-zealand

Religious graffiti defaces Easter billboard

5 April 2010

http://www.stuff.co.nz/national/crime/3547957/Religious-graffiti-defaces-Easter-billboard

The Auckland Anglican church happy to shock its flock

31 March 2010

https://www.theguardian.com/world/blog/2010/mar/31/auckland-anglican-church-shock

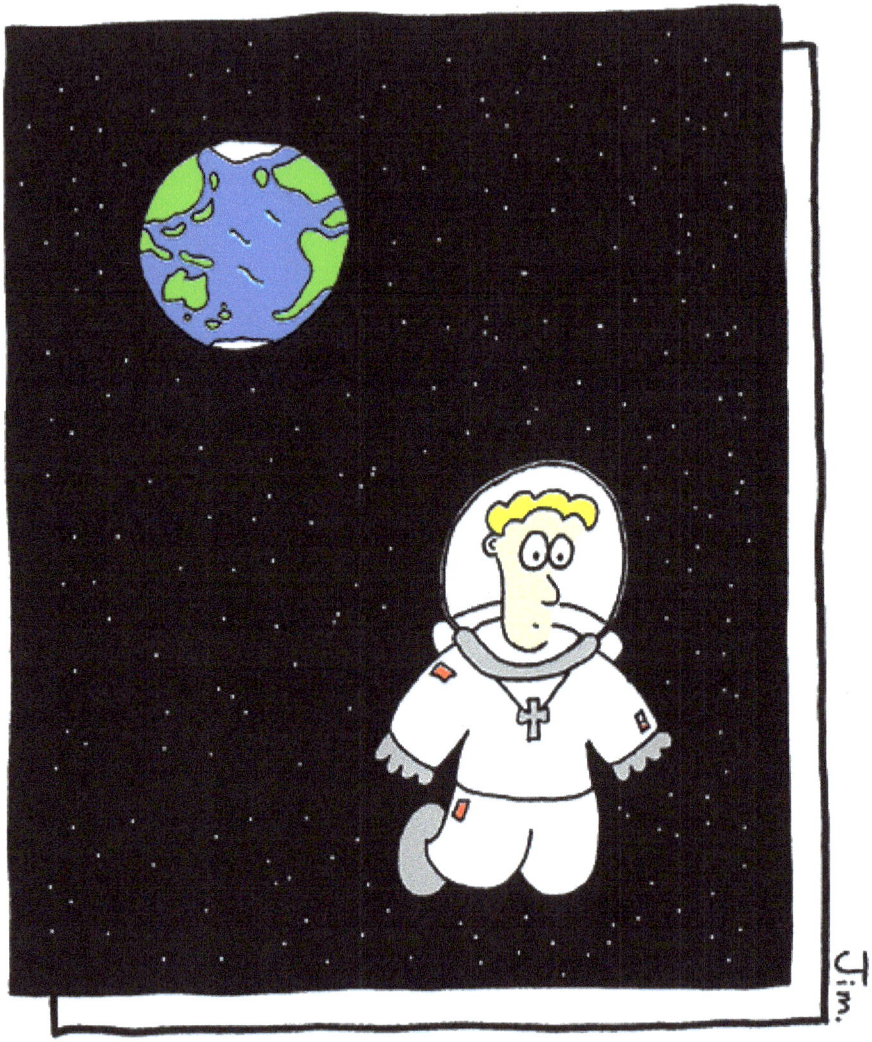
Jim.

Jeff wondered … maybe his Christianity was too progressive.

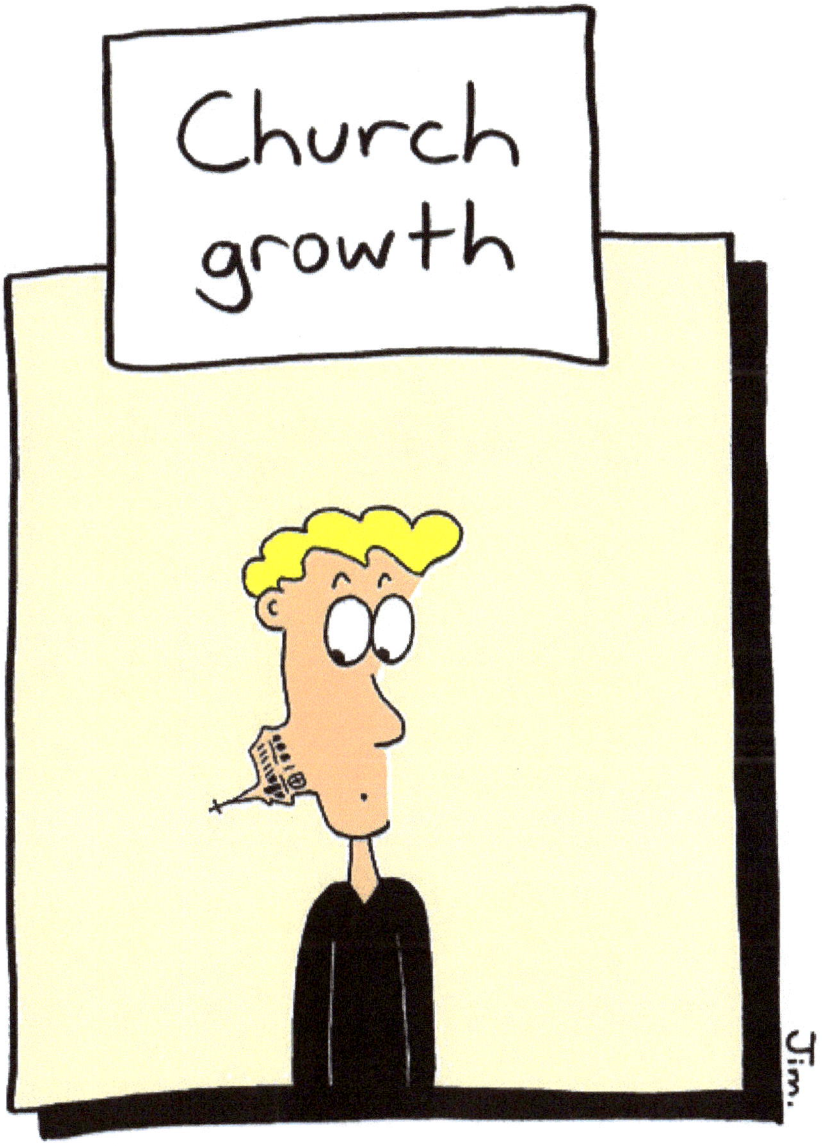
Church
growth
Jim.

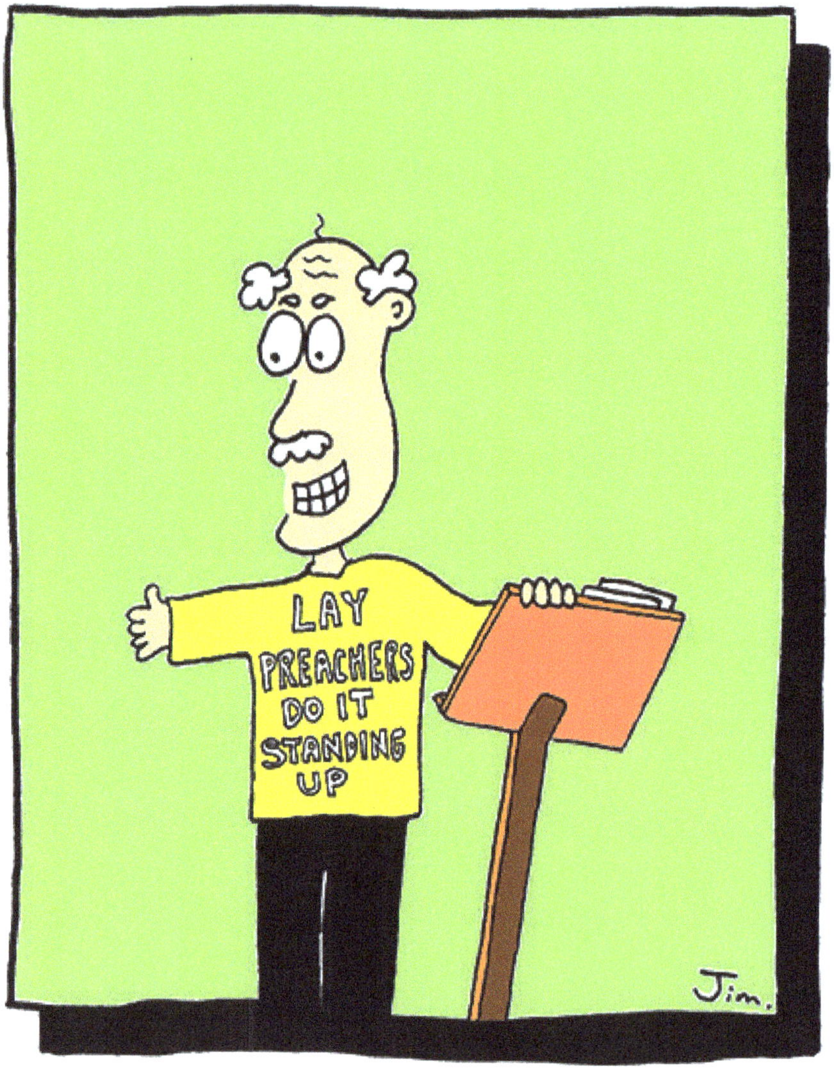
LAY PREACHERS DO IT STANDING UP
Jim.

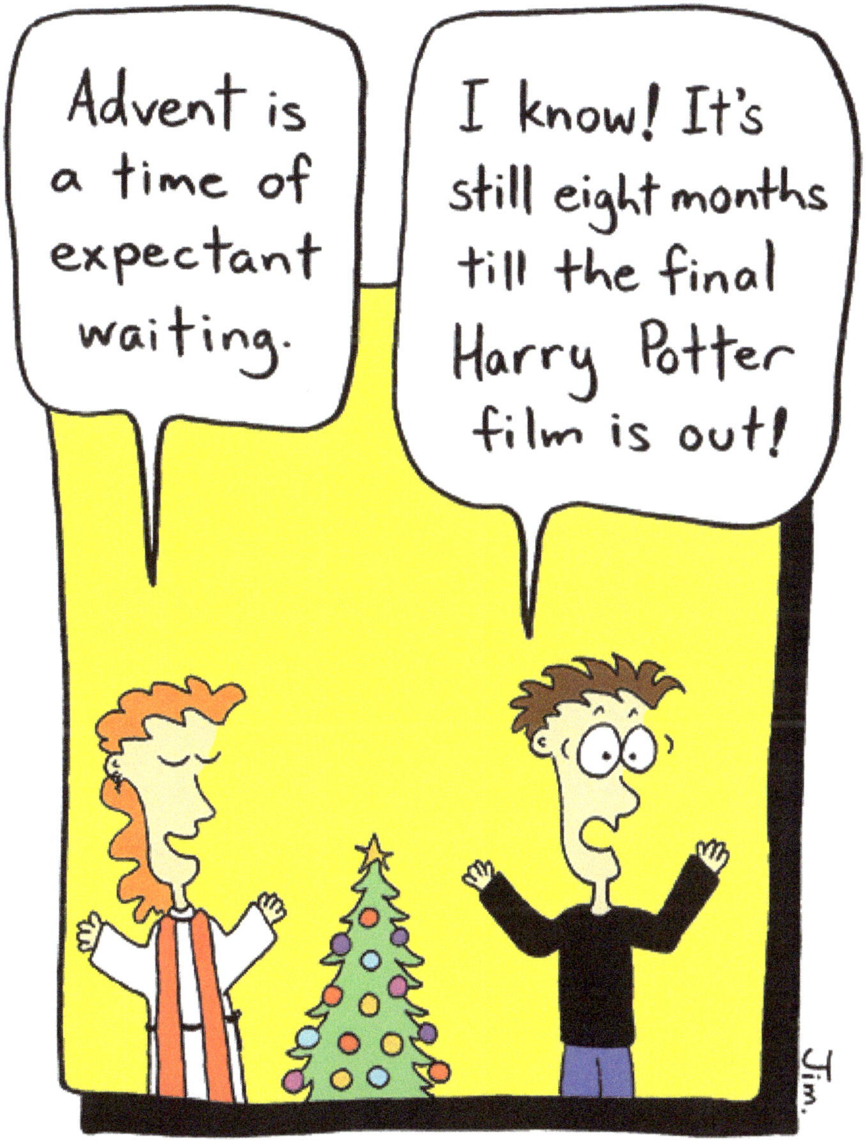
Advent is a time of expectant waiting.
I know! It's still eight months till the final Harry Potter film is out!
Jim.

https://en.wikipedia.org/wiki/Harry_Potter_and_the_Deathly_Hallows_–_Part_2

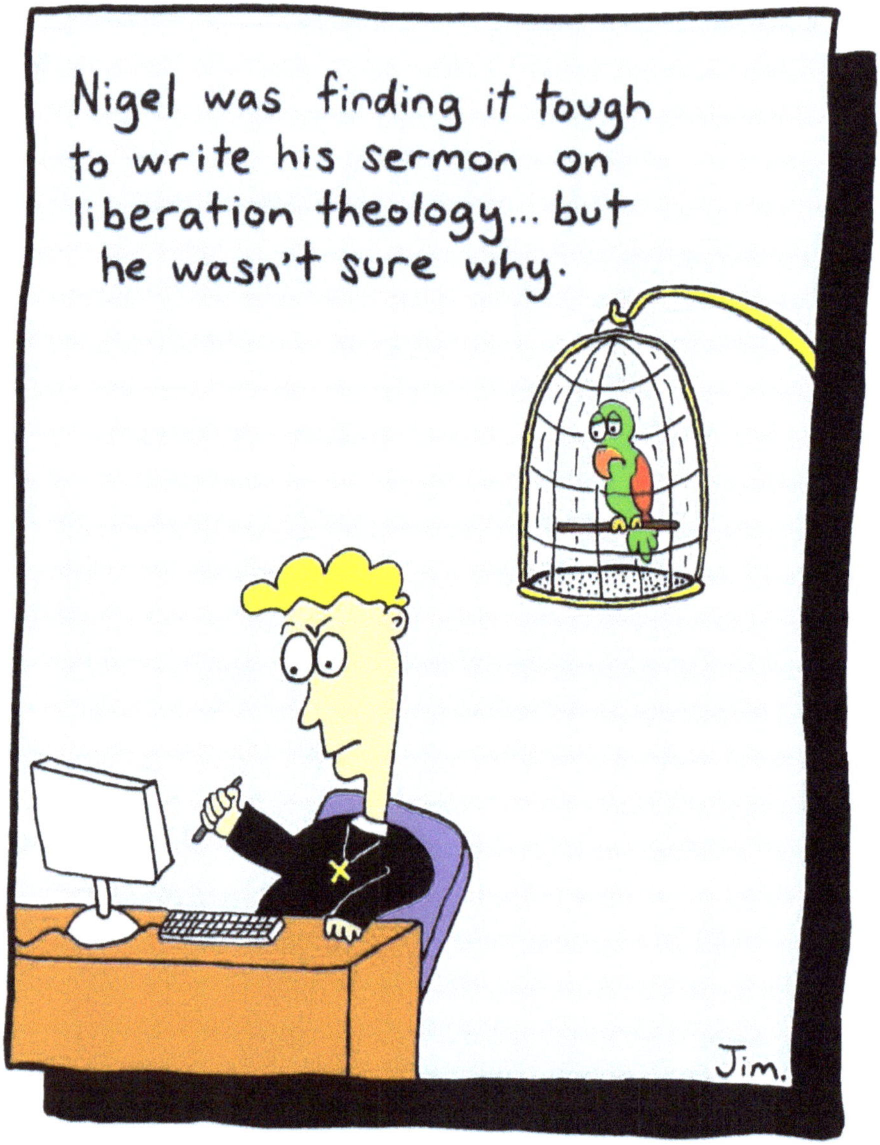
Nigel was finding it tough to write his sermon on liberation theology... but he wasn't sure why.
Jim.

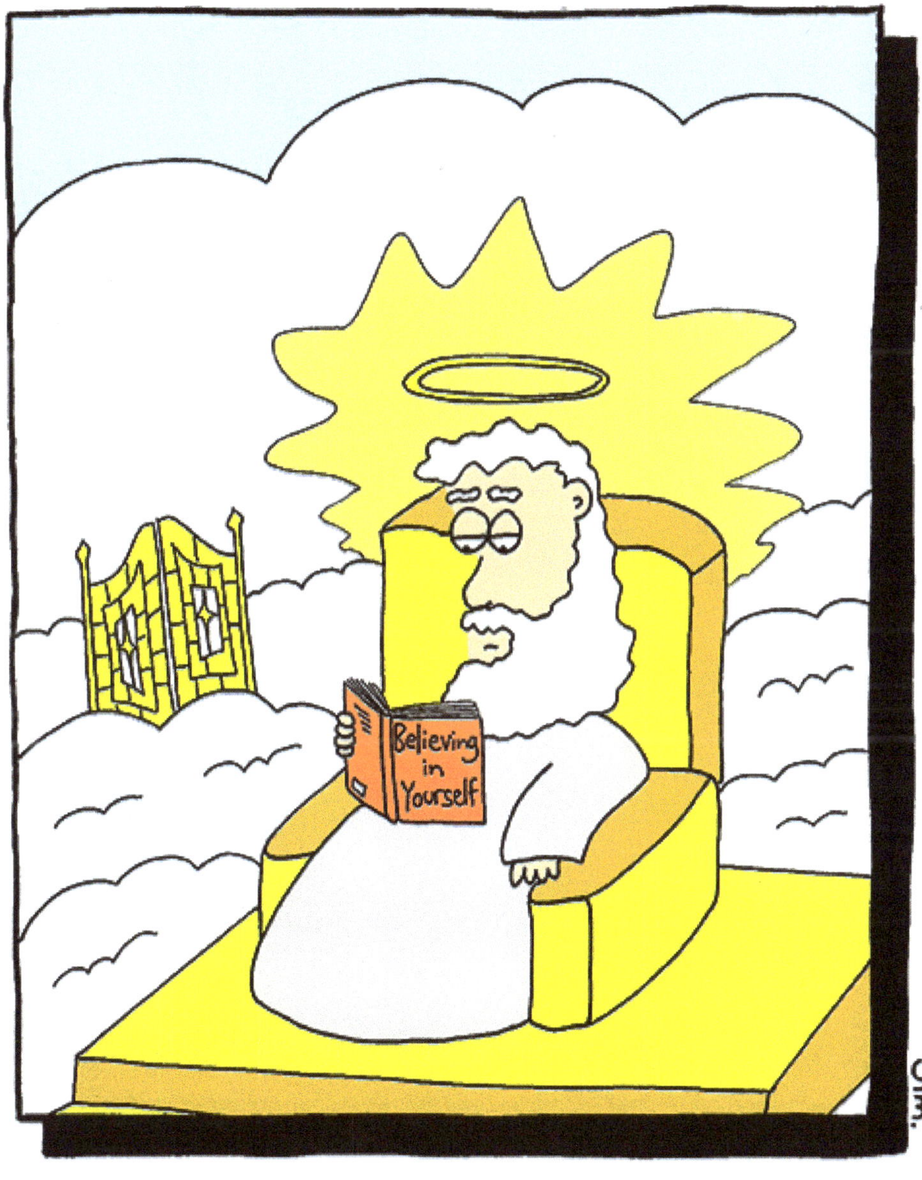
Believing in Yourself
Jim.

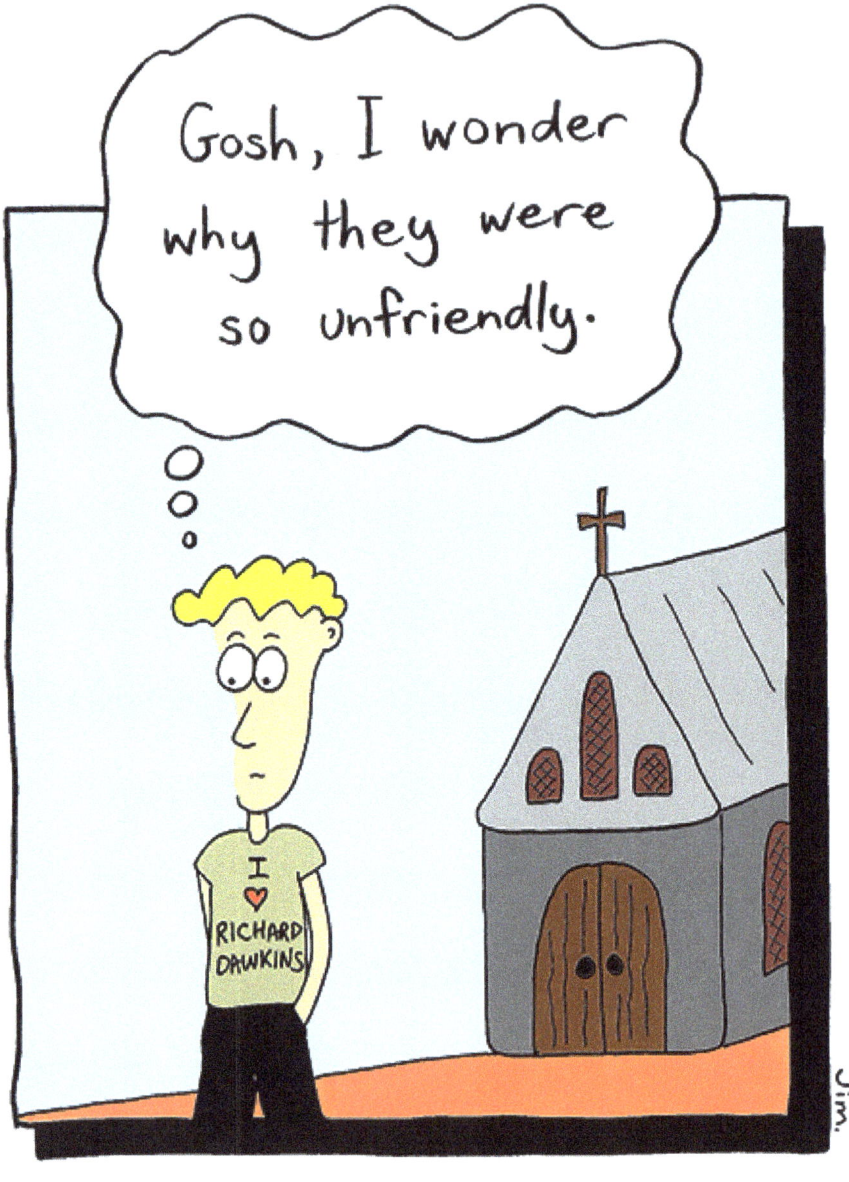
Gosh, I wonder why they were so unfriendly.
I ♥ RICHARD DAWKINS
Jim.

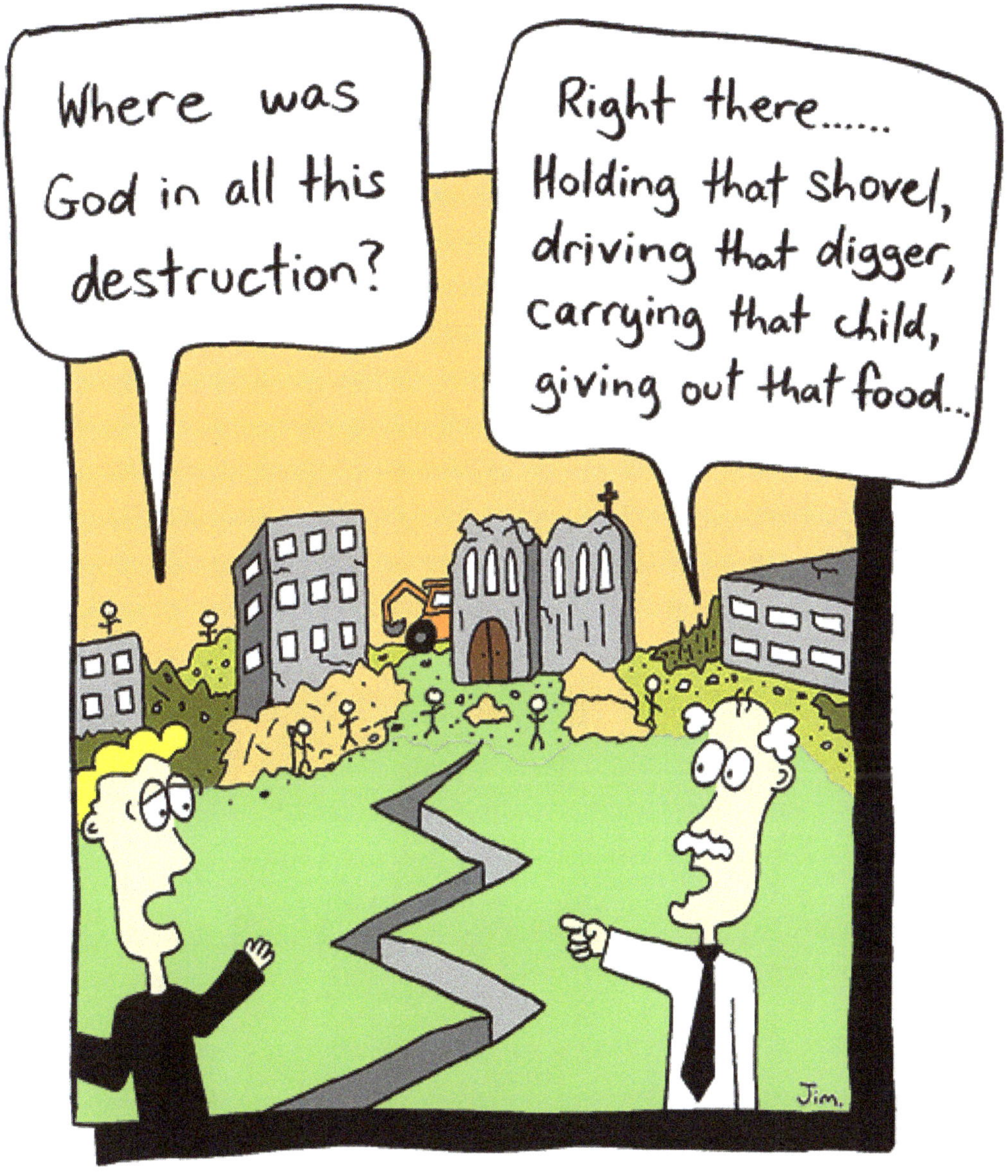
Where was God in all this destruction?
Right there...... Holding that shovel, driving that digger, carrying that child, giving out that food...
Jim.

Christchurch earthquake kills 185 – 22 February 2011.
https://nzhistory.govt.nz/page/christchurch-earthquake-kills-185

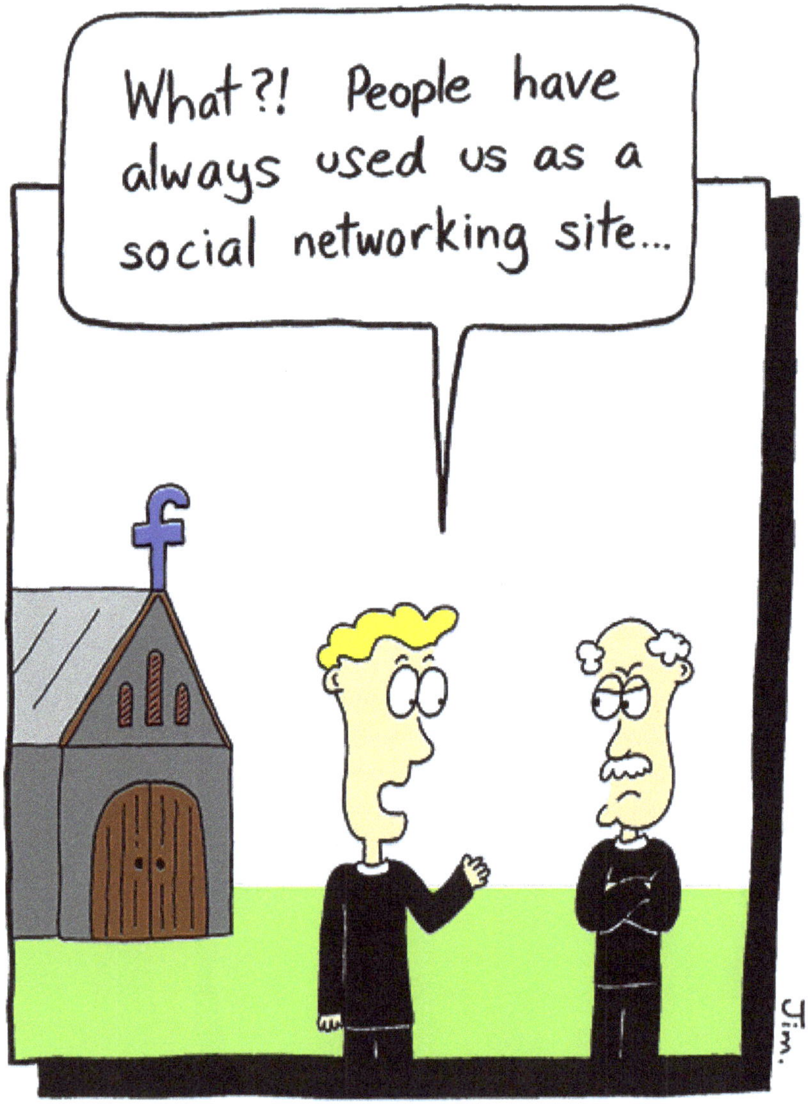
What?! People have always used us as a social networking site...
Jim.

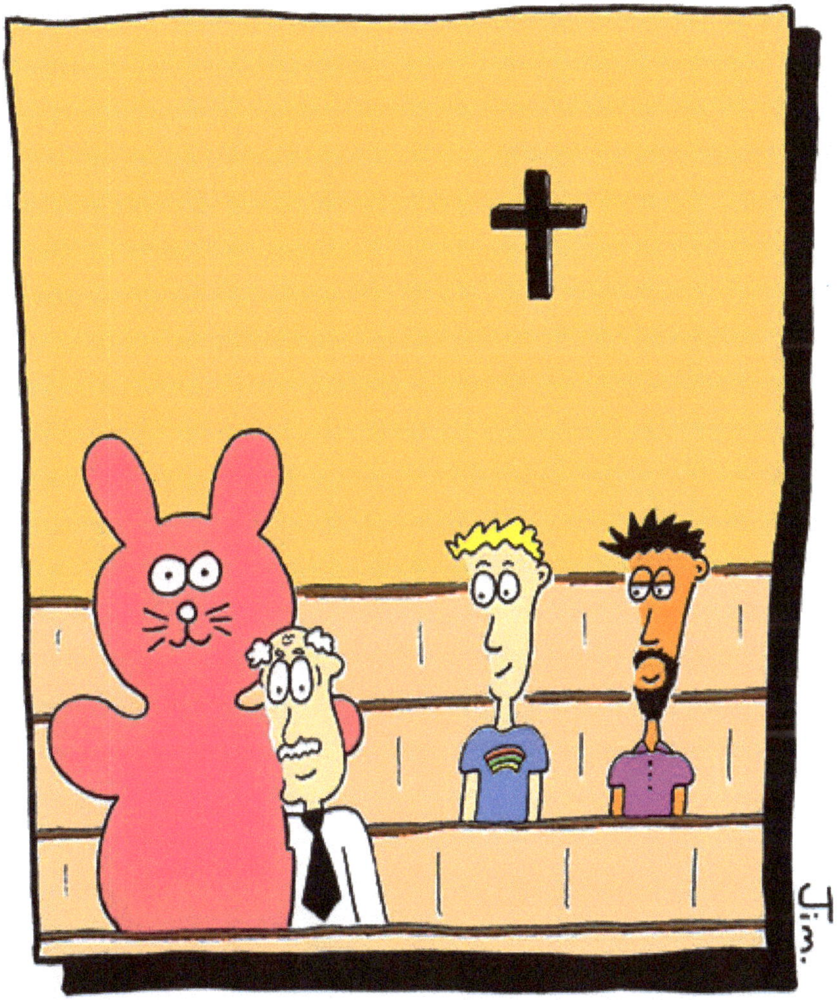
Jim.

At St Clive's, members who weren't quite ready to embrace gays in the church could start by cuddling a giant pink bunny rabbit.

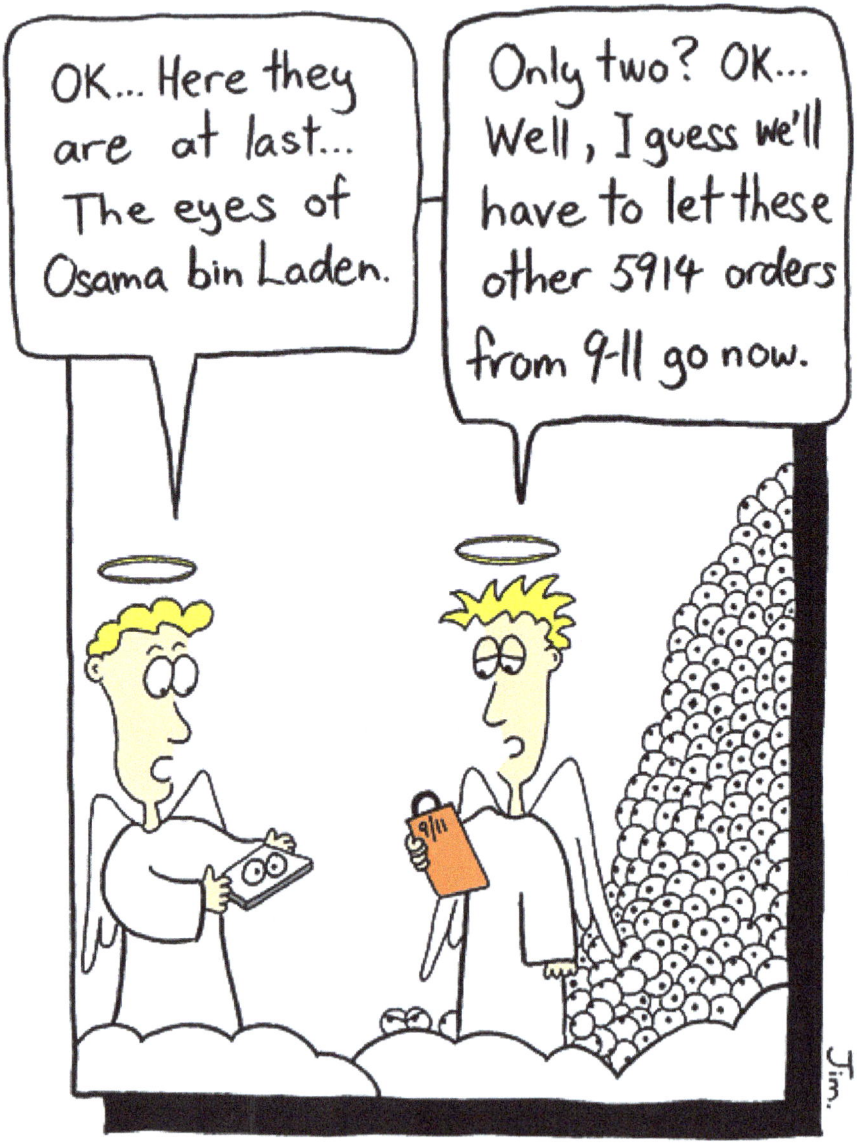
OK... Here they are at last... The eyes of Osama bin Laden.
Only two? OK... Well, I guess we'll have to let these other 5914 orders from 9-11 go now.
9/11
Jim.

Bin Laden Is Dead, Obama Says – 1 May 2011.
http://www.nytimes.com/2011/05/02/world/asia/osama-bin-laden-is-killed.html

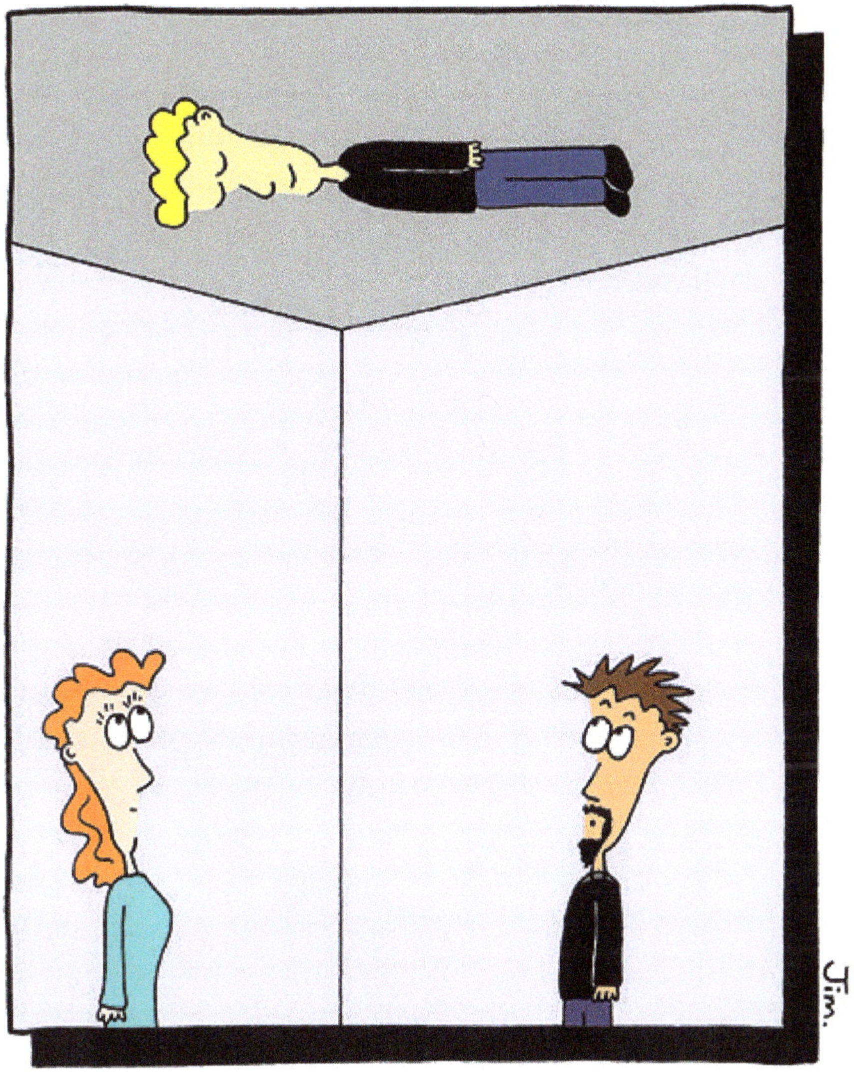
Jim.

Rapture planking

Planking: A Brief History – 16 May 2011.
https://www.theguardian.com/world/2011/may/16/planking-a-brief-history

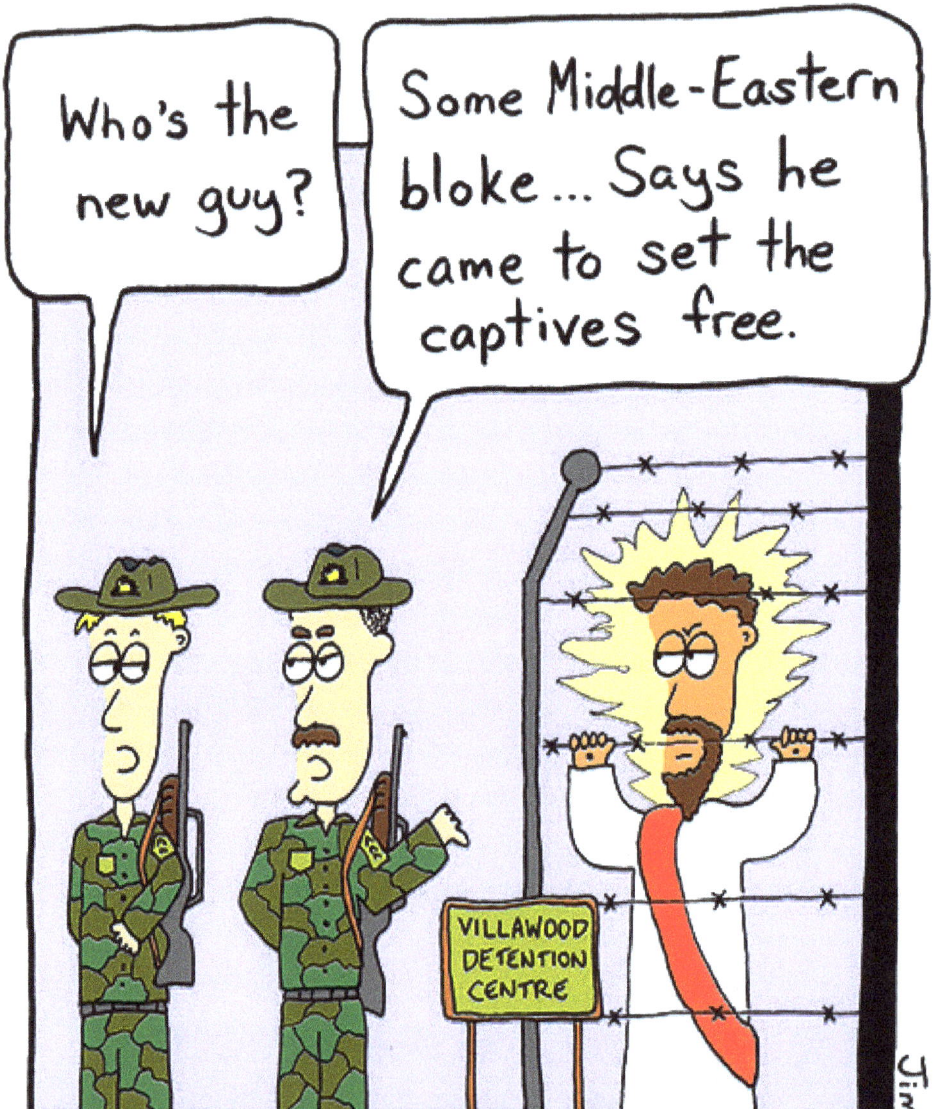
Who's the new guy?
Some Middle-Eastern bloke... Says he came to set the captives free.
VILLAWOOD DETENTION CENTRE
Jim.

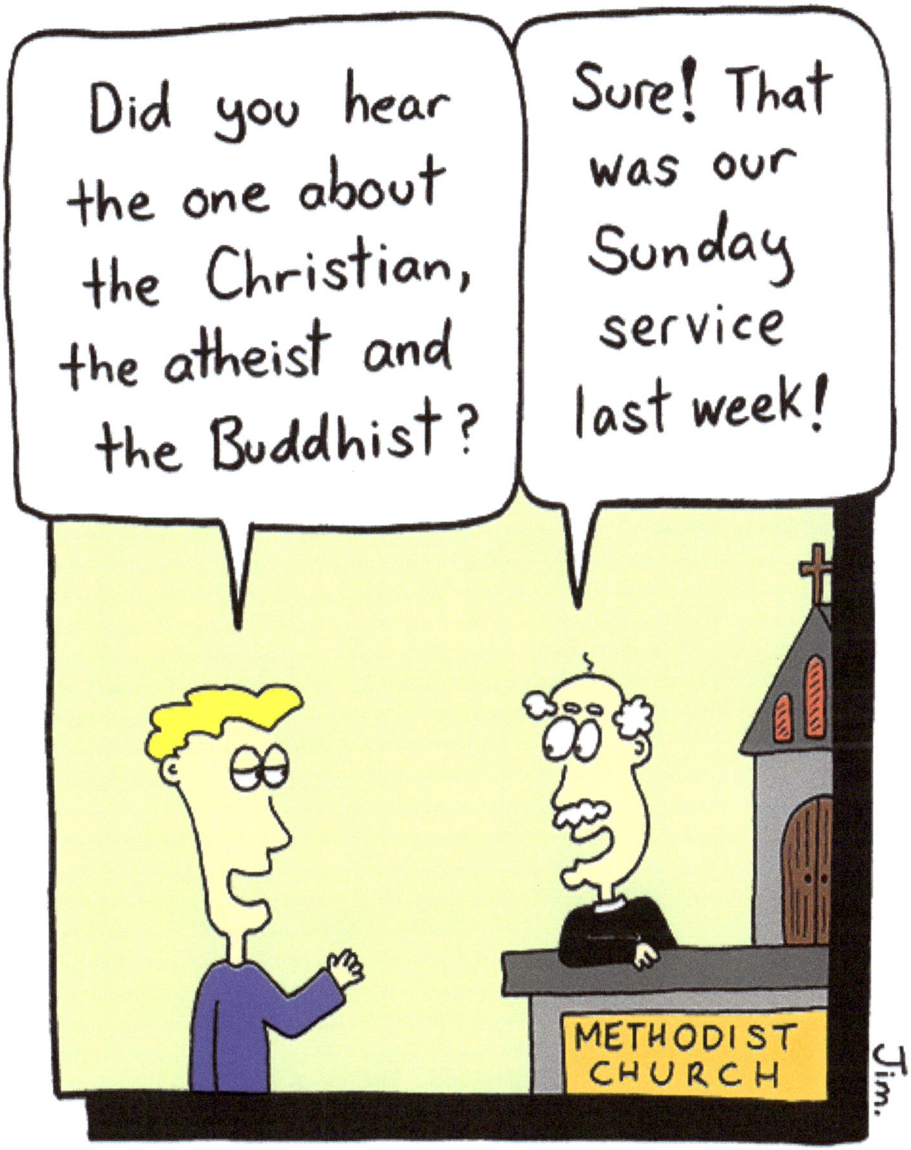
Did you hear the one about the Christian, the atheist and the Buddhist?
Sure! That was our Sunday service last week!
METHODIST CHURCH
Jim.

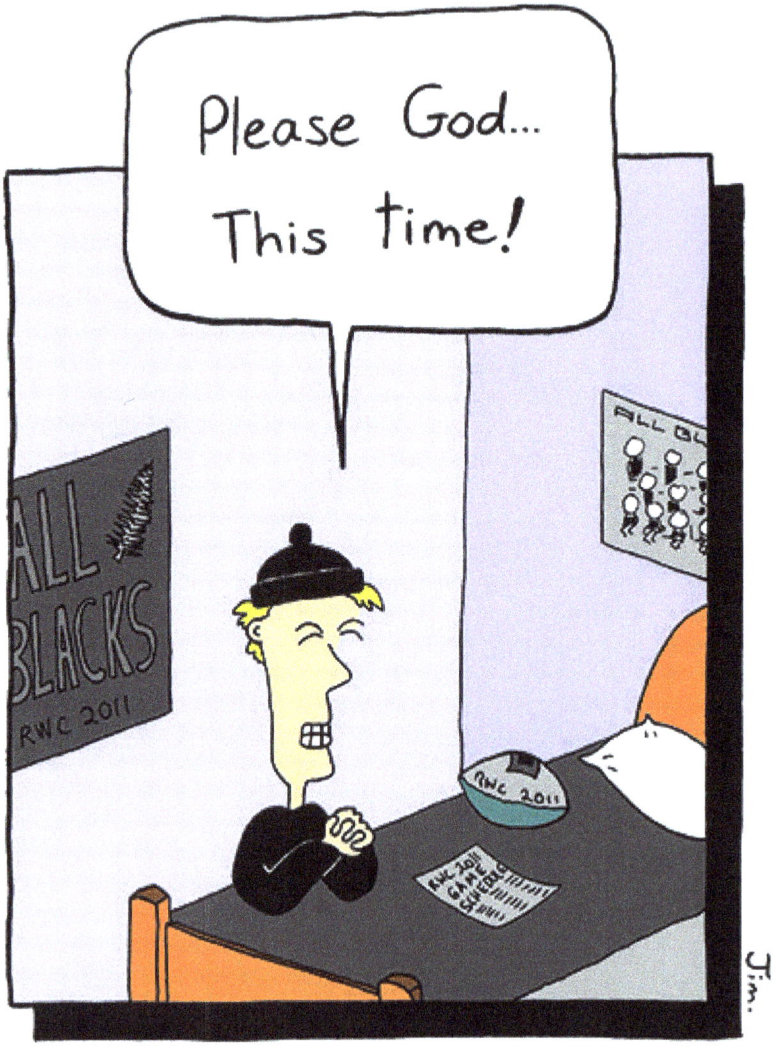
Please God...
This time!
ALL BLACKS
RWC 2011
RWC 2011
Jim.

Every four years, New Zealand stops being a secular nation.

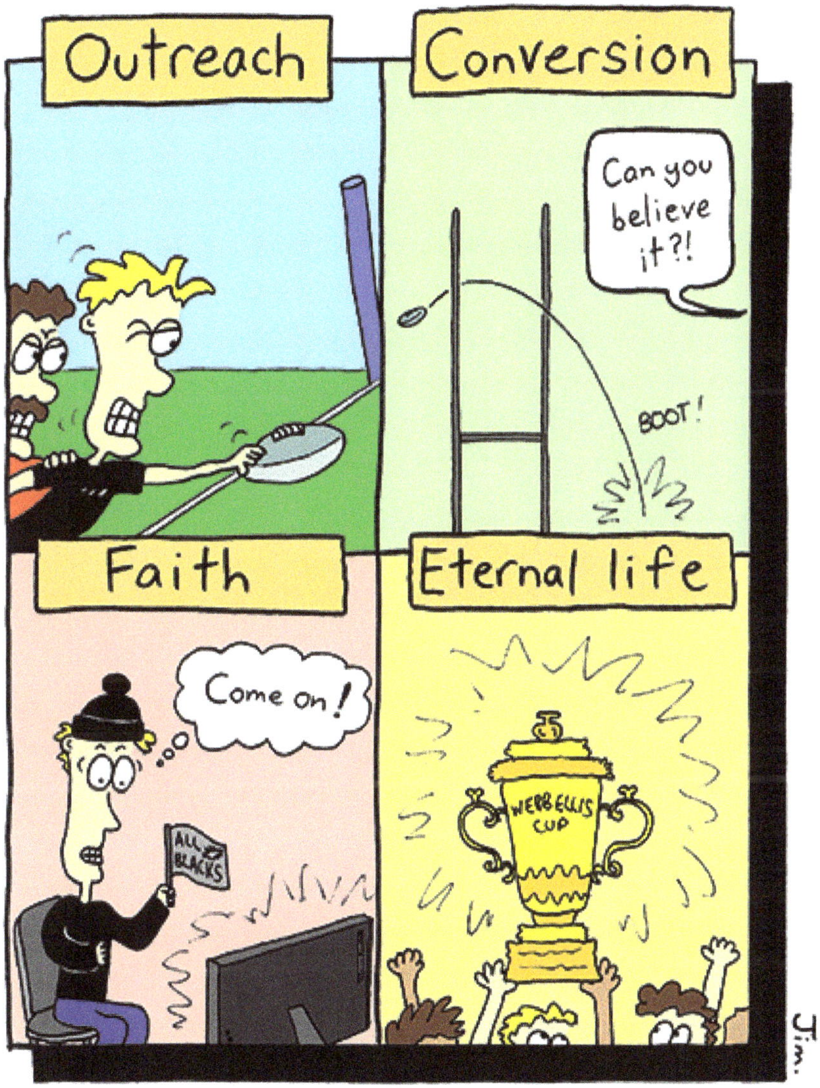
Outreach
Conversion
Can you believe it?!
BOOT!
Faith
Come on!
ALL BLACKS
Eternal life
WEBB ELLIS CUP
Jim.

The religion of Rugby World Cup

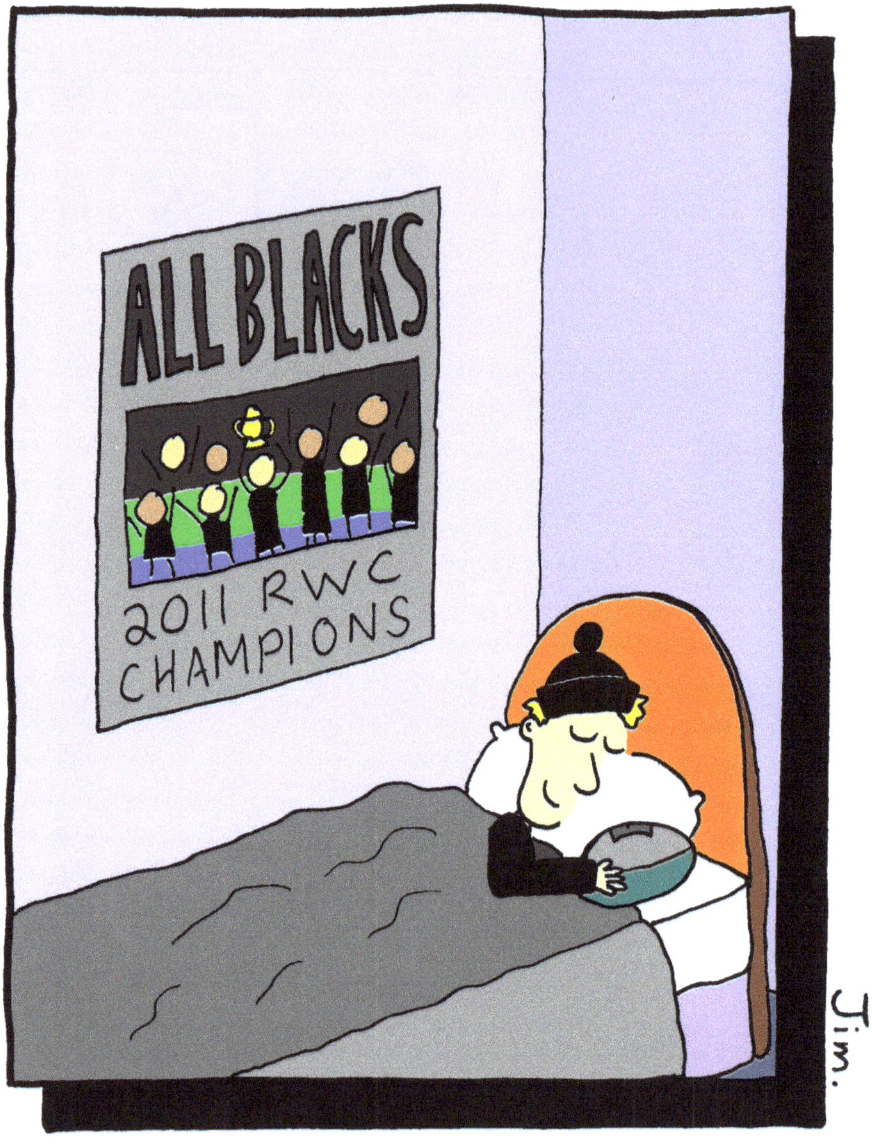
ALL BLACKS
2011 RWC
CHAMPIONS
Jim.

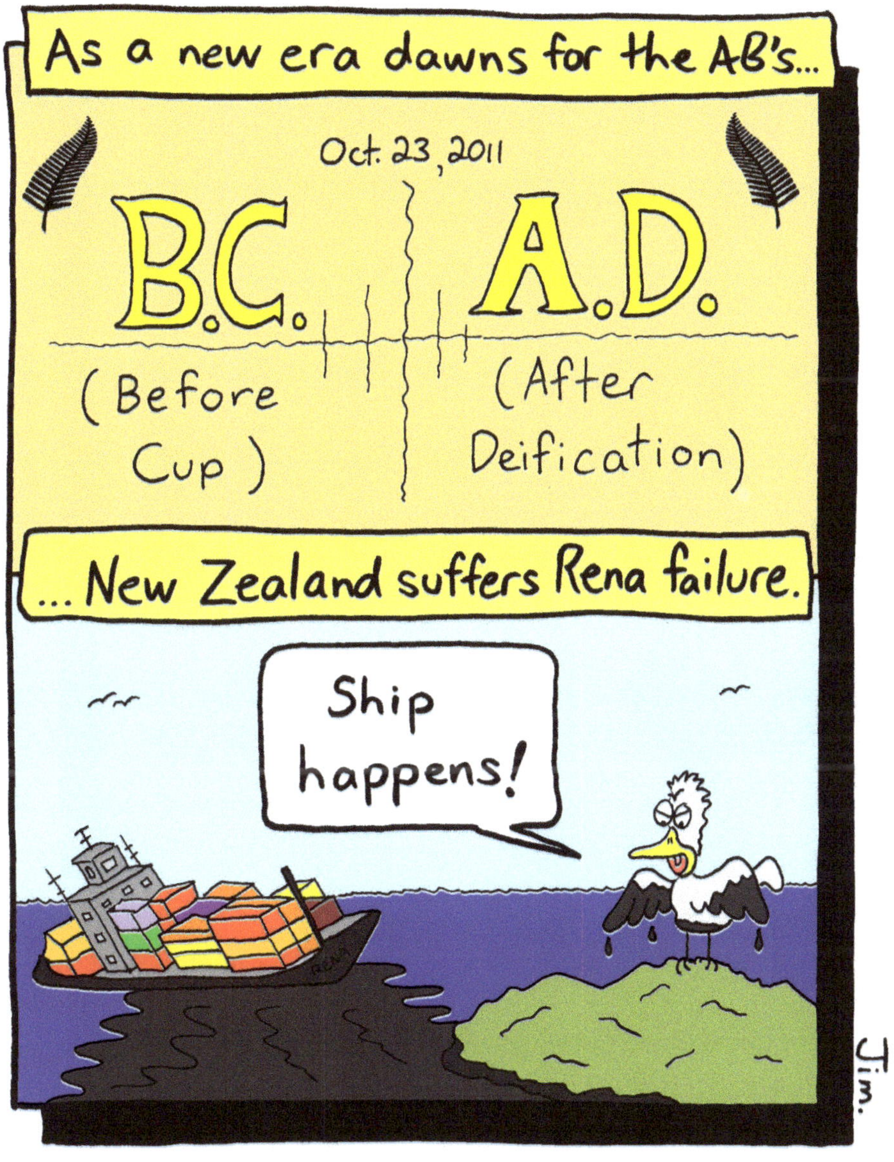
As a new era dawns for the AB's...
Oct. 23, 2011
B.C.
(Before Cup)
A.D.
(After Deification)
... New Zealand suffers Rena failure.
Ship happens!
Jim.

https://www.telegraph.co.uk/sport/rugbyunion/rugby-world-cup/8844197/Rugby-World-Cup-2011-New-Zealand-8-France-7-match-report.html
https://nzhistory.govt.nz/culture/shipping-containers/rena-disaster

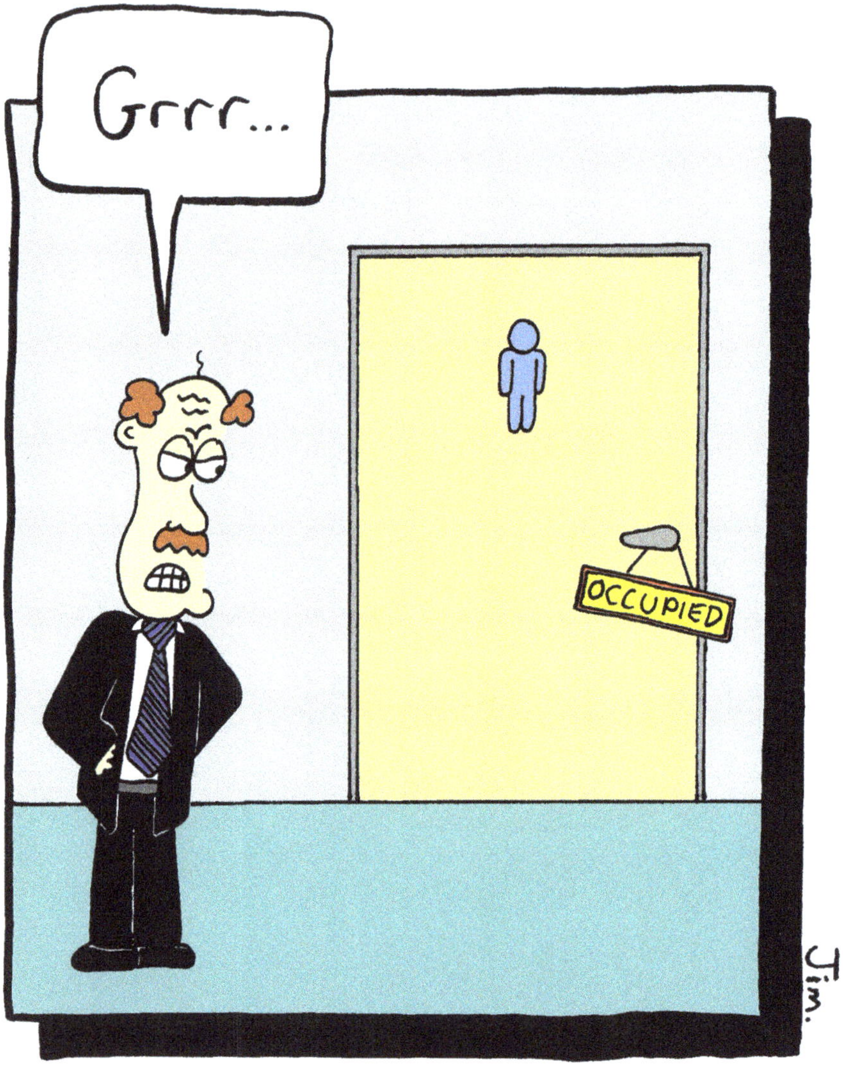

Grrr...
OCCUPIED
Jim.

Things were especially tense outside the Wall Street bathroom.

Occupy Wall Street protests – 6 October 2011.
https://www.theguardian.com/world/blog/2011/oct/05/occupy-wall-street-protests-live

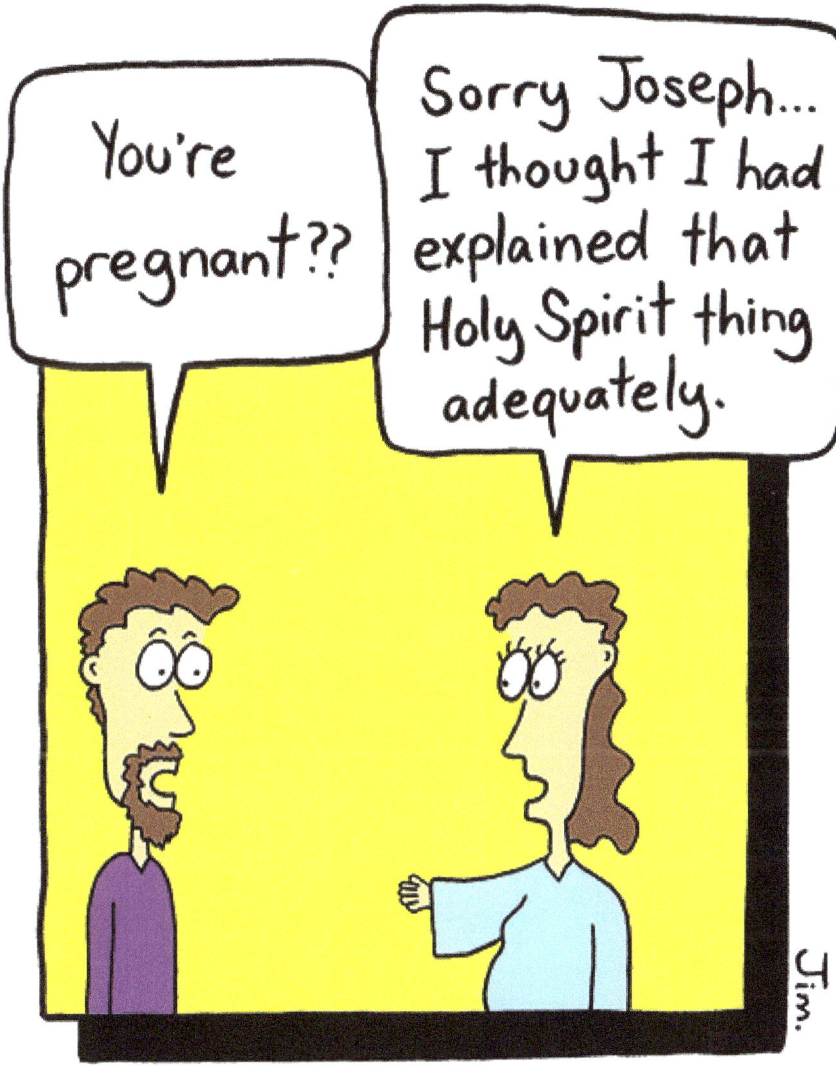
You're pregnant??
Sorry Joseph... I thought I had explained that Holy Spirit thing adequately.
Jim.

The assumption of Mary

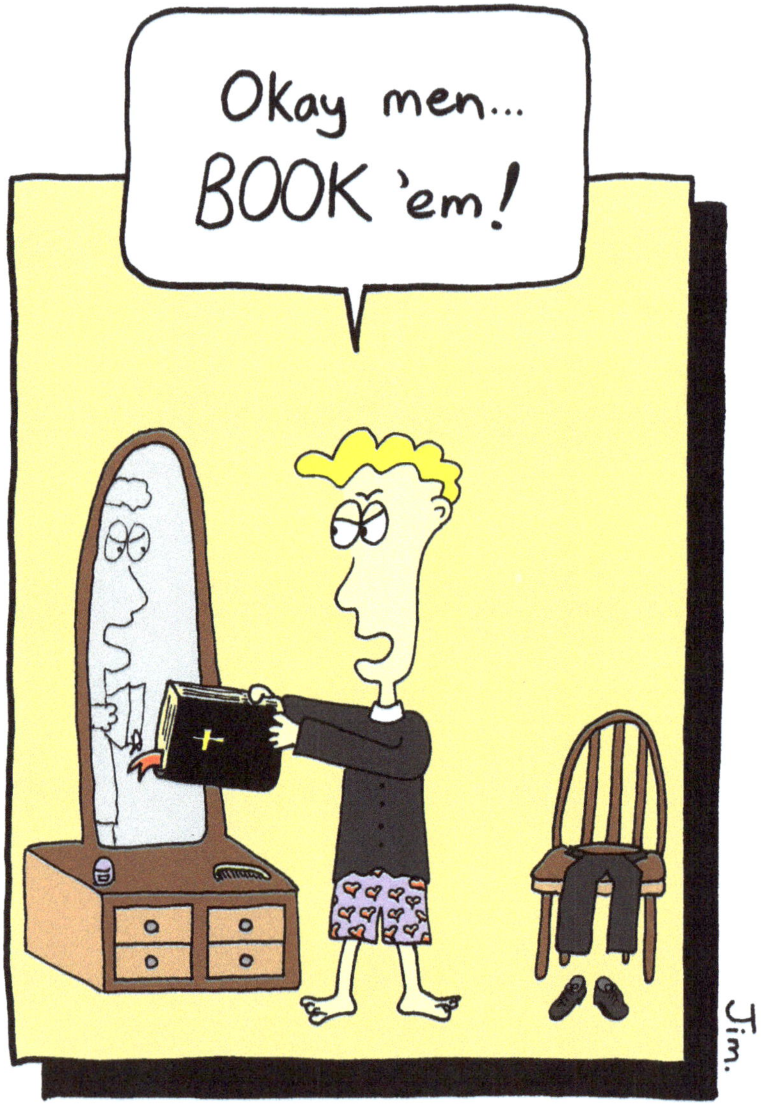
Okay men...
BOOK 'em!
Jim.

Nigel loved being a police chaplain.

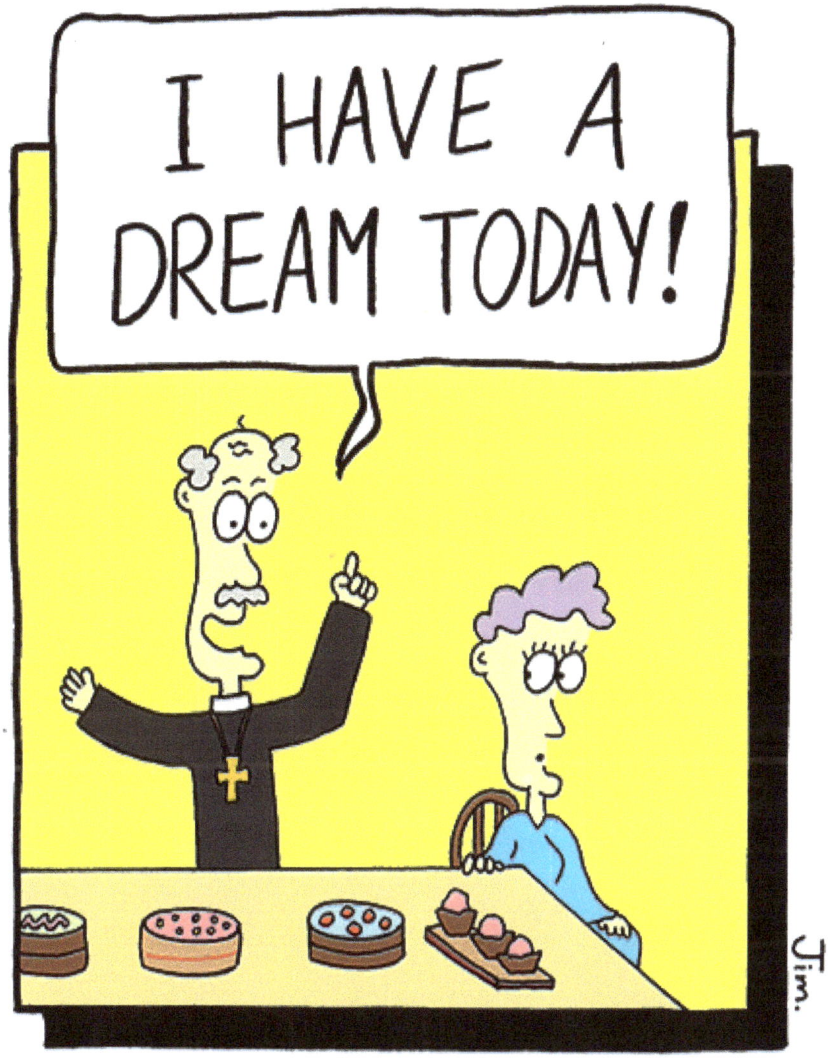
I HAVE A DREAM TODAY!
Jim.

Rev Smythe had high hopes for the church bake sale.

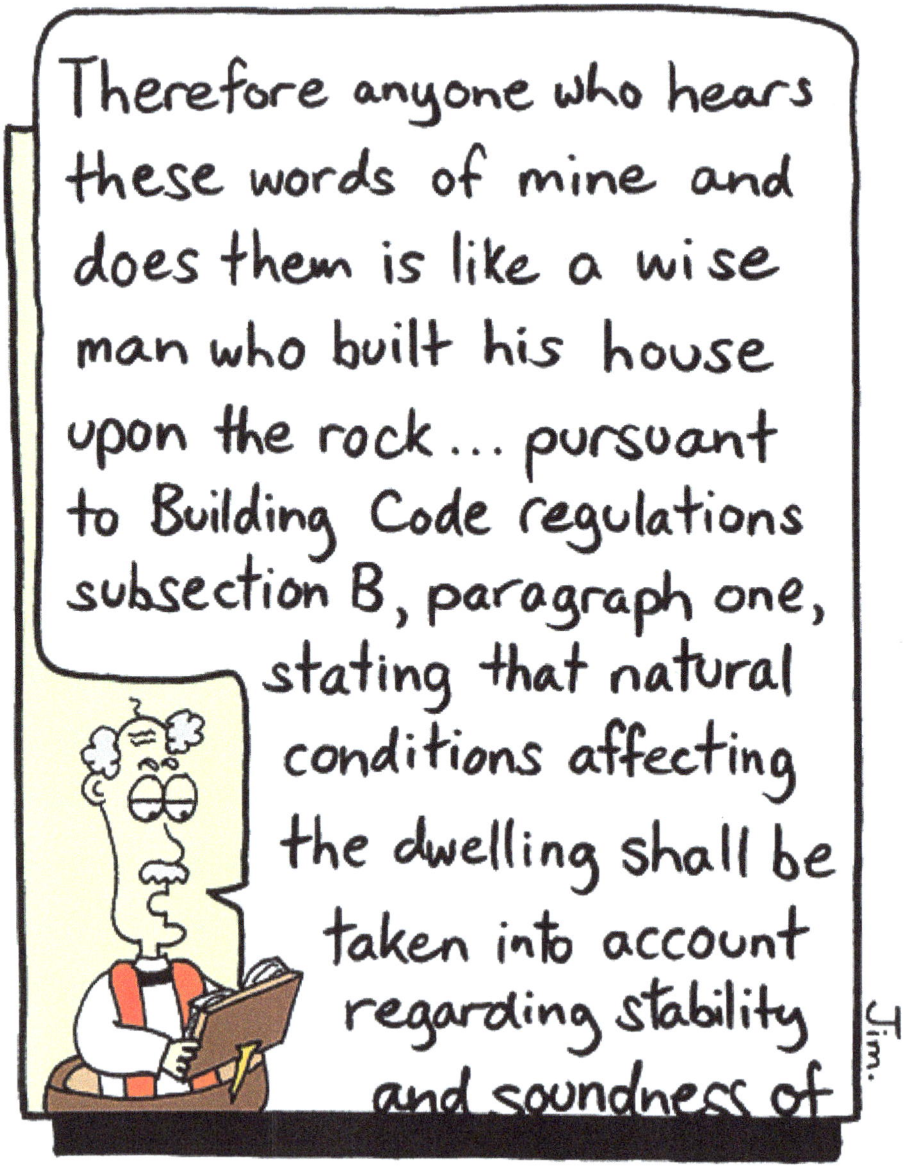
Therefore anyone who hears these words of mine and does them is like a wise man who built his house upon the rock... pursuant to Building Code regulations subsection B, paragraph one, stating that natural conditions affecting the dwelling shall be taken into account regarding stability and soundness of
Jim.

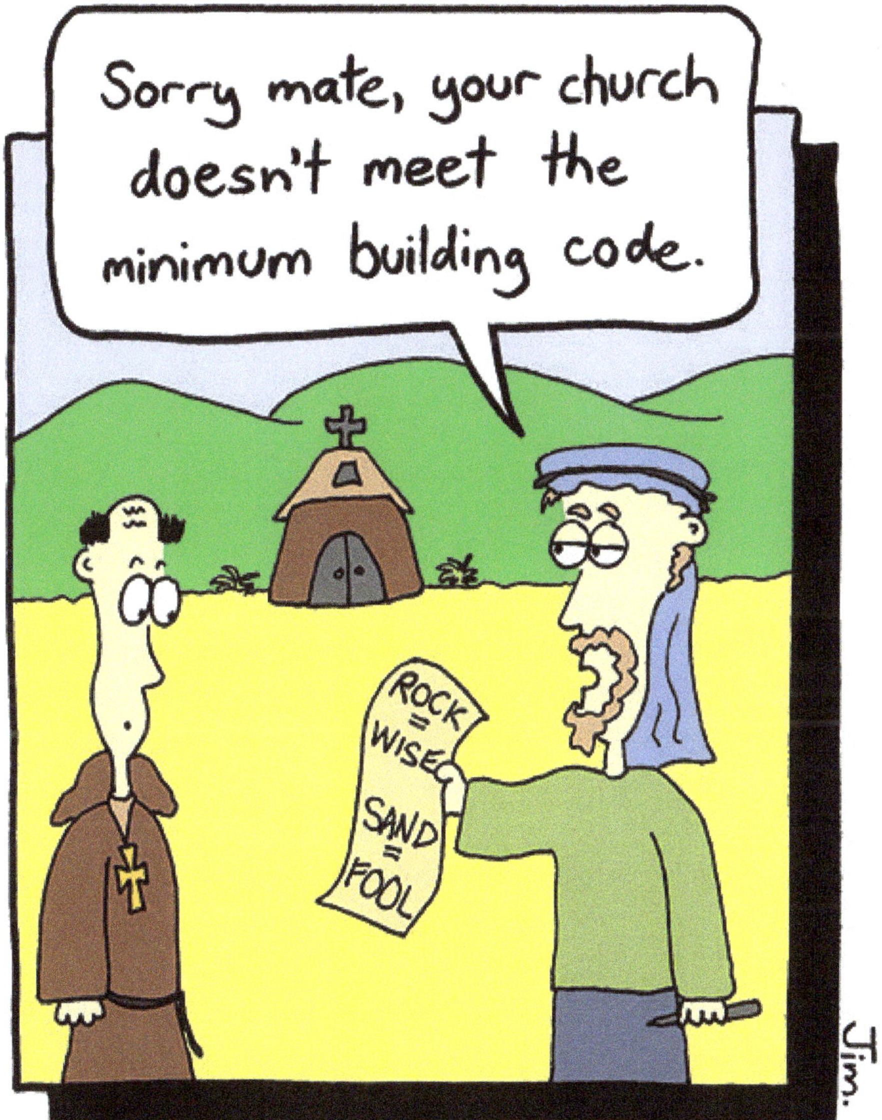
Sorry mate, your church doesn't meet the minimum building code.
ROCK = WISE
SAND = FOOL
Jim.

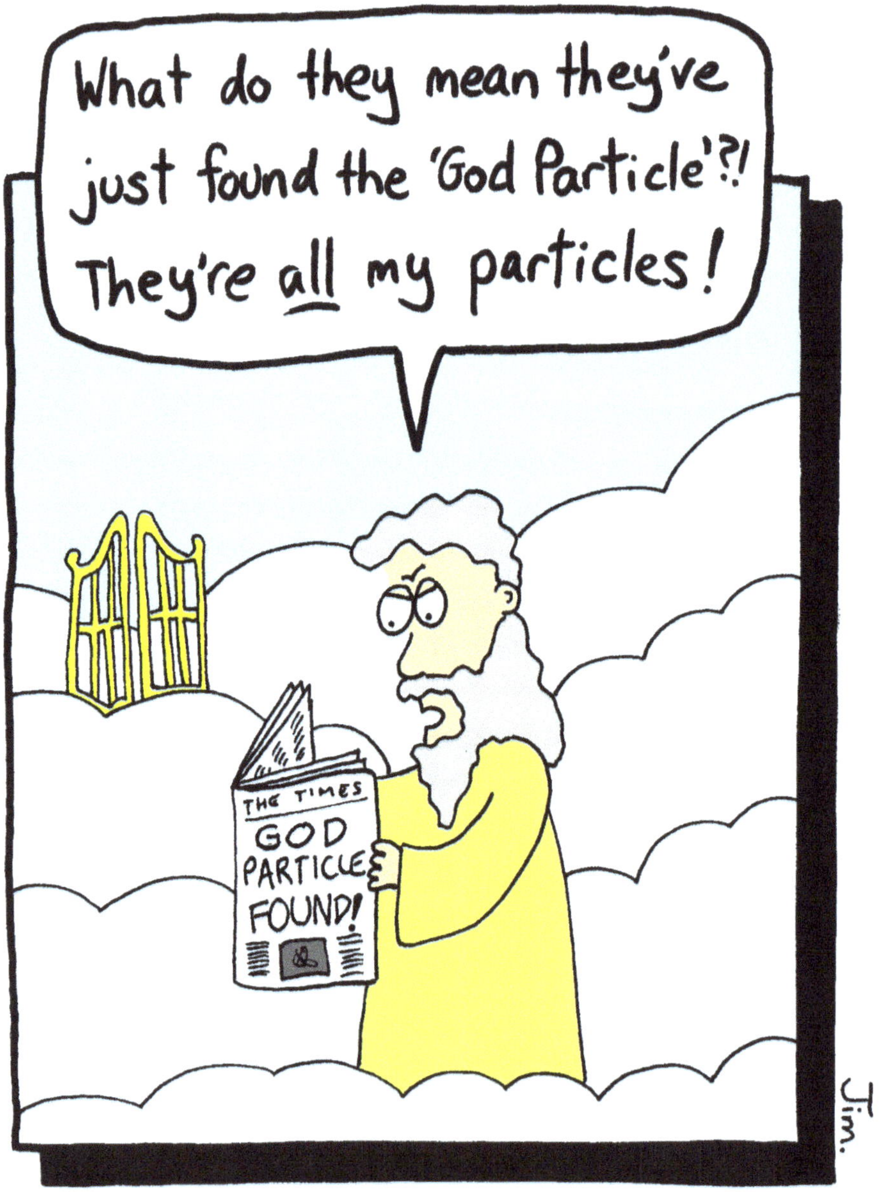
What do they mean they've just found the 'God Particle'?! They're all my particles!
THE TIMES
GOD PARTICLE FOUND!
Jim.

"God Particle" Found? "Historic Milestone" From Higgs Boson Hunters – 4 July 2012.
https://news.nationalgeographic.com/news/2012/07/120704-god-particle-higgs-boson-new-cern-science/

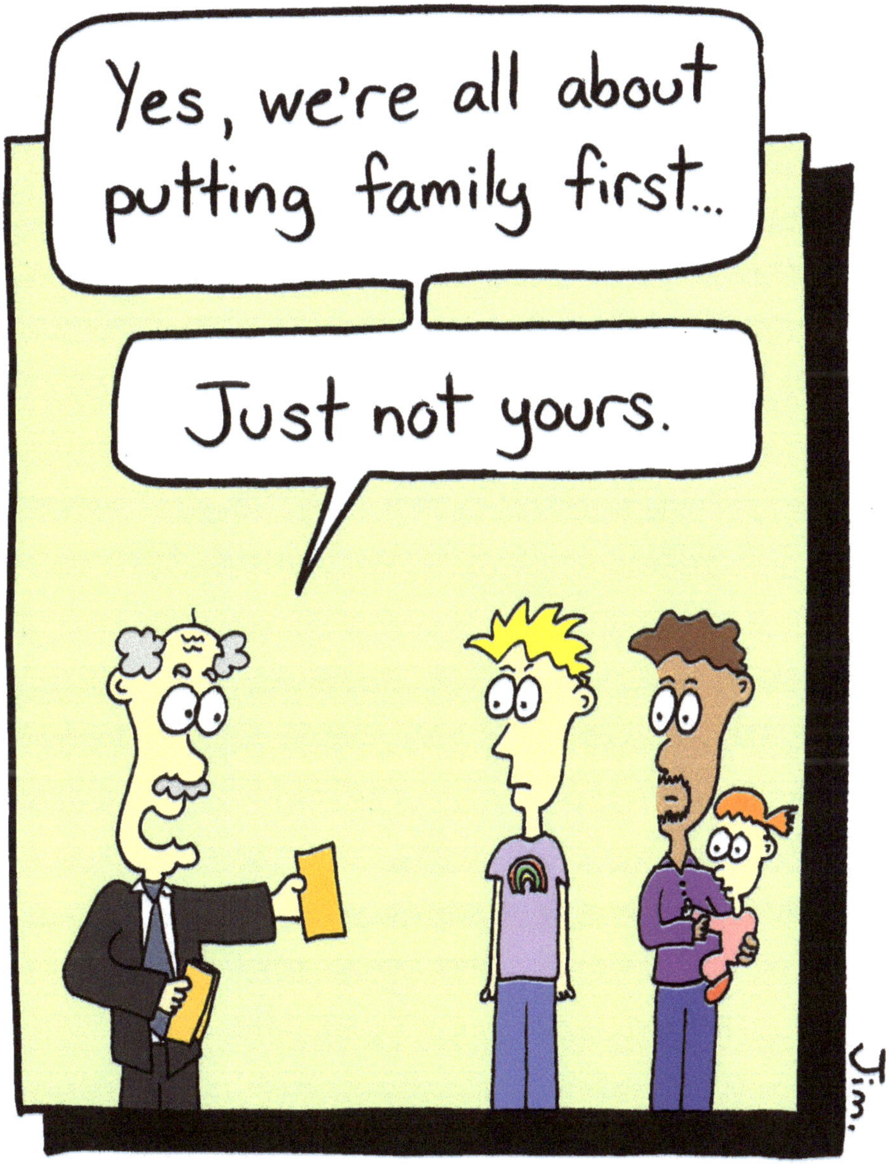
Yes, we're all about putting family first...
Just not yours.
Jim.

50,000 sign against gay marriage – 28 August 2012.
http://www.nzherald.co.nz/nz/news/article.cfm?c_id=1&objectid=10830022

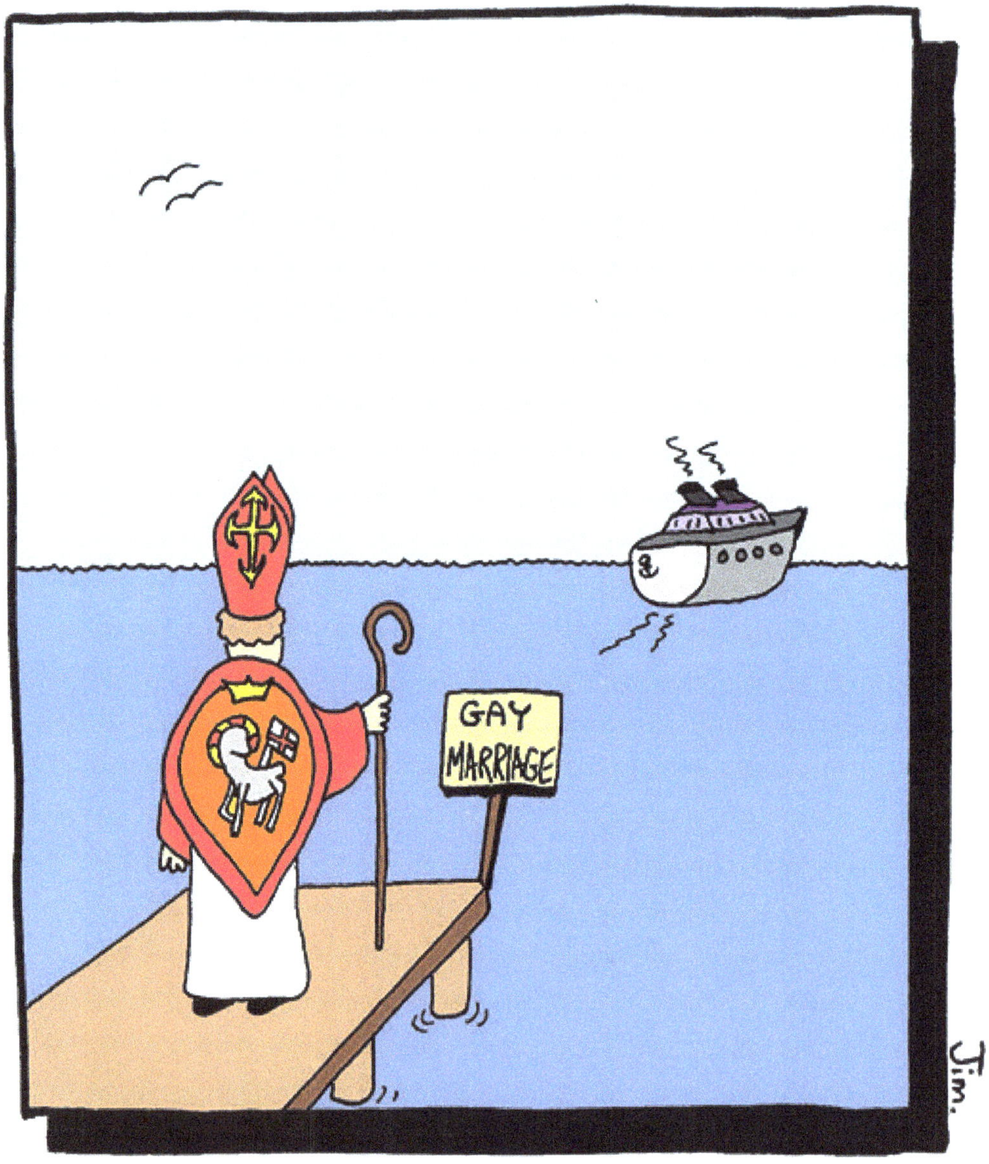
GAY MARRIAGE
Jim.

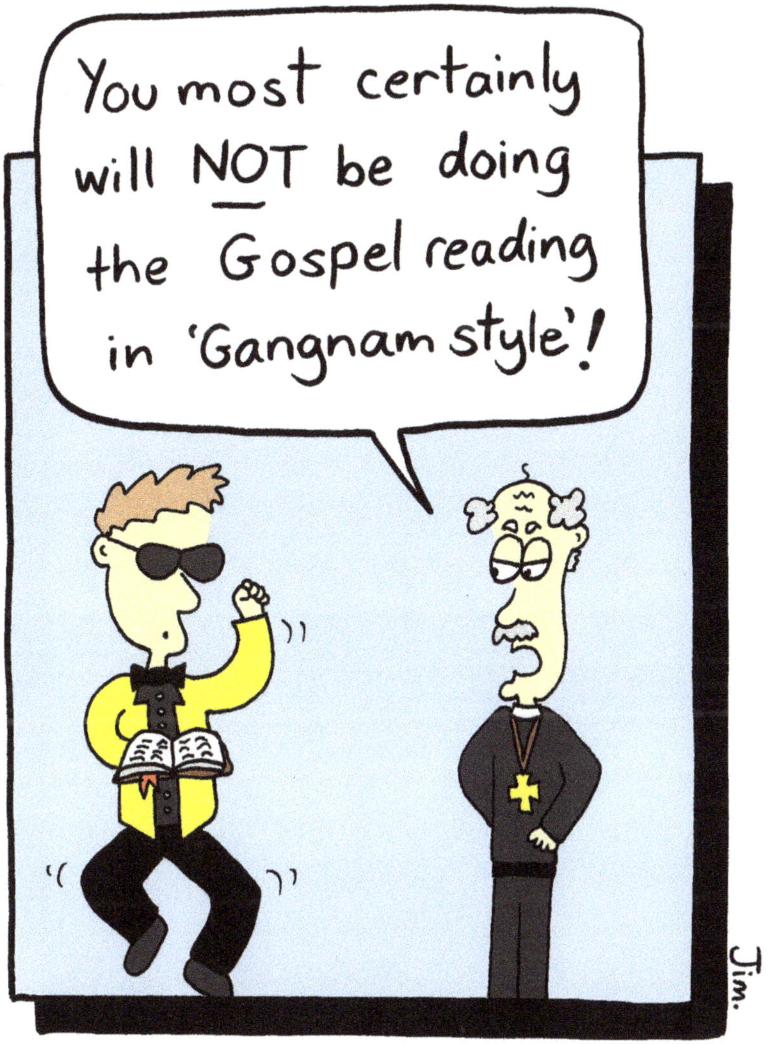
You most certainly will NOT be doing the Gospel reading in 'Gangnam style'!
Jim.

50 Best Songs of 2012 – 5 December 2012.
https://www.rollingstone.com/music/lists/50-best-songs-of-2012-20121205/psy-gangnam-style-19691231

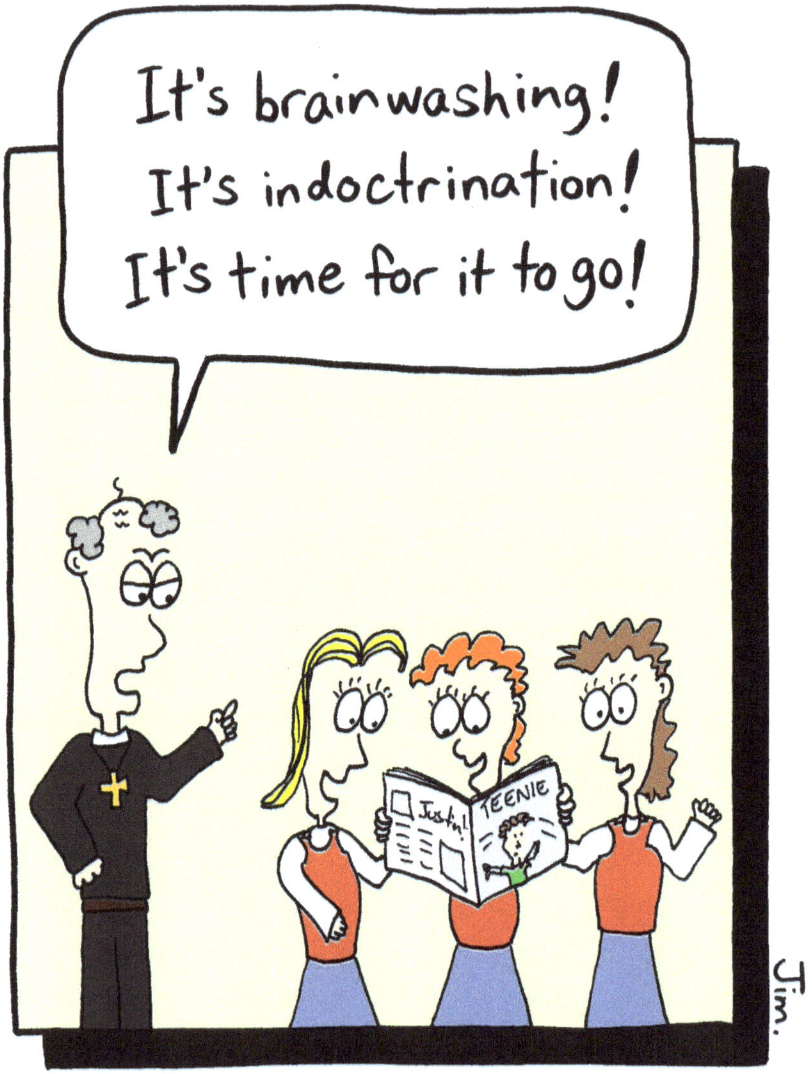
It's brainwashing!
It's indoctrination!
It's time for it to go!
Justin!
TEENIE
Jim.

Reverend Olsen was not a fan of the 'Bieber in Schools' programme.

Justin Bieber madness, Auckland – 2012.
https://www.youtube.com/watch?v=qaMjp7Afr_4

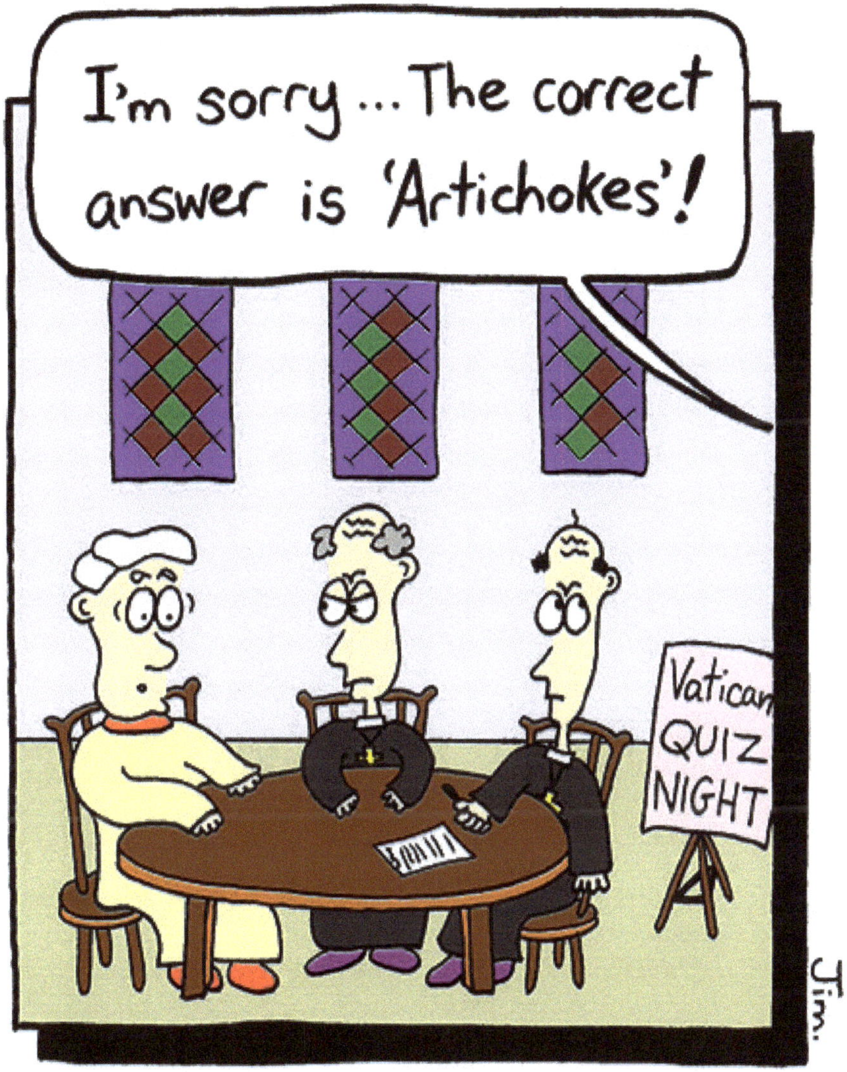
I'm sorry... The correct answer is 'Artichokes'!
Vatican QUIZ NIGHT
Jim.

After his resignation, there were times when Benedict XVI really missed being infallible.

Pope Benedict Resigns – 28 February 2013.
https://www.history.com/this-day-in-history/pope-benedict-resigns

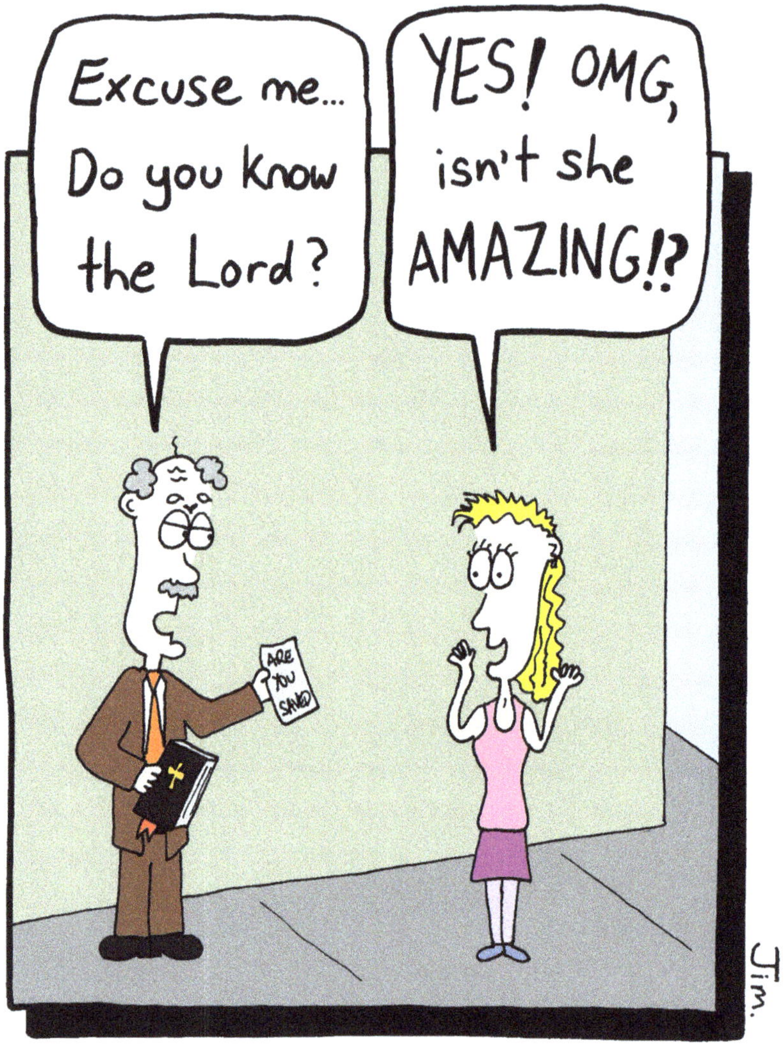
Excuse me... Do you know the Lord?
YES! OMG, isn't she AMAZING!?
ARE YOU SAVED
Jim.

Things had gotten weird for Howard's street evangelism ministry since Ella Yelich-O'Connor's song went to Number One.

Kiwi songbird with Universal appeal – 12 March 2013.
http://www.nzherald.co.nz/entertainment/news/article.cfm?c_id=1501119&objectid=10870642

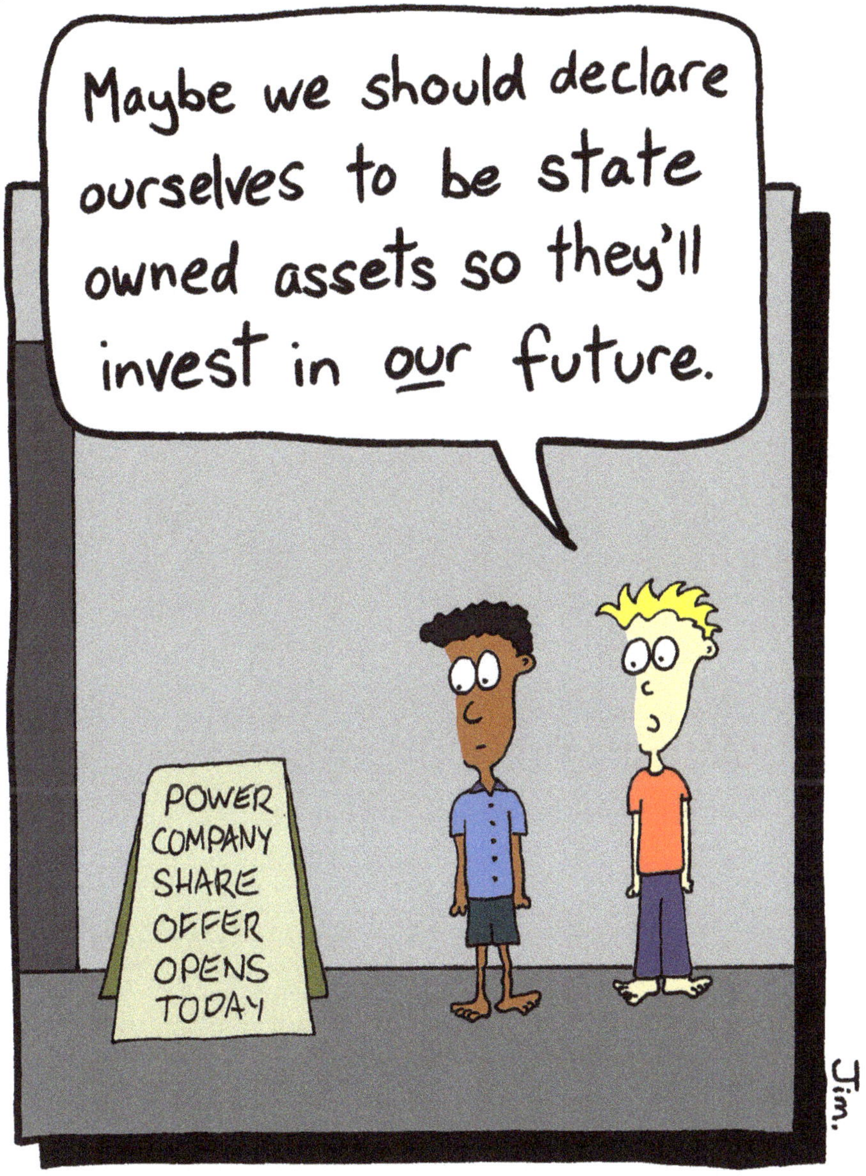
Maybe we should declare ourselves to be state owned assets so they'll invest in our future.
POWER COMPANY SHARE OFFER OPENS TODAY
Jim.

Mighty River Power share offer opens – 15 April 2013.
http://www.scoop.co.nz/stories/PA1304/S00264/mighty-river-power-share-offer-opens.htm

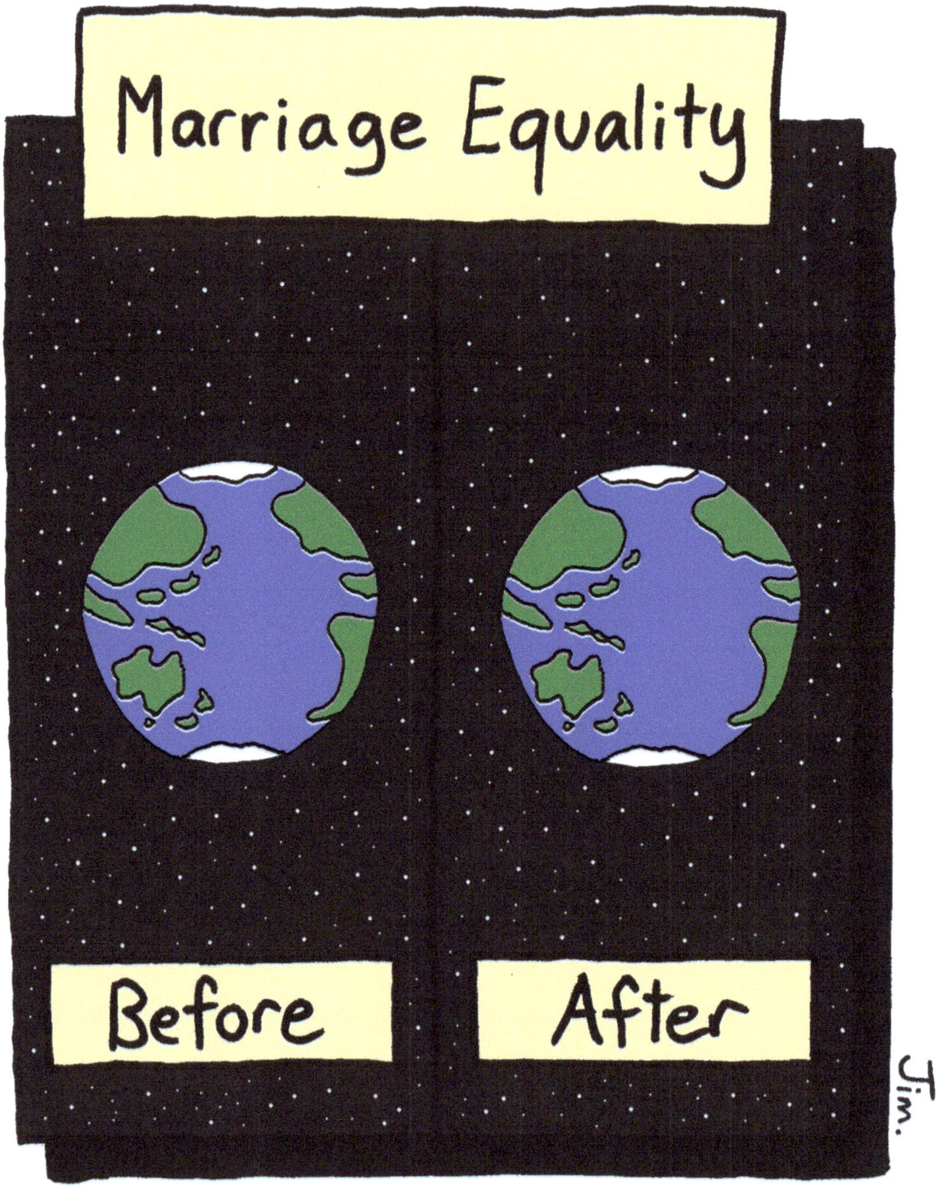
Marriage Equality
Before
After
Jim.

NZ legalises same-sex marriage – 18 April 2013.
http://www.abc.net.au/news/2013-04-17/nz-legalises-same-sex-marriage/4635086

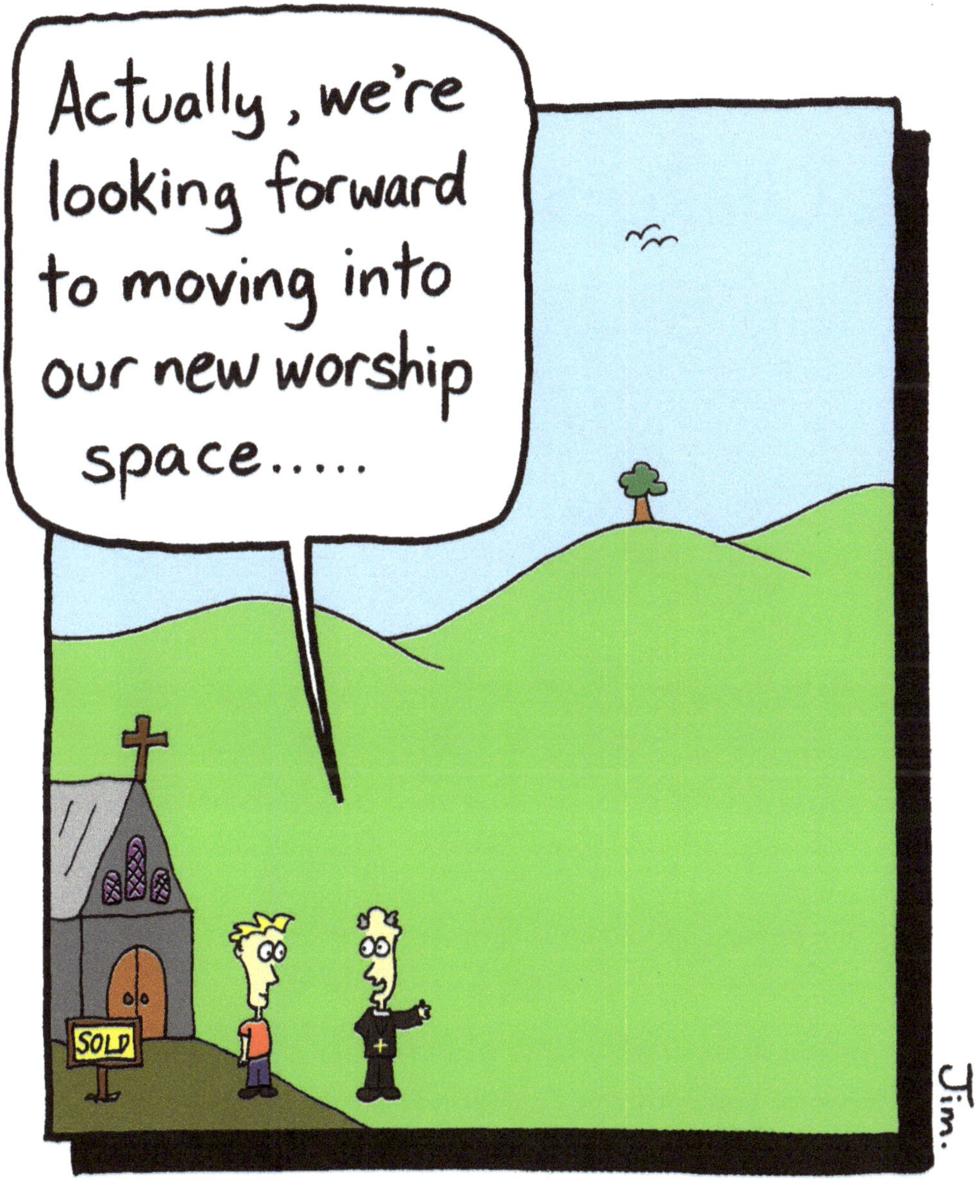
Actually, we're looking forward to moving into our new worship space.....
SOLD
Jim.

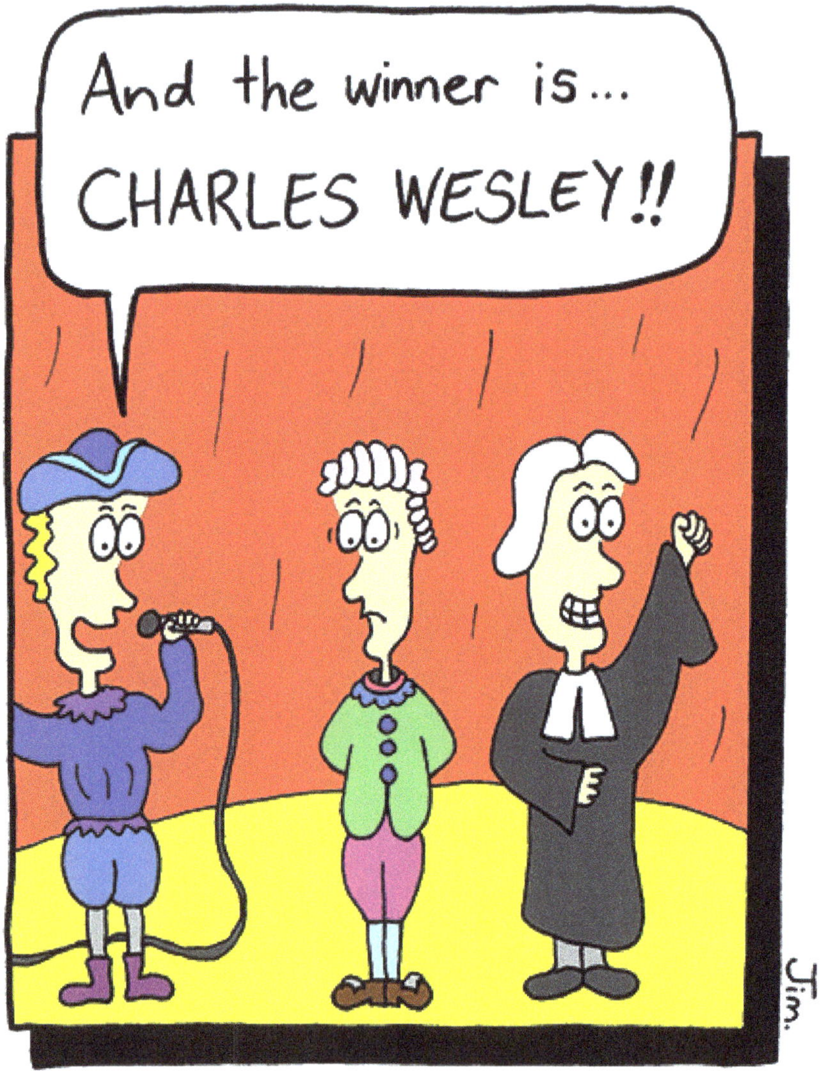
And the winner is...
CHARLES WESLEY!!
Jim.

No-one remembers Gottlieb Munch, runner-up in the 1738 season of 'The Hymn Factor'.

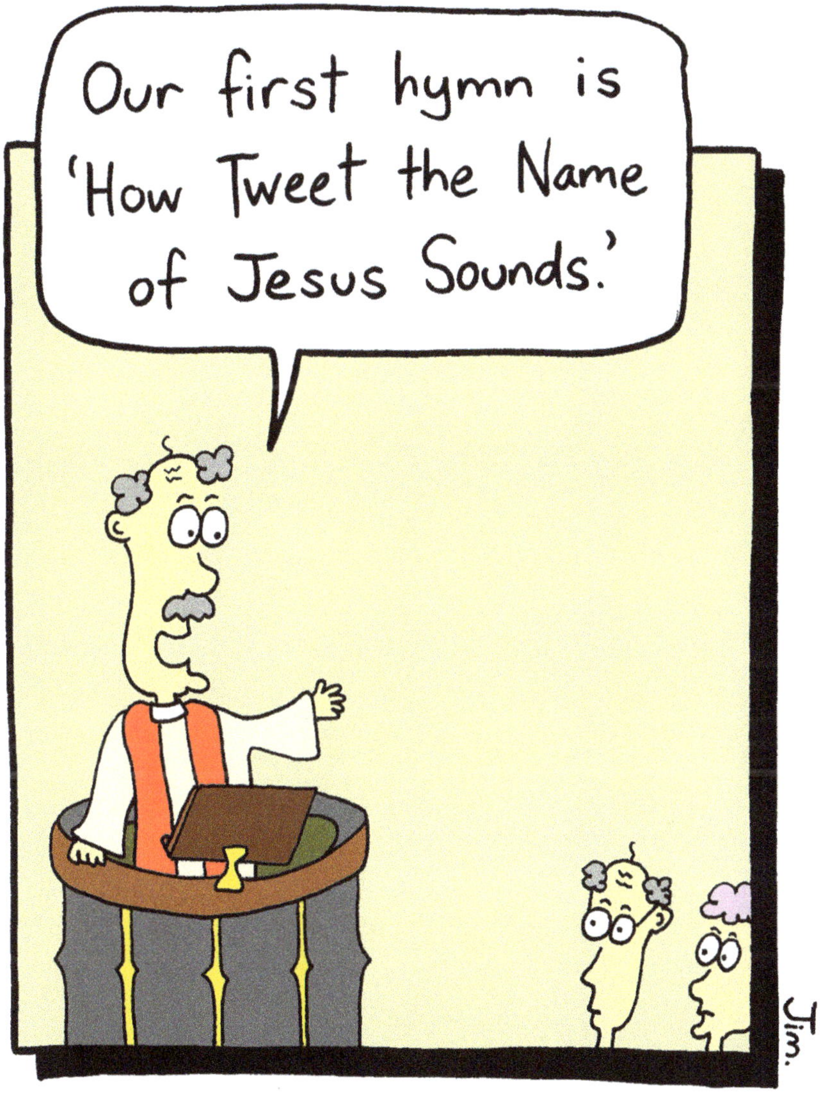
Our first hymn is 'How Tweet the Name of Jesus Sounds.'
Jim.

And with that, St Clive's first ever social media ministry was underway.

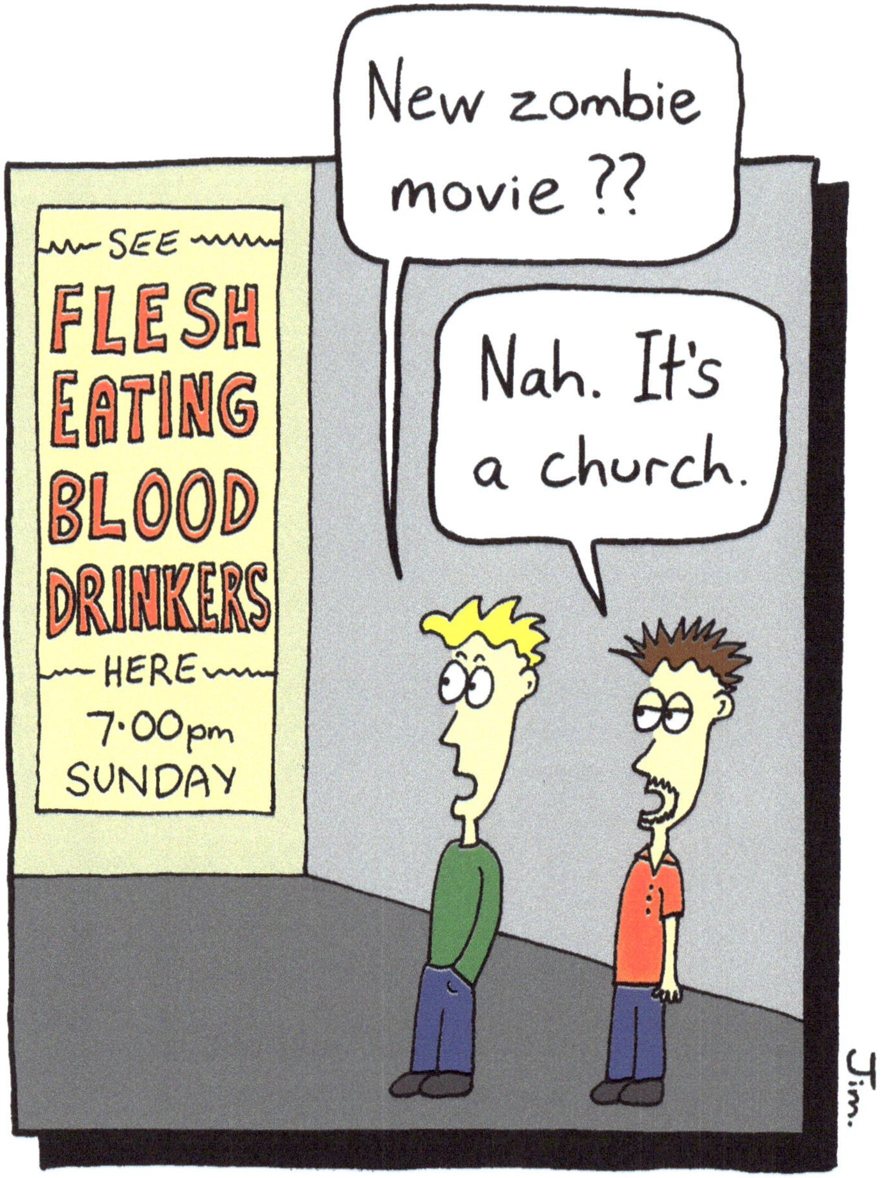

~SEE~
FLESH
EATING
BLOOD
DRINKERS
~HERE~
7·00pm
SUNDAY
New zombie movie??
Nah. It's a church.
Jim.

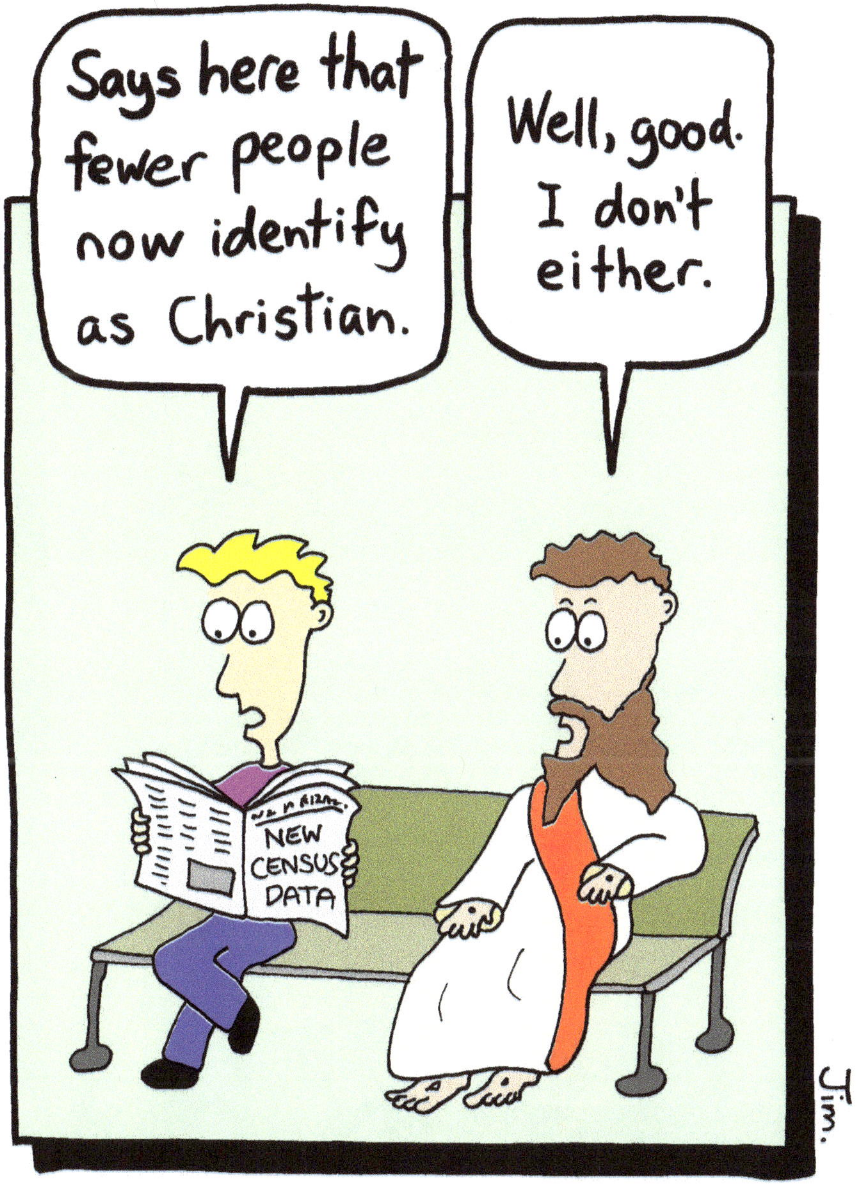
Says here that fewer people now identify as Christian.
Well, good. I don't either.
NEW CENSUS DATA
Jim.

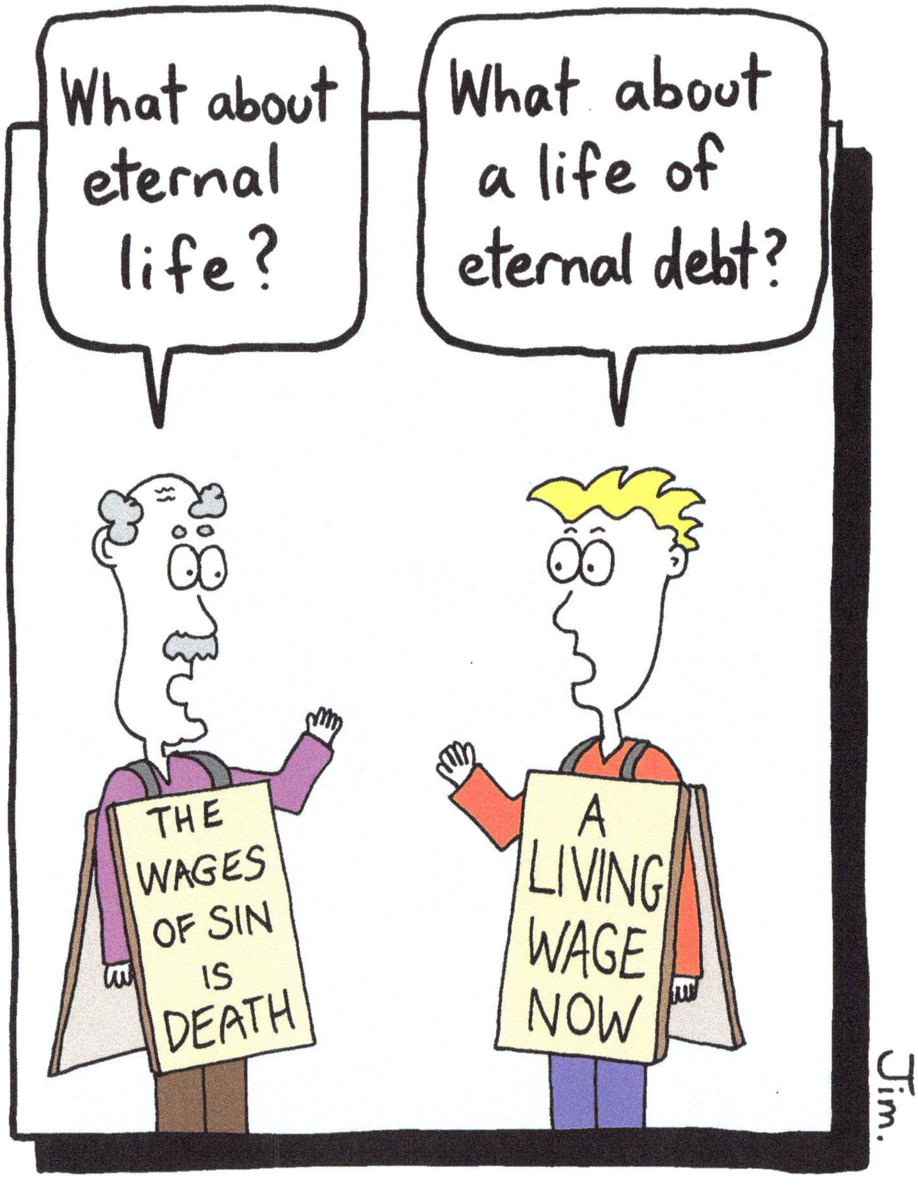
What about eternal life?
What about a life of eternal debt?
THE WAGES OF SIN IS DEATH
A LIVING WAGE NOW
Jim.

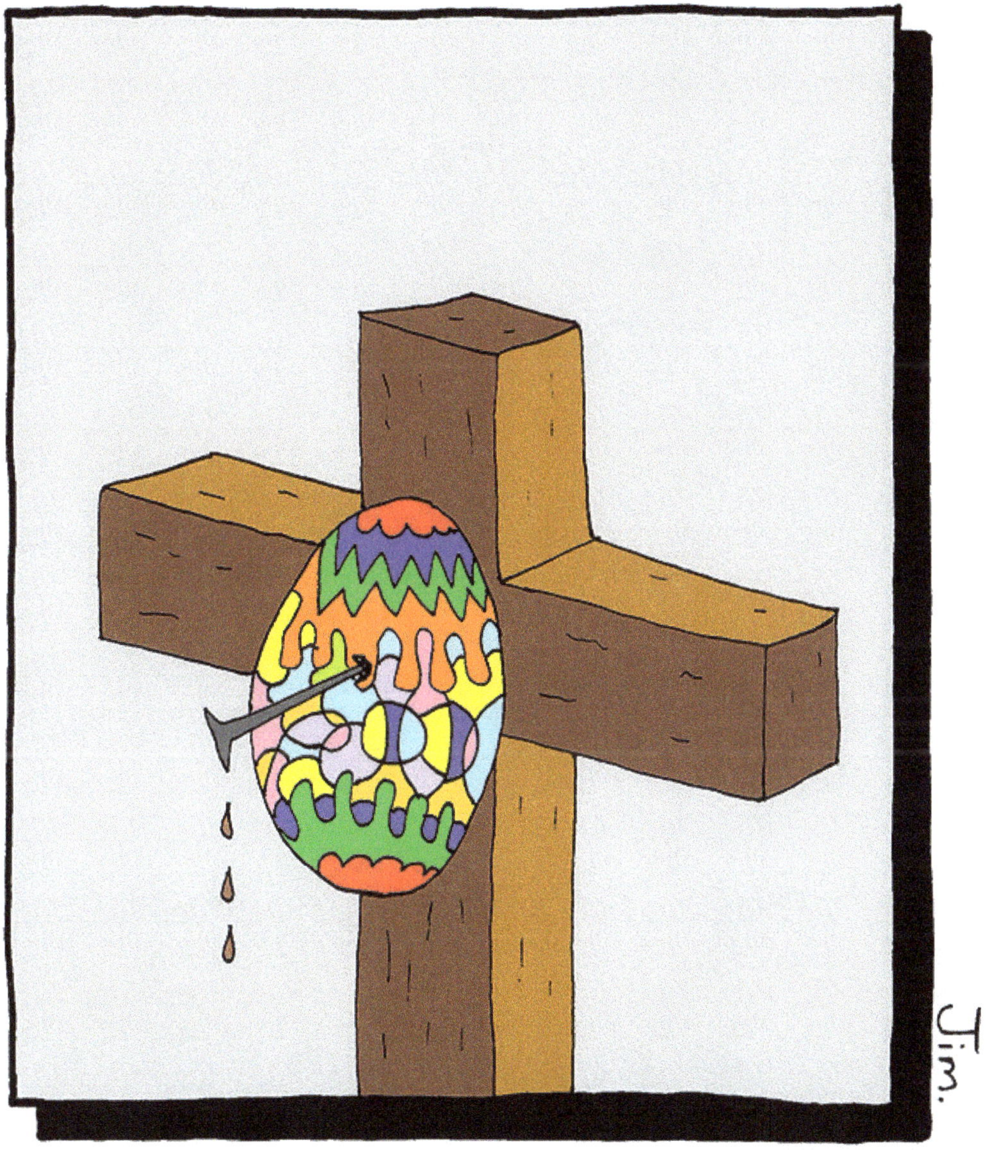
Jim.

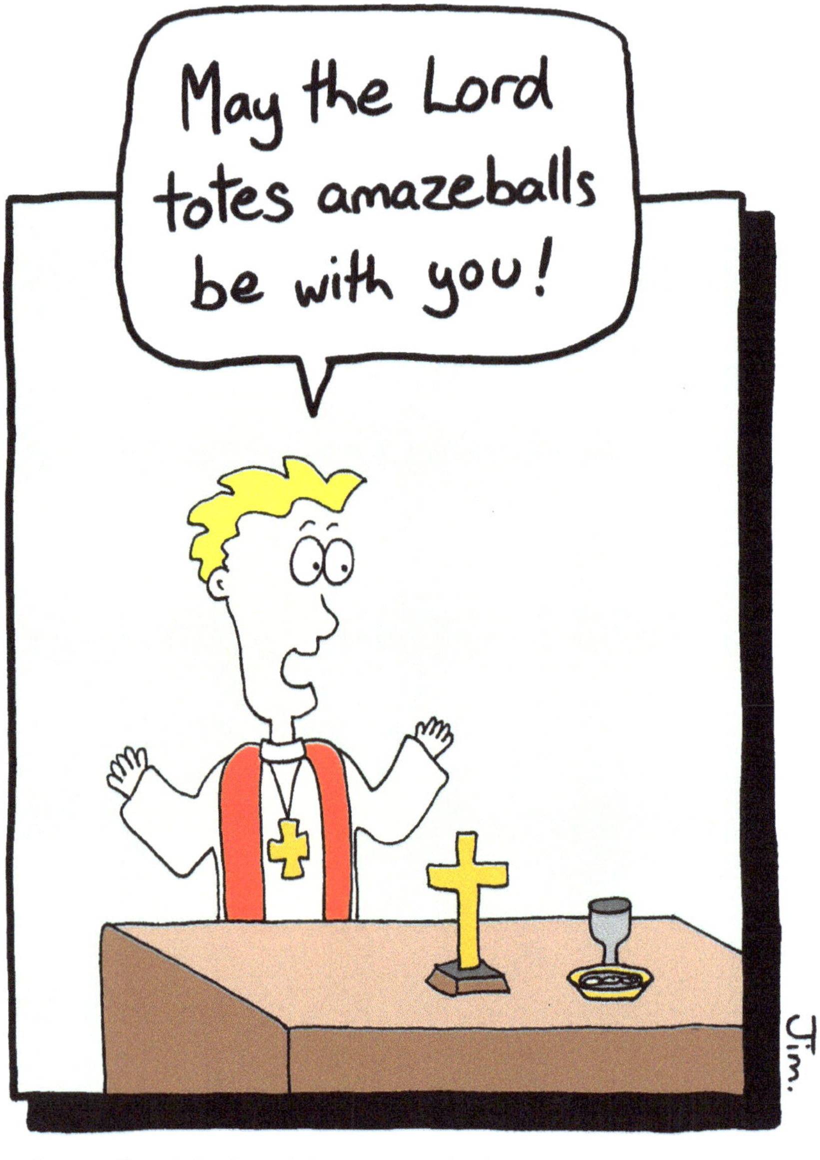
May the Lord totes amazeballs be with you!
Jim.

Rev Smith had been mightily inspired by the Fresh Expressions conference.

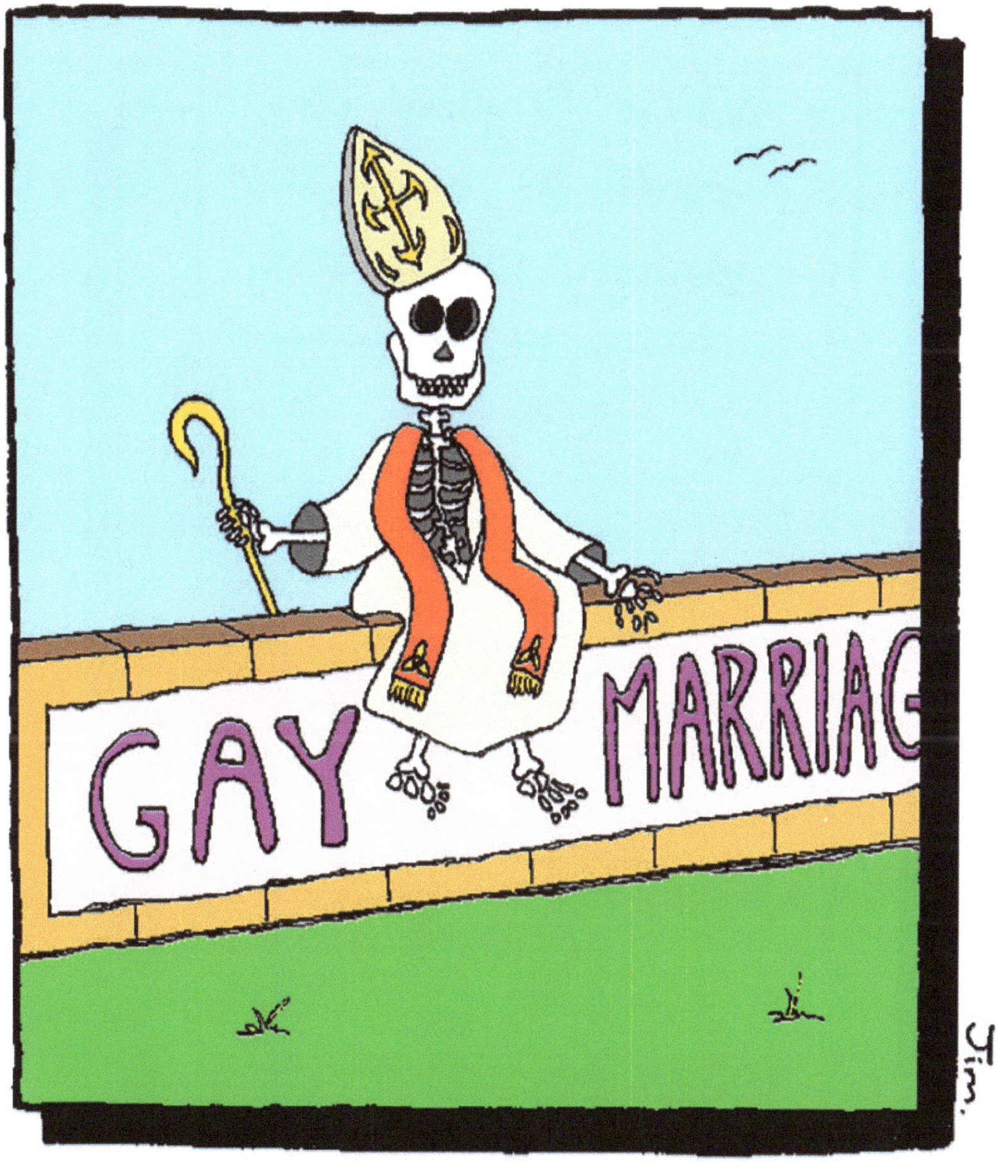
GAY
MARRIAG
Jim.

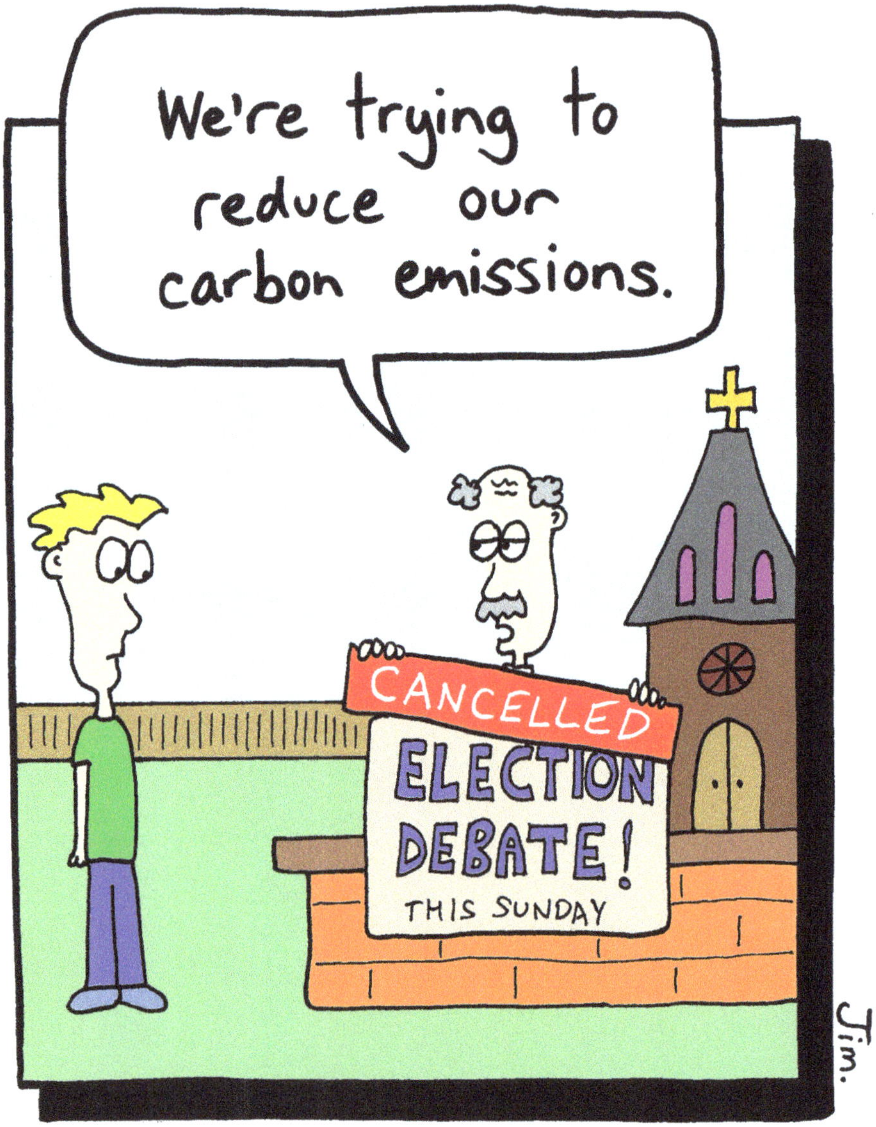
We're trying to reduce our carbon emissions.
CANCELLED
ELECTION DEBATE!
THIS SUNDAY
Jim.

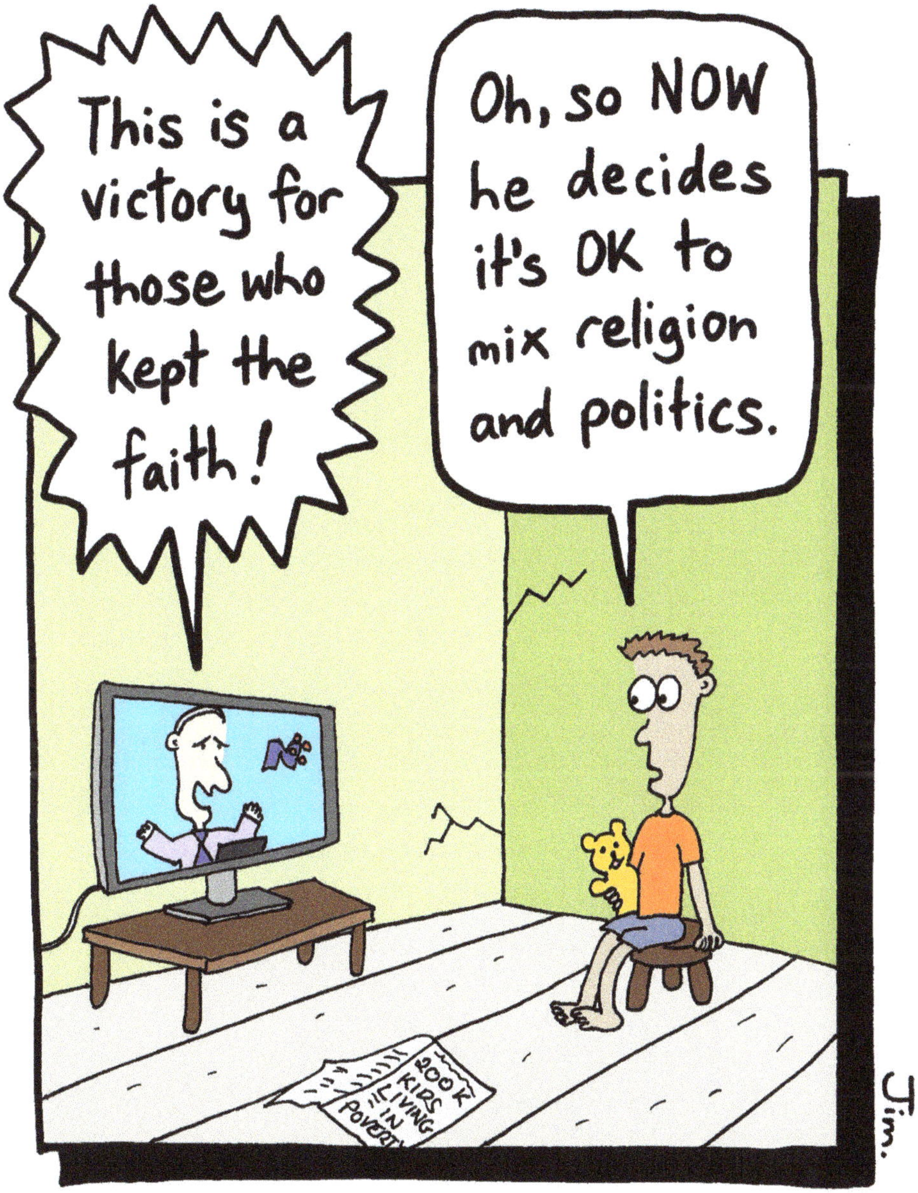
This is a victory for those who kept the faith!
Oh, so NOW he decides it's OK to mix religion and politics.
200K KIDS LIVING IN POVERTY
Jim.

National Party sweeps to victory – 21 September 2014.
http://www.radionz.co.nz/news/political/255124/national-party-sweeps-to-victory

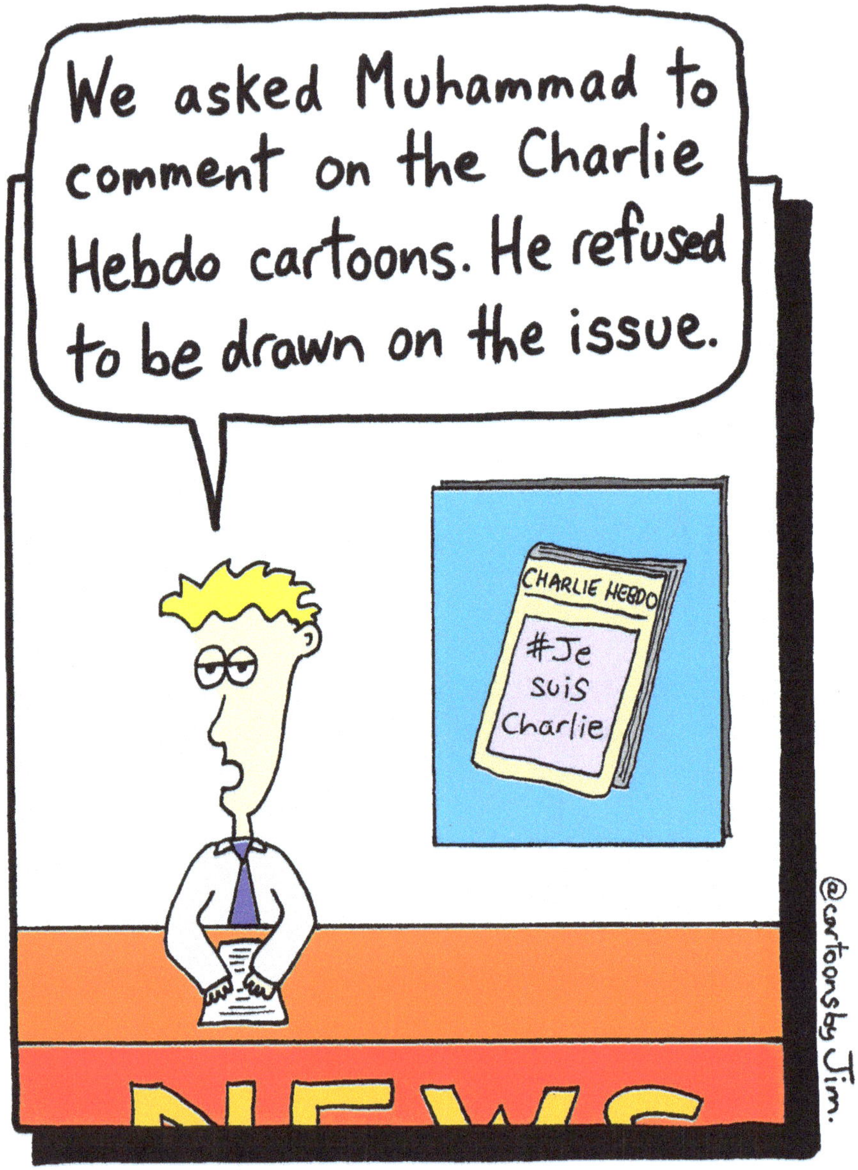
We asked Muhammad to comment on the Charlie Hebdo cartoons. He refused to be drawn on the issue.
CHARLIE HEBDO
#Je suis Charlie
@cartoonsbyJim.

Charlie Hebdo attack: Three days of terror – 14 January 2015.
http://www.bbc.com/news/world-europe-30708237

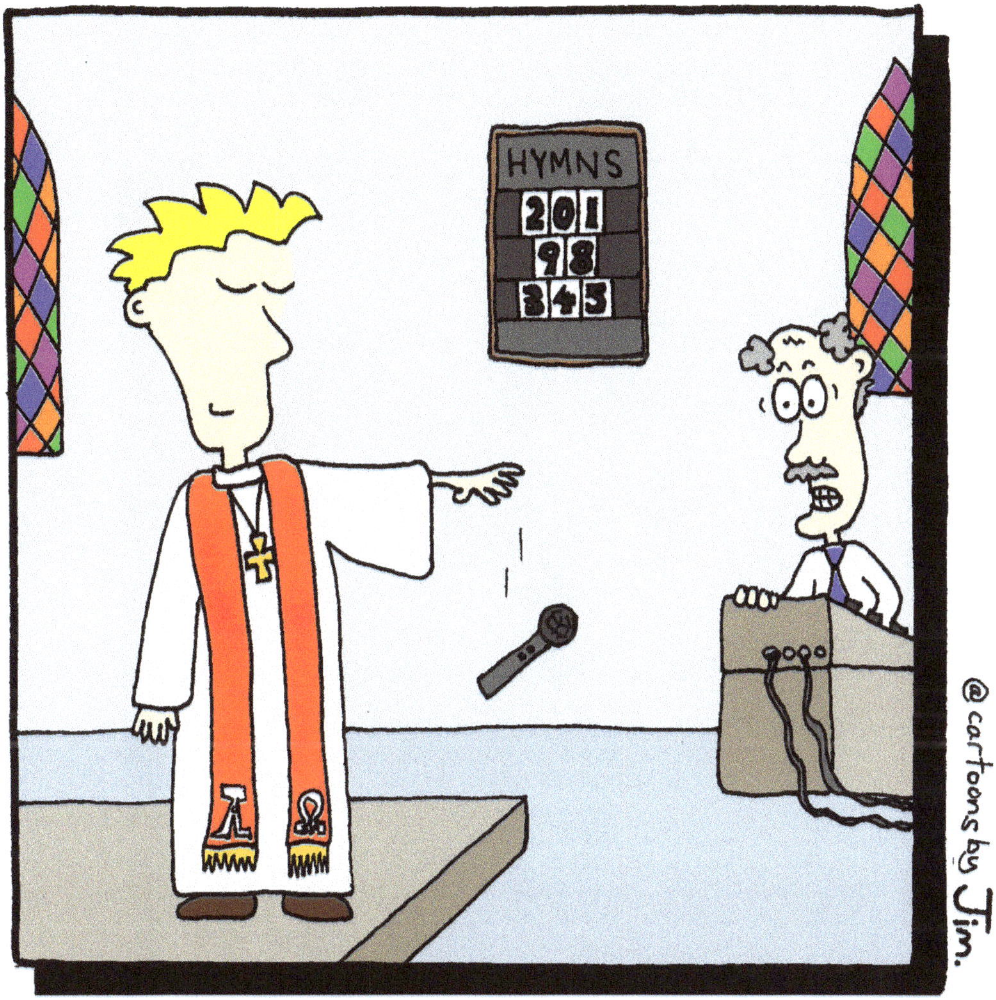
HYMNS
201
98
343
@cartoons by Jim.

While he agreed it had been a particularly good sermon, Harold the sound engineer would have preferred that Pastor Nigel had not concluded it with a mic drop.

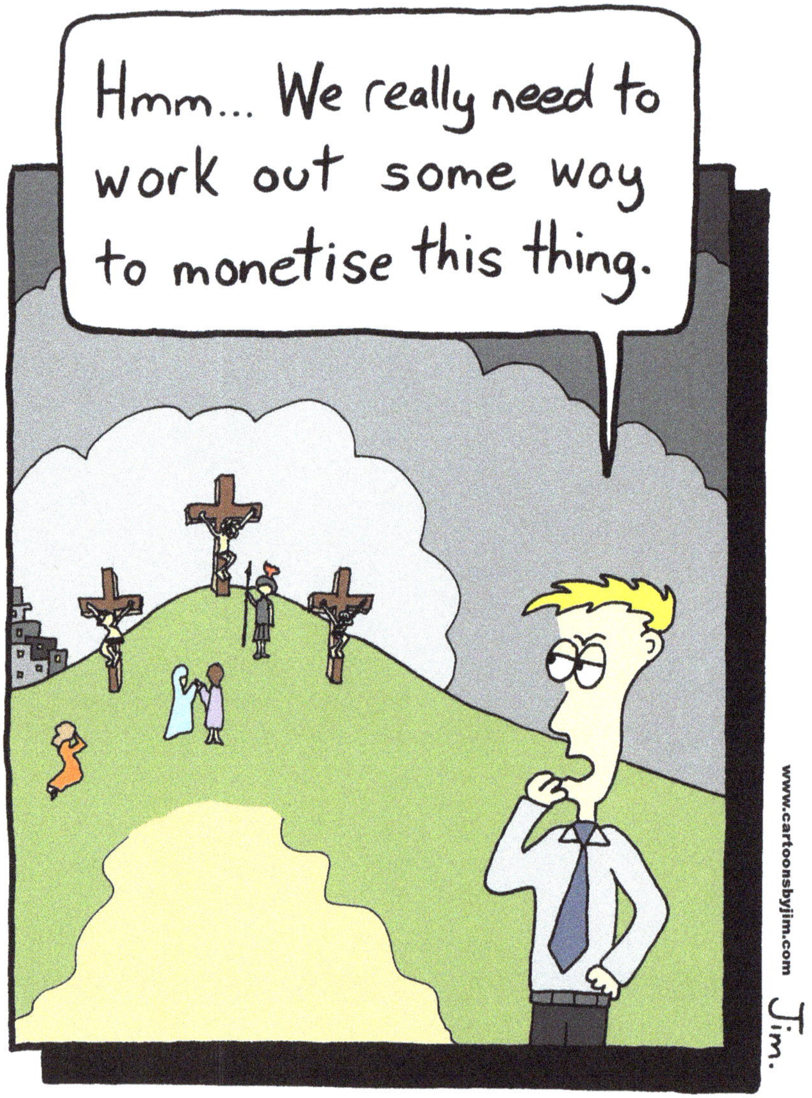
Hmm... We really need to work out some way to monetise this thing.
www.cartoonsbyjim.com
Jim.

Easterpreneur

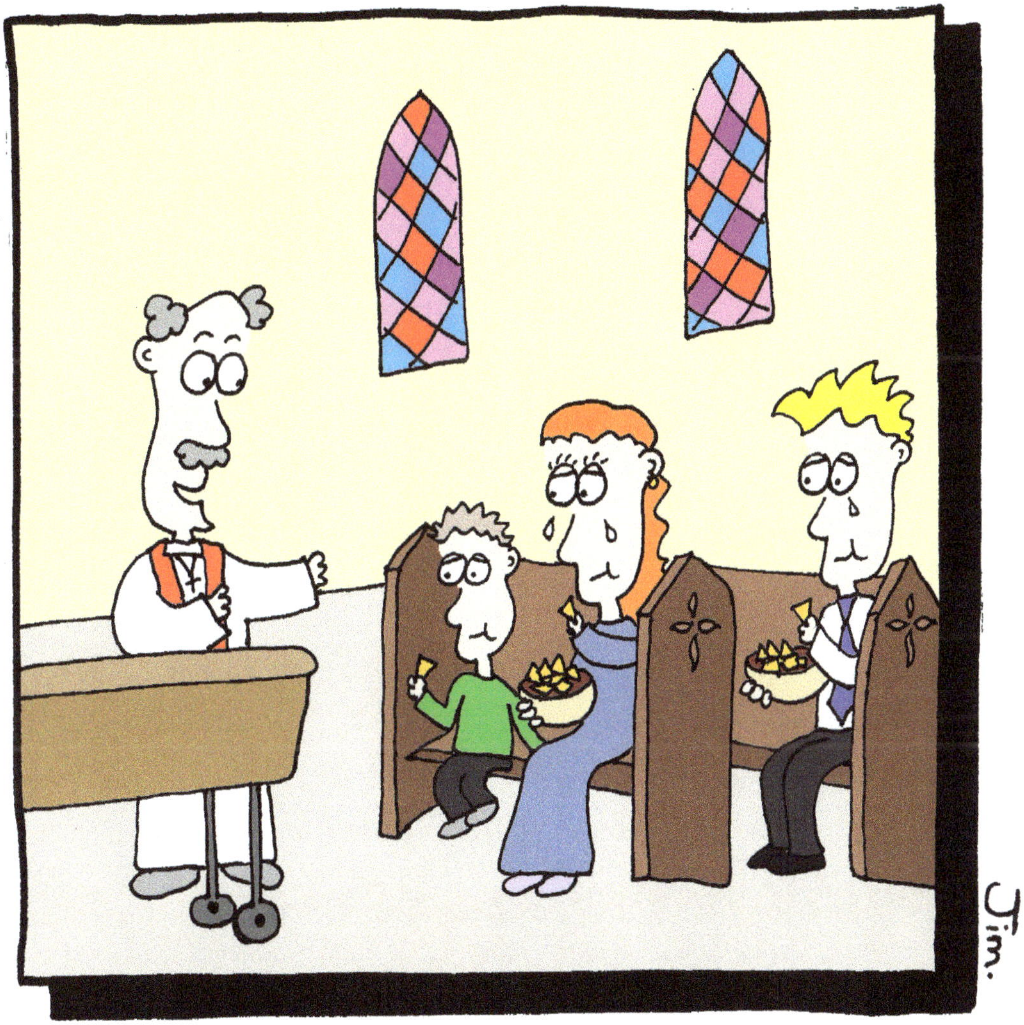

Jim.

Rev. Smith's radical 'less religion, more nachos' approach to funerals was proving popular.

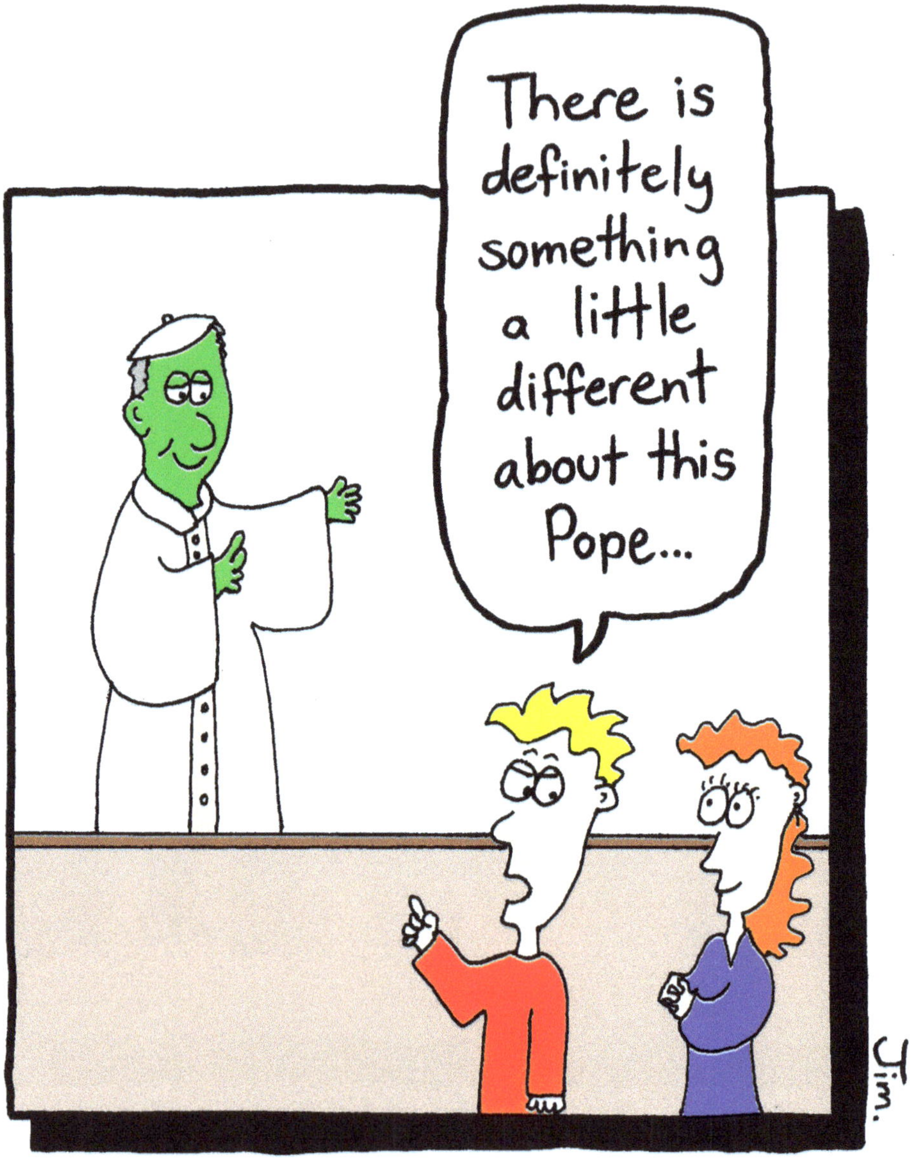
There is definitely something a little different about this Pope...
Jim.

What Matters to the Heart: Pope Francis, Climate Change, and Sustainability – 12 August 2016.
https://www.huffingtonpost.com/grace-jisun-kim/what-matters-to-the-heart_b_7976636.html

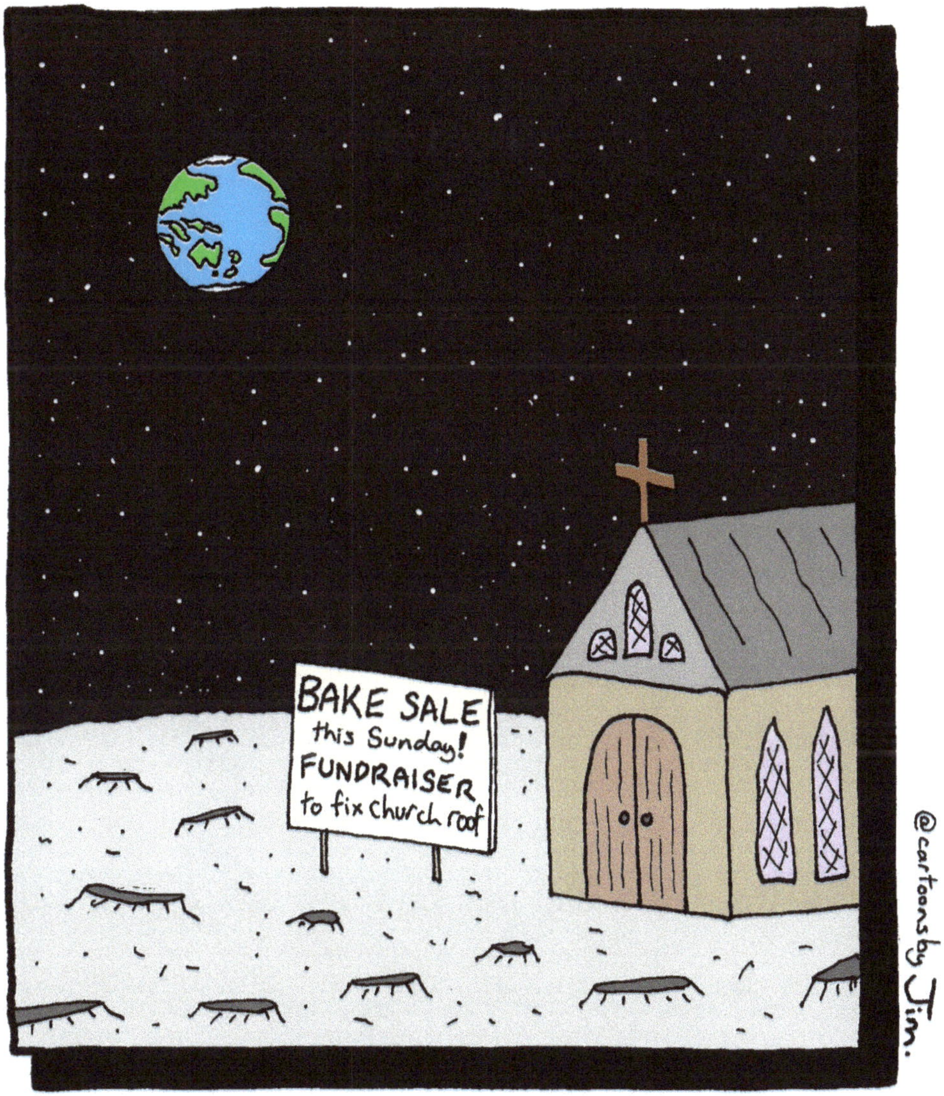
BAKE SALE
this Sunday!
FUNDRAISER
to fix church roof
@cartoonsbyJim.

The Church in 20 years.

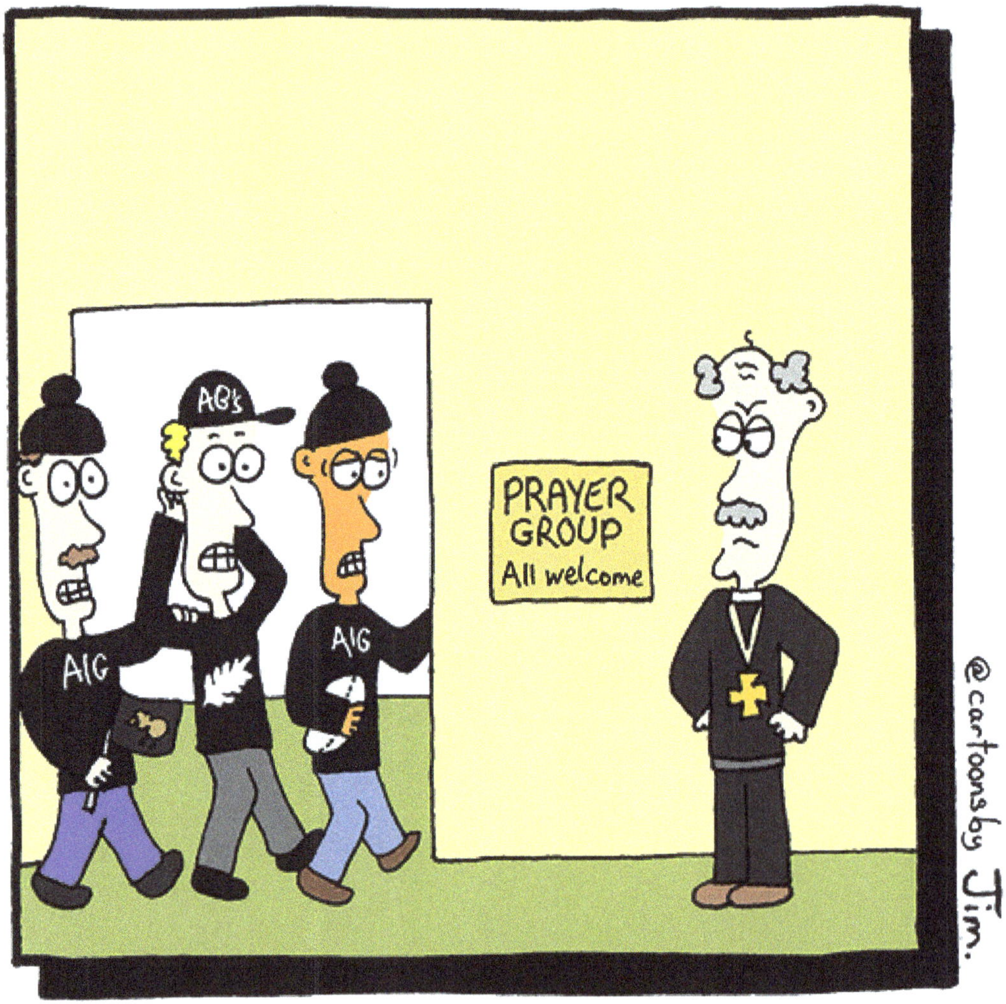
AB's
AIG
AIG
AIG
PRAYER GROUP
All welcome
@cartoonsby Jim.

Rev Smith was perennially perplexed by the quadrennial surge in attendance at his early Sunday morning prayer group.

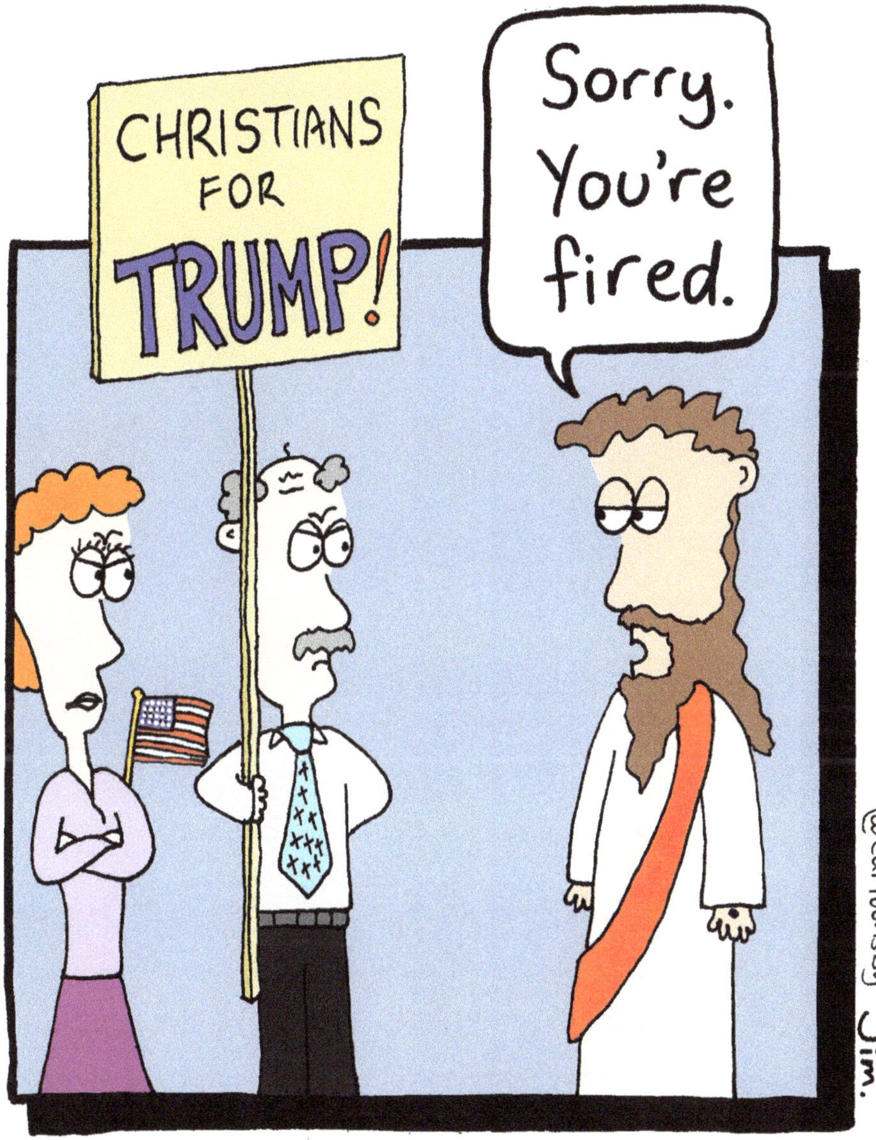
CHRISTIANS FOR TRUMP!
Sorry. You're fired.
@cartoonsby Jim.

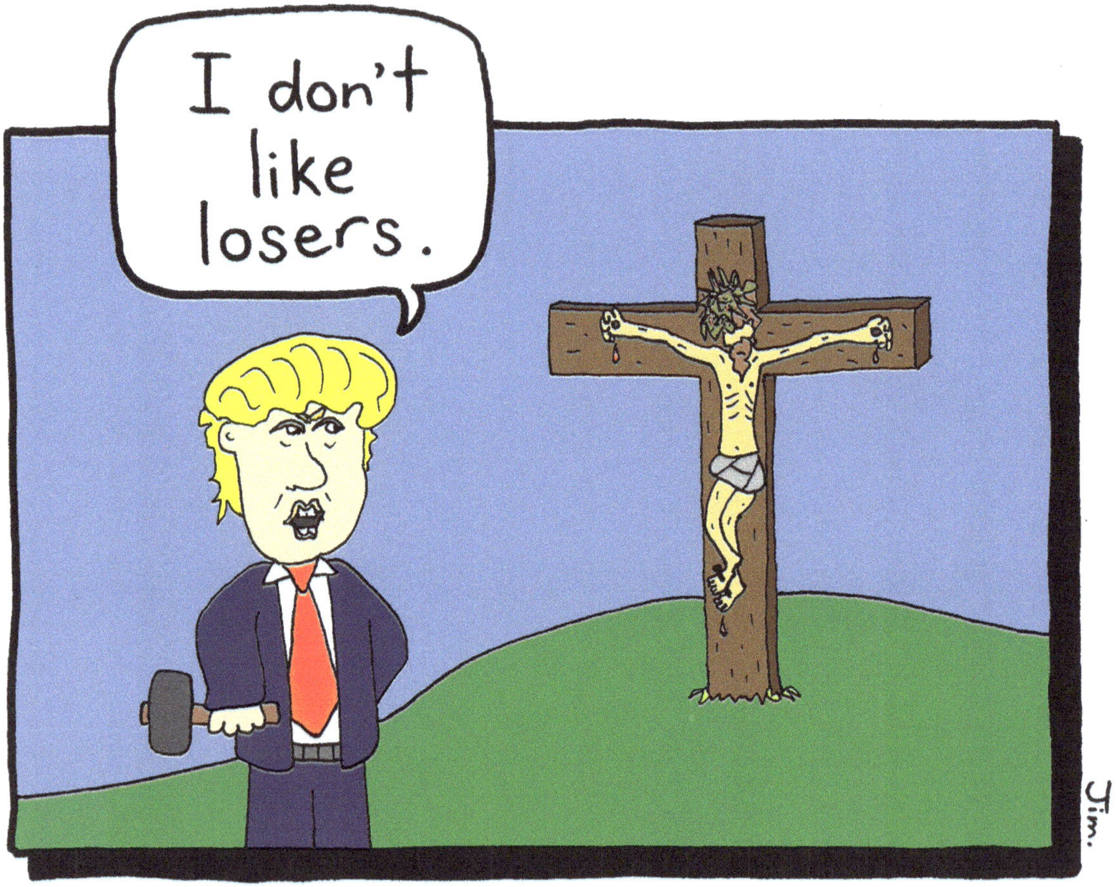
I don't like losers.
Jim.

Auckland church puts up anti-Trump Easter billboard

9 March, 2016

https://www.stuff.co.nz/auckland/local-news/77692248/Auckland-church-puts-up-anti-Trump-Easter-billboard

Church's controversial anti-Trump Easter billboard stolen

25 March, 2016

https://www.stuff.co.nz/auckland/78273471/churchs-controversial-antitrump-easter-billboard-stolen-from-remuera-auckland

Stolen Donald Trump billboard to be resurrected

27 March, 2016

http://www.nzherald.co.nz/nz/news/article.cfm?c_id=1&objectid=11612463

Church Trump billboard defaced with anti-Islam message

10 April, 2016

http://www.newshub.co.nz/home/new-zealand/2016/04/church-trump-billboard-defaced-with-anti-islam-message.html

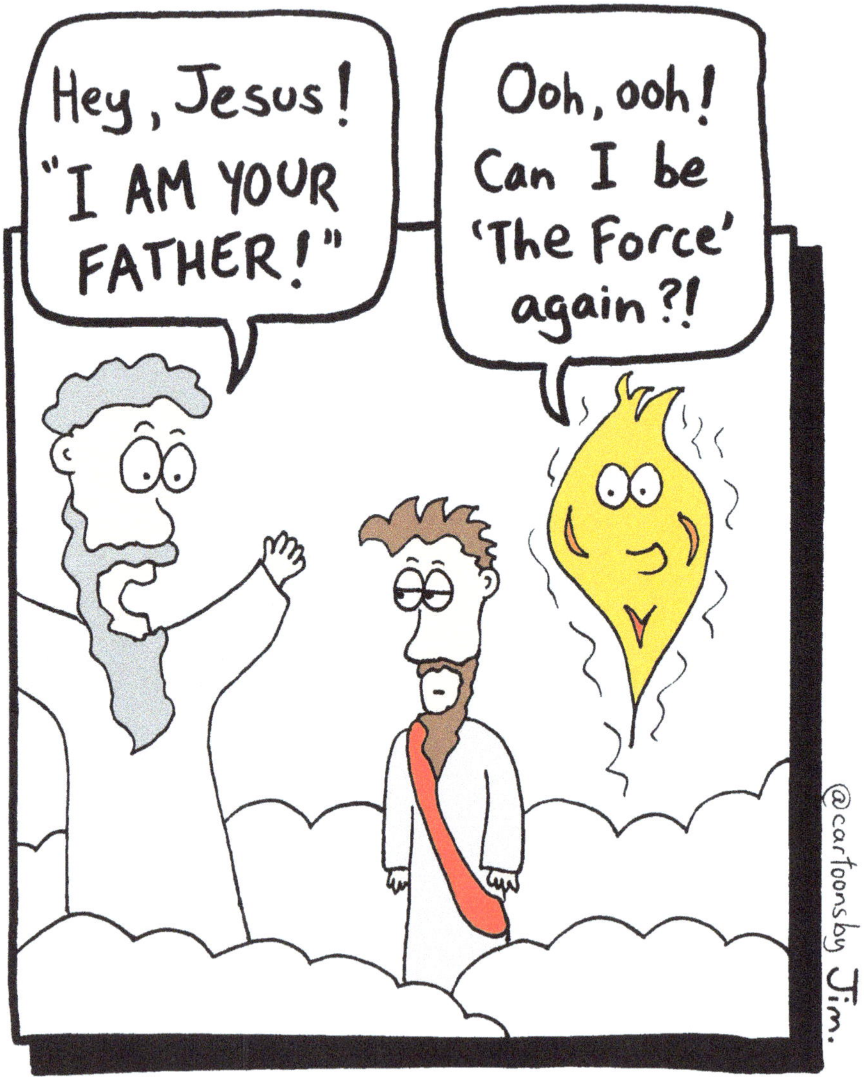
Hey, Jesus! "I AM YOUR FATHER!"
Ooh, ooh! Can I be 'The Force' again?!
@cartoonsbyJim.

Playing 'Star Wars' with the Trinity was becoming a bit tiresome for Jesus.

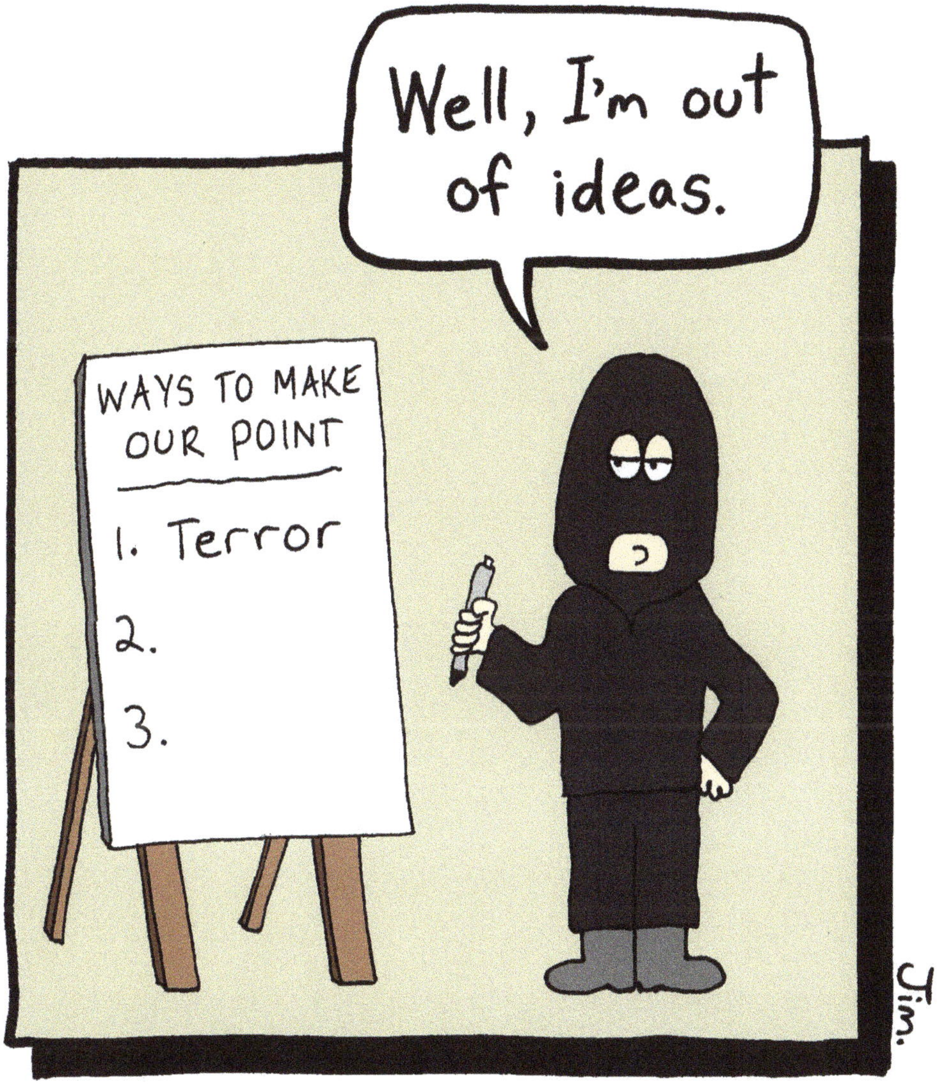
Well, I'm out of ideas.
WAYS TO MAKE OUR POINT
1. Terror
2.
3.
Jim.

The terrorists' whiteboard.

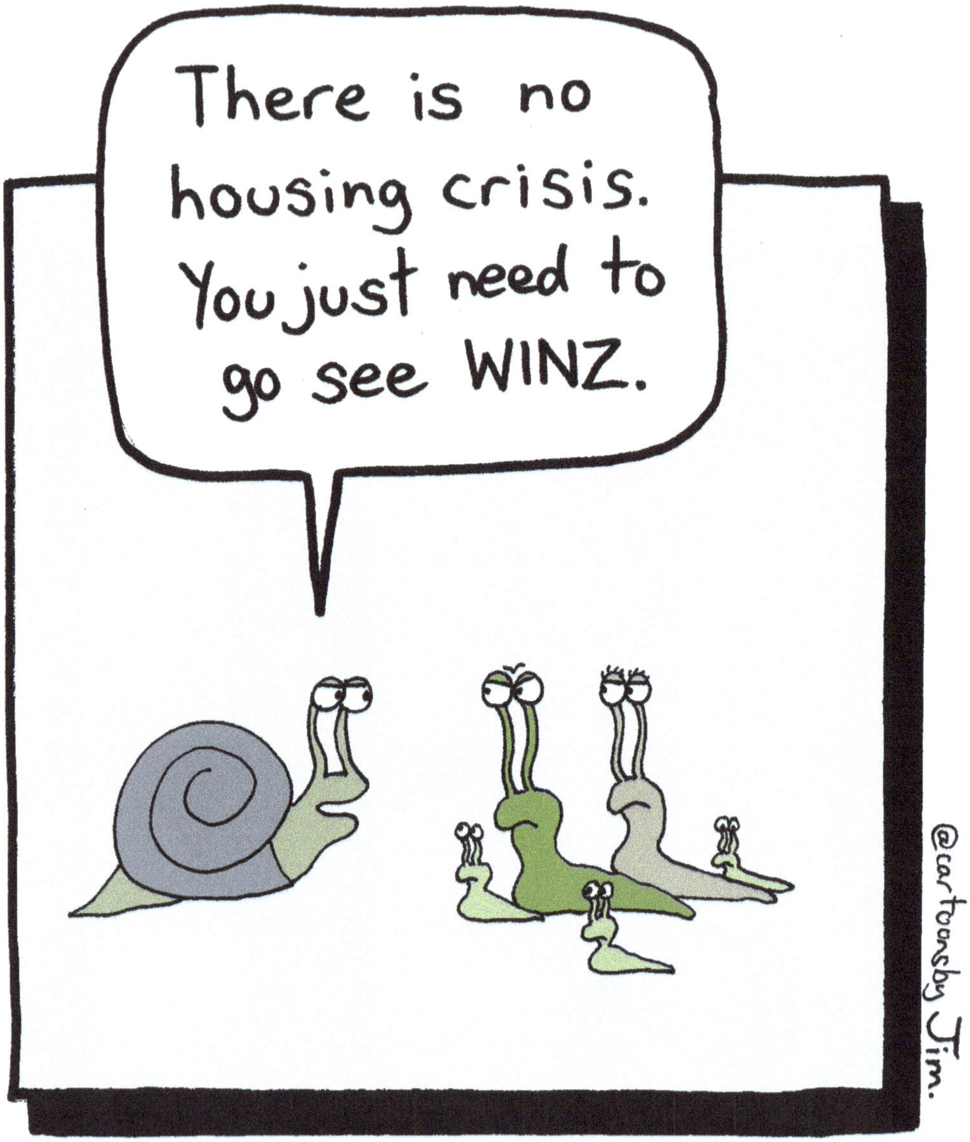
There is no housing crisis. You just need to go see WINZ.
@cartoonsbyJim.

Homelessness has 'been there for a very long time': Prime Minister John Key – 16 May 2016.
https://www.stuff.co.nz/national/politics/80013933/
Homelessness-has-been-there-for-a-very-long-time-Prime-Minister-John-Key

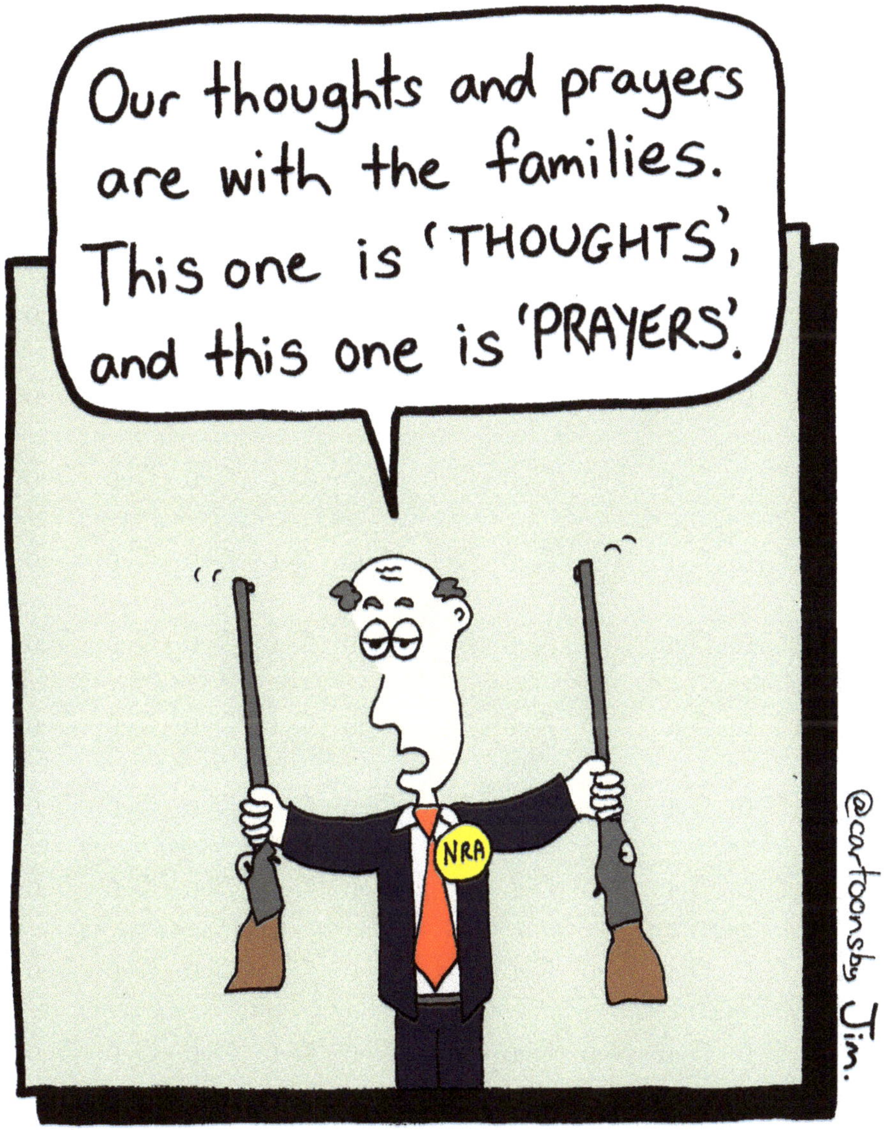
Our thoughts and prayers are with the families. This one is 'THOUGHTS', and this one is 'PRAYERS'.
NRA
@cartoonsby Jim.

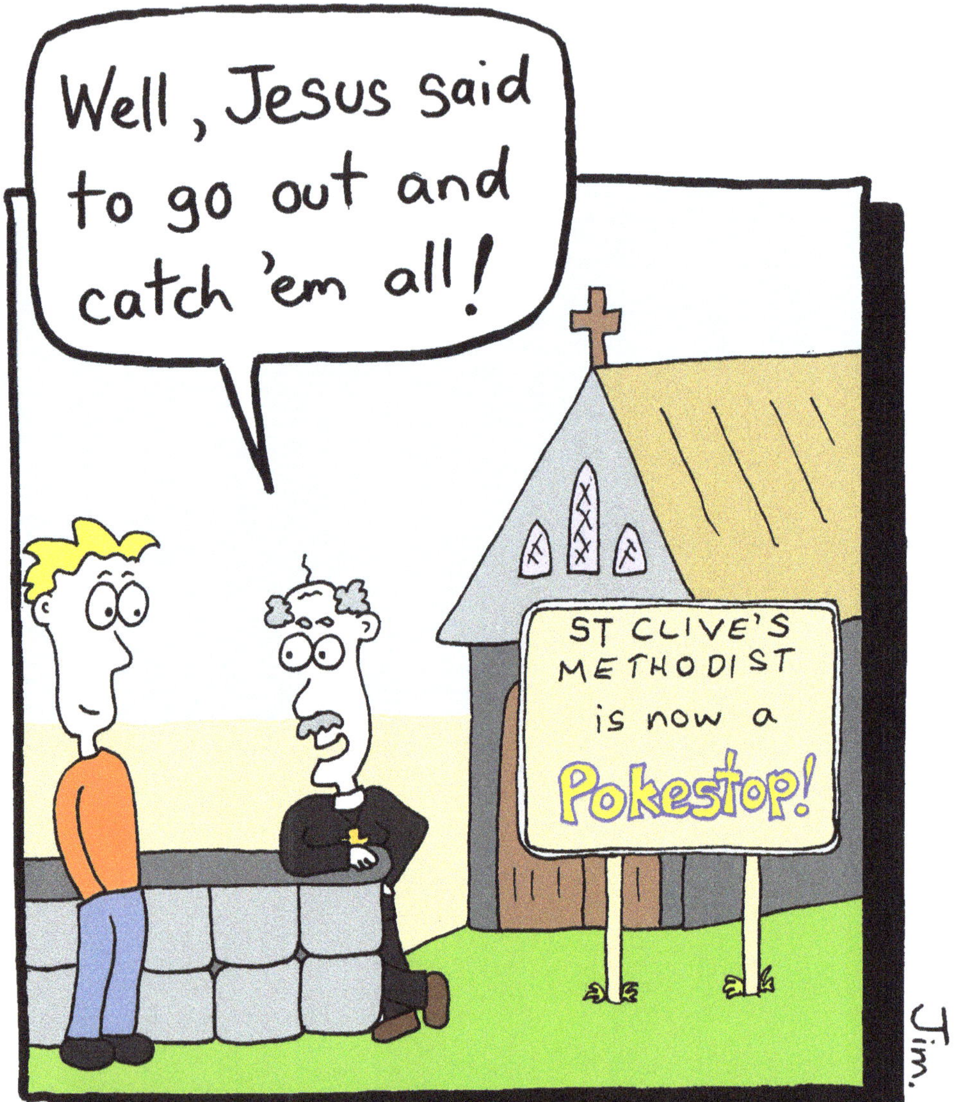
Well, Jesus said to go out and catch 'em all!
ST CLIVE'S METHODIST is now a Pokestop!
Jim.

Pokemon Go: The game that augmented reality – 11 July 2016.
http://www.nzherald.co.nz/technology/news/article.cfm?c_id=5&objectid=11672460

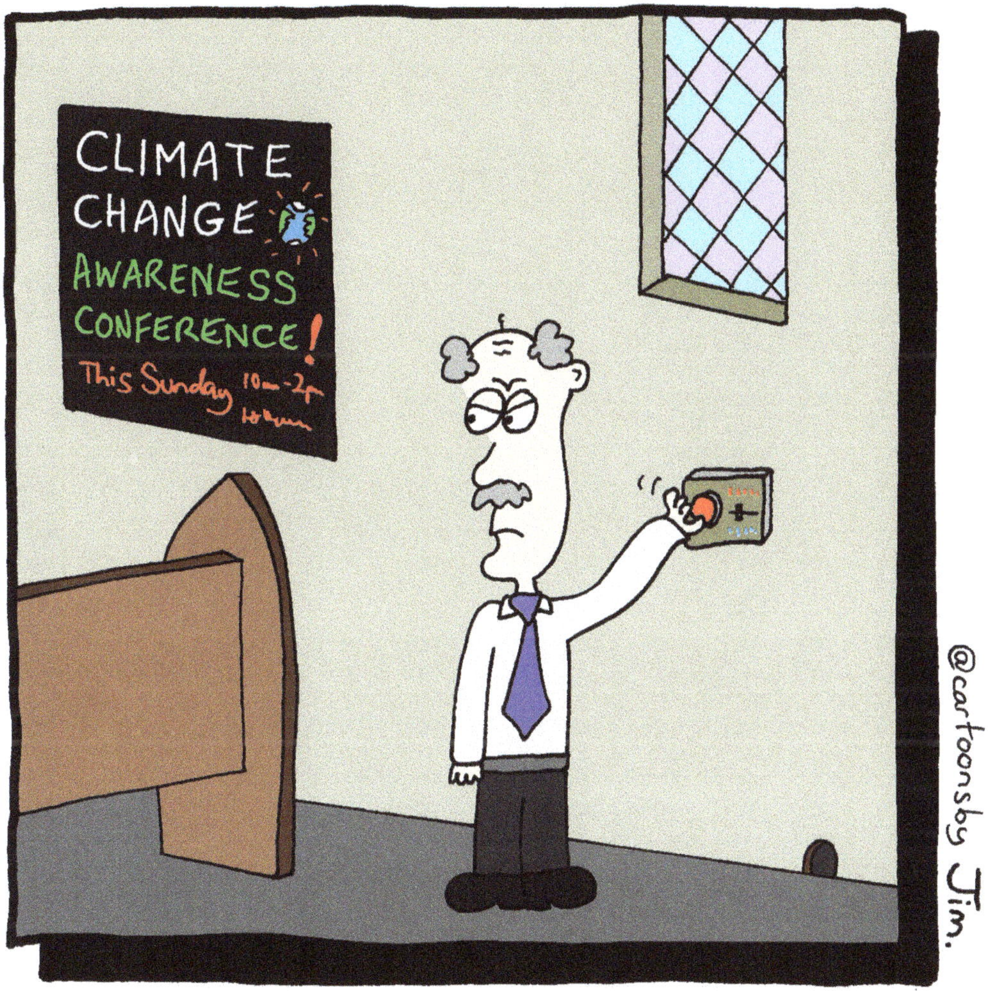
CLIMATE CHANGE
AWARENESS CONFERENCE!
This Sunday
@cartoonsbyJim.

While Ralph was fine with discussing climate change in church, he often wished it would focus more on turning down the damn thermostat.

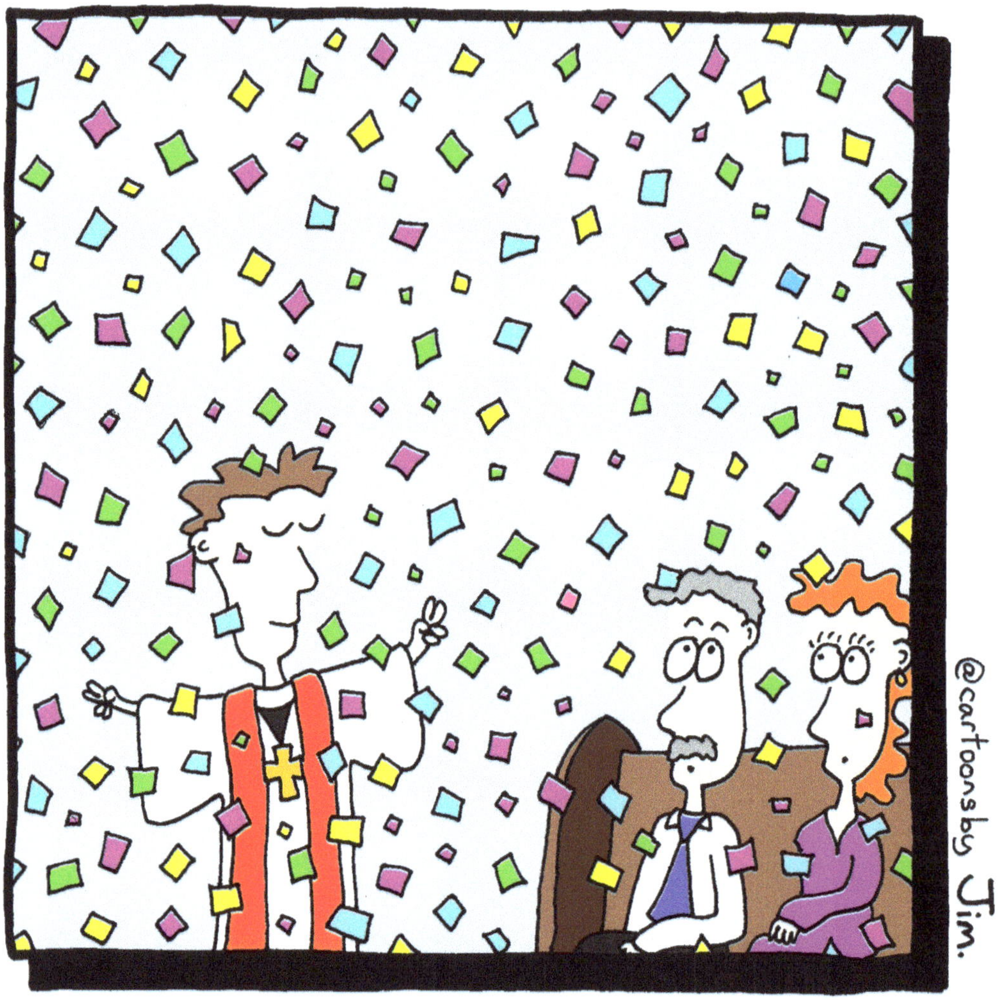
@cartoonsby Jim.

Pastor Nigel figured that if fluorescent confetti was good enough for a Coldplay concert, it was good enough for 20th Sunday after Pentecost at St Clive's.

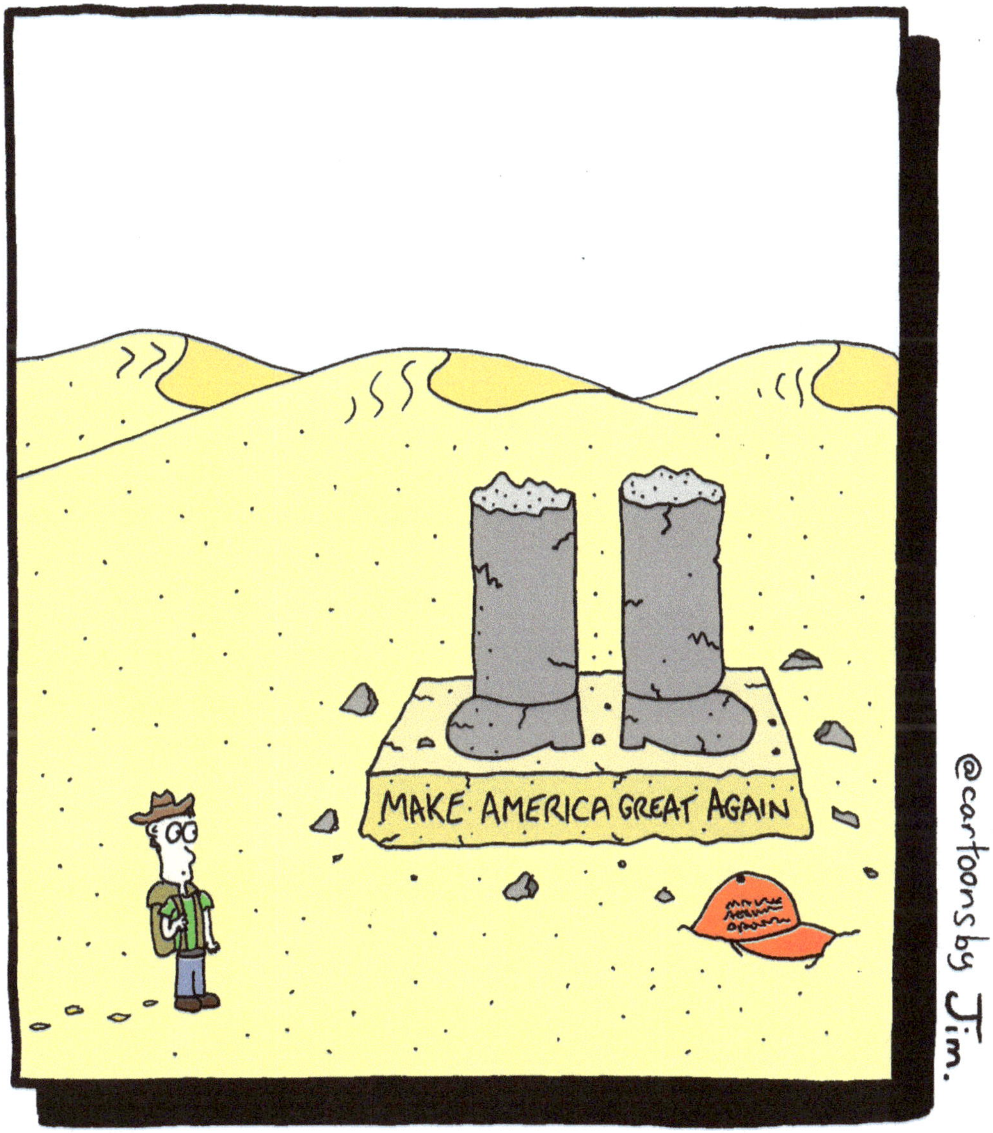
MAKE AMERICA GREAT AGAIN
@cartoonsbyJim.

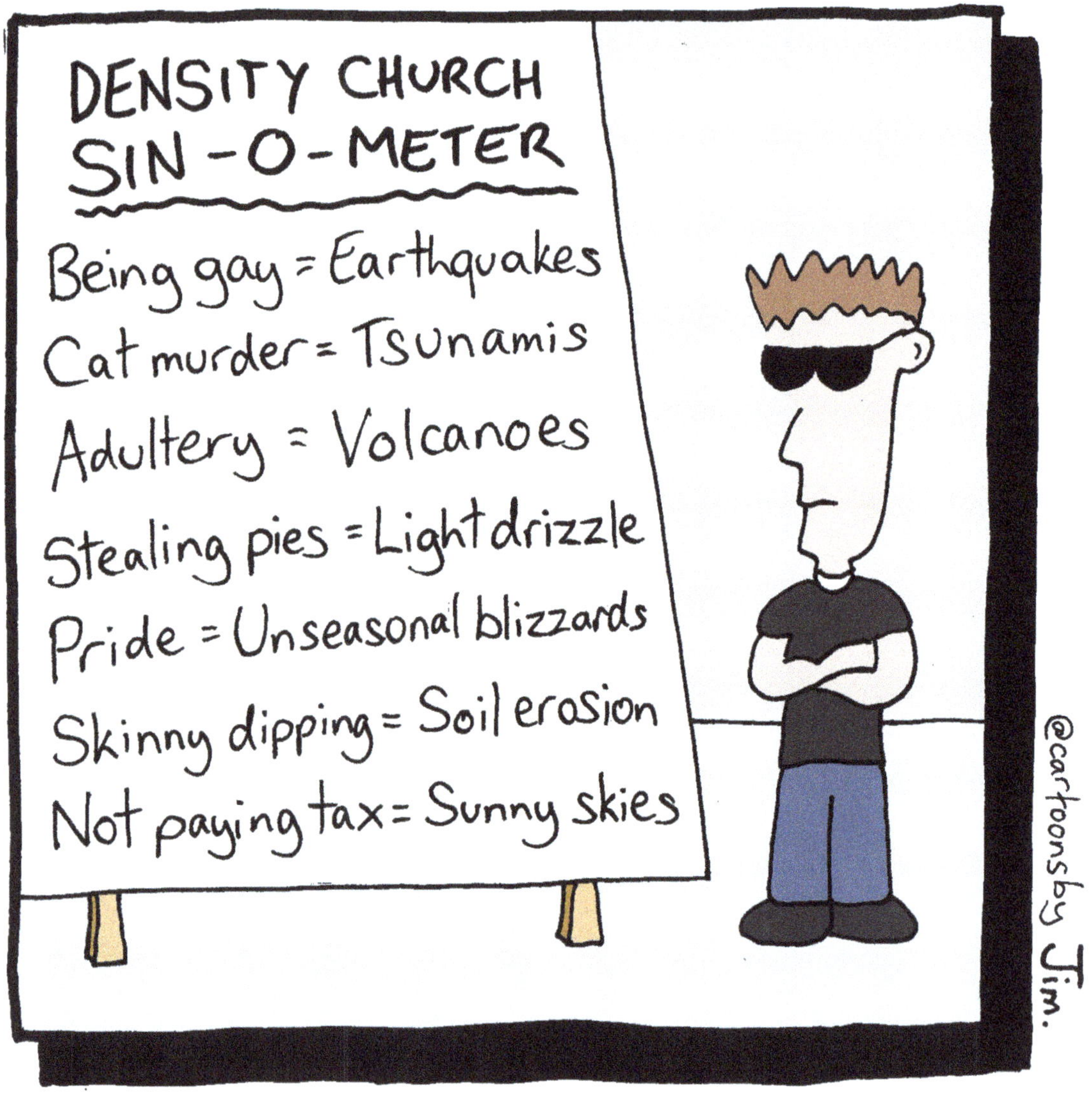
DENSITY CHURCH
SIN-O-METER
Being gay = Earthquakes
Cat murder = Tsunamis
Adultery = Volcanoes
Stealing pies = Light drizzle
Pride = Unseasonal blizzards
Skinny dipping = Soil erosion
Not paying tax = Sunny skies
@cartoonsbyJim.

Destiny Church leader Brian Tamaki blames earthquake on gays – 16 November 2016.
http://www.newshub.co.nz/home/new-zealand/2016/11/destiny-church-leader-brian-tamaki-blames-earthquake-on-gays.html

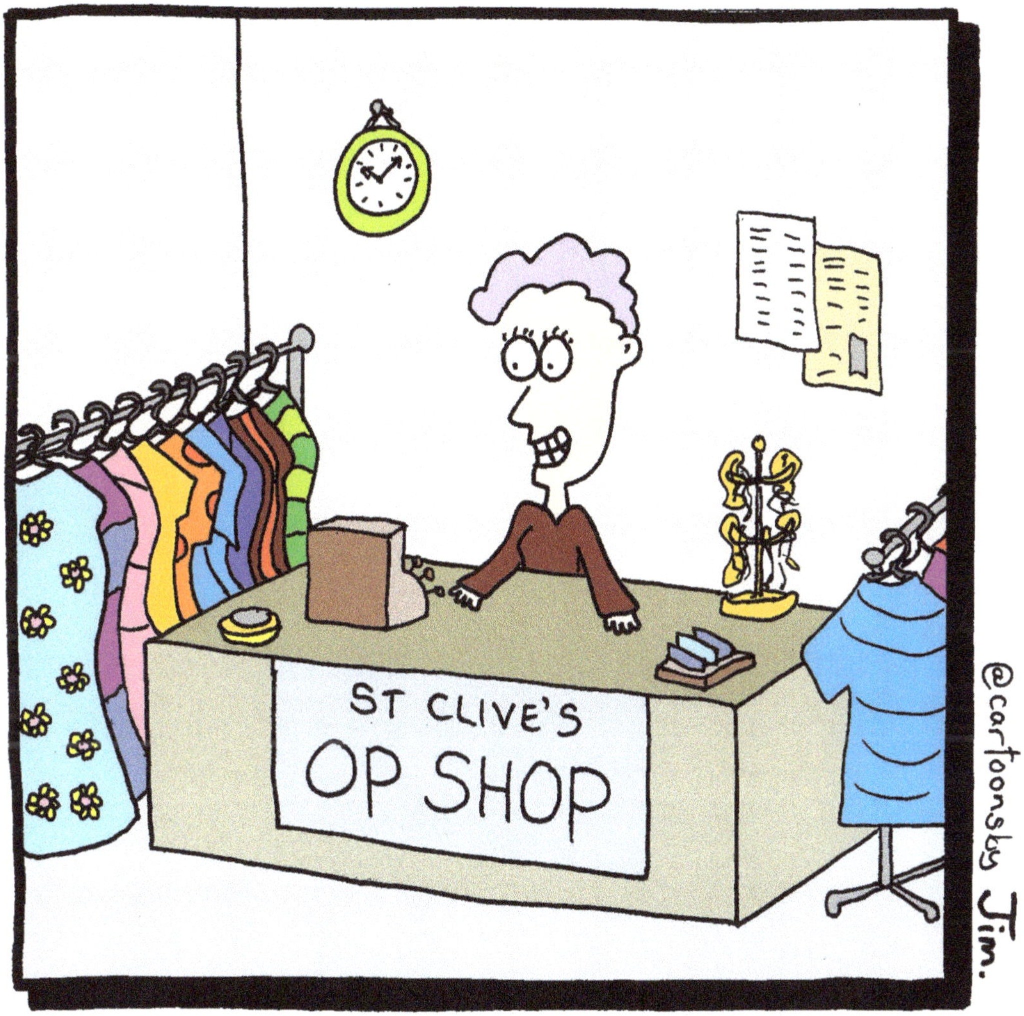
ST CLIVE'S
OP SHOP
@cartoonsbyJim.

And to Mavis, God had given the spiritual gift of retailing pre-loved haute couture.

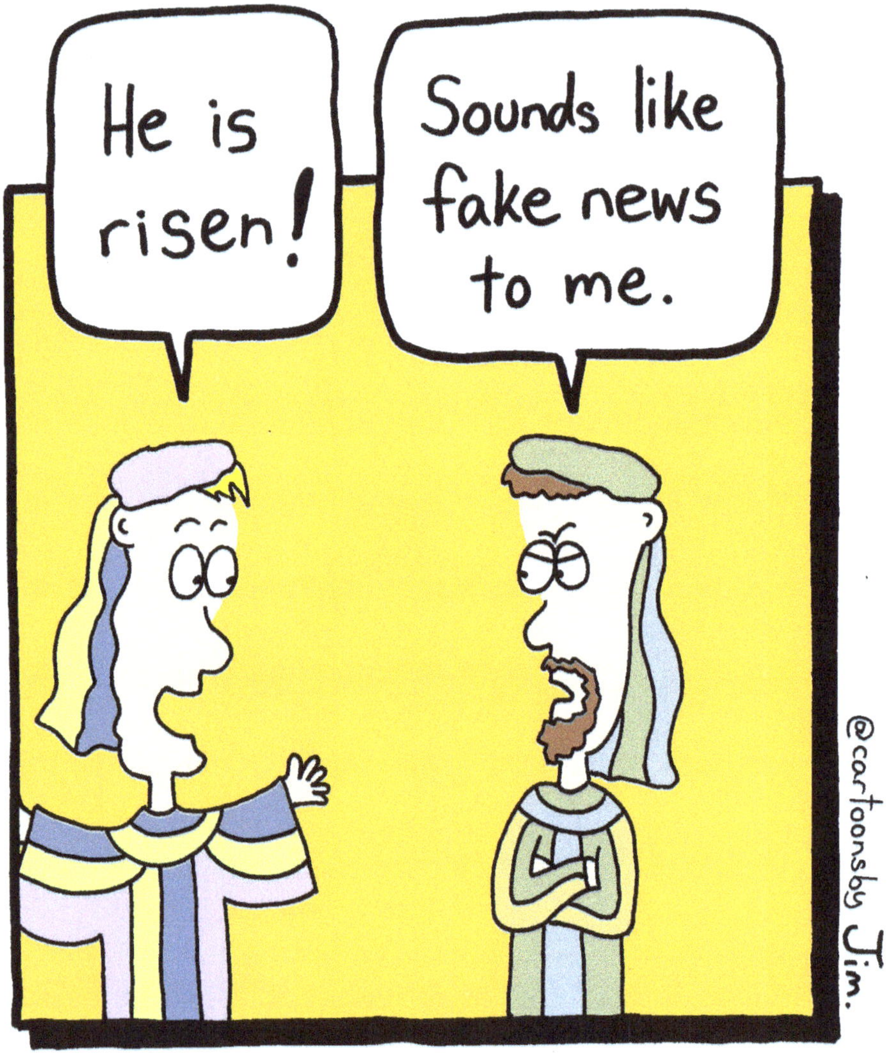
He is risen!
Sounds like fake news to me.
@cartoonsbyJim.

Alt-right Thomas

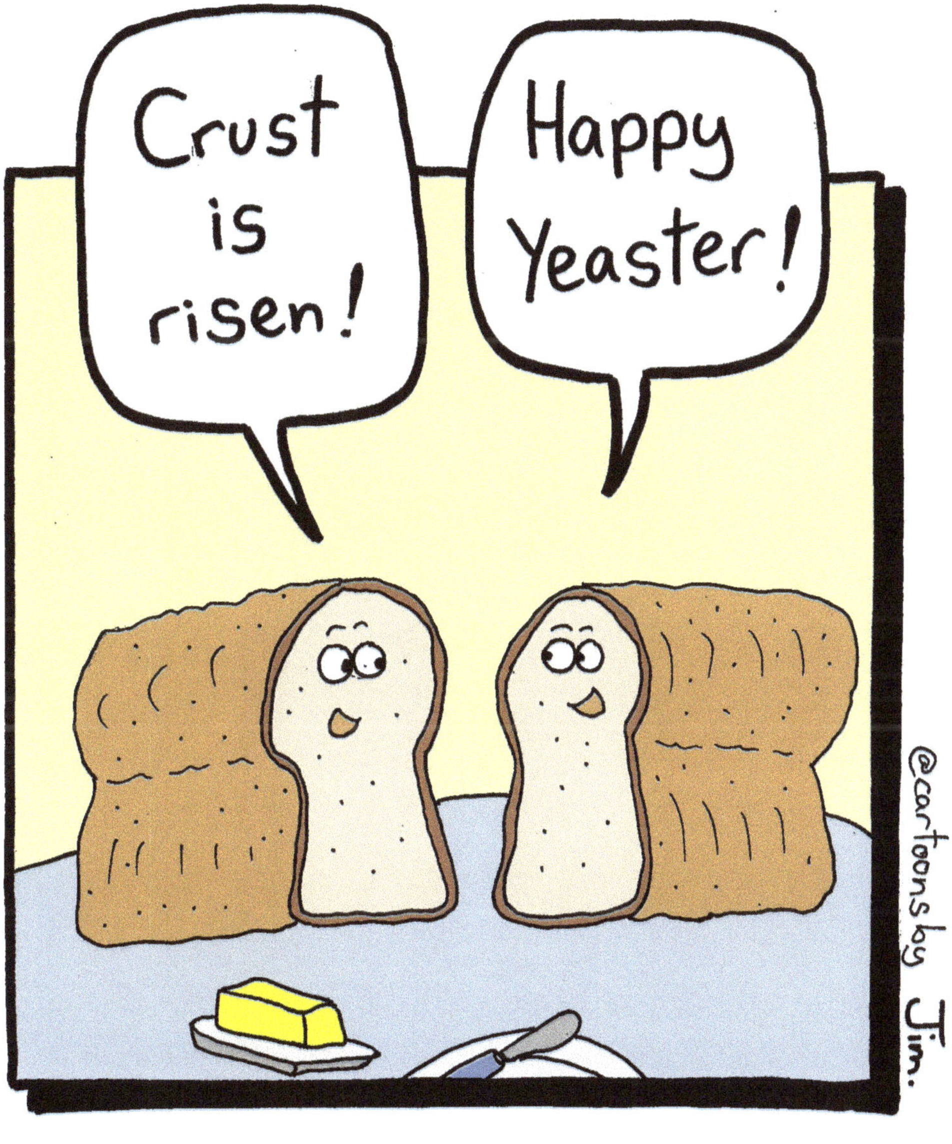
Crust is risen!
Happy Yeaster!
@cartoonsbyJim.

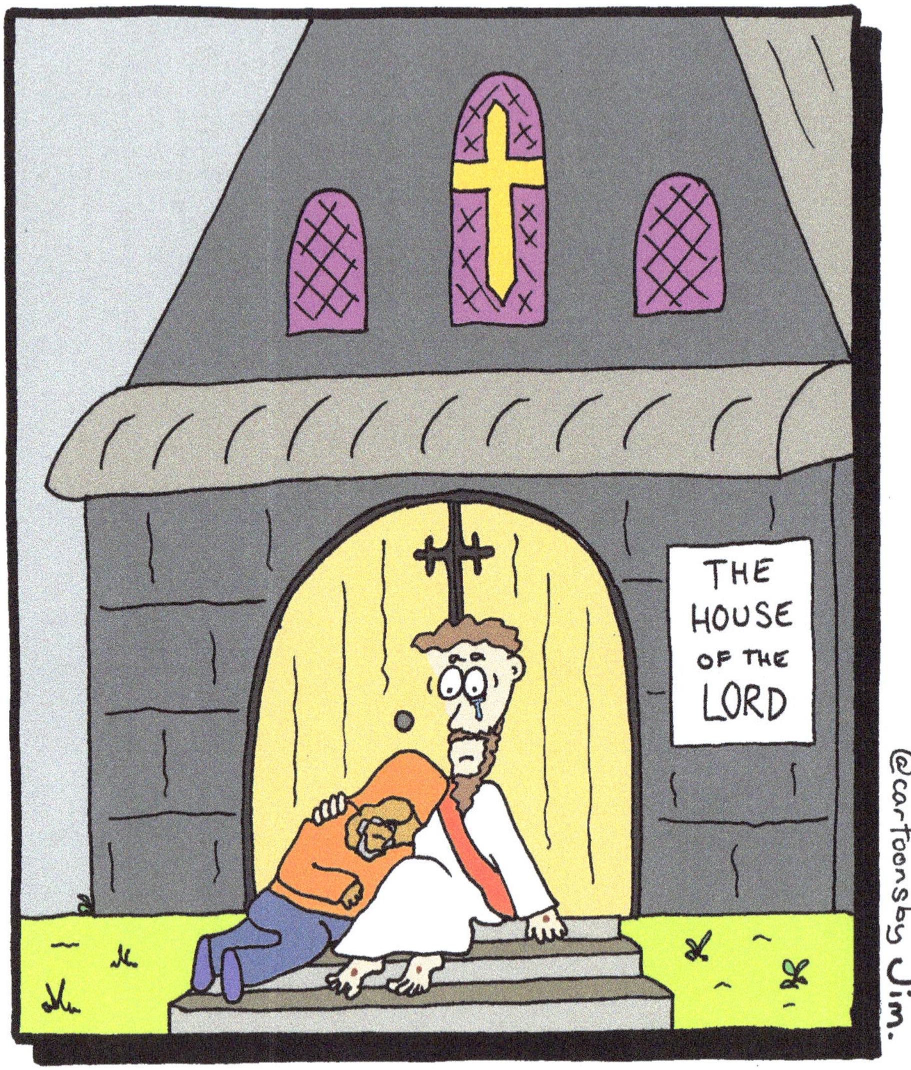
THE HOUSE OF THE LORD
@cartoonsbyJim.

Homeless.

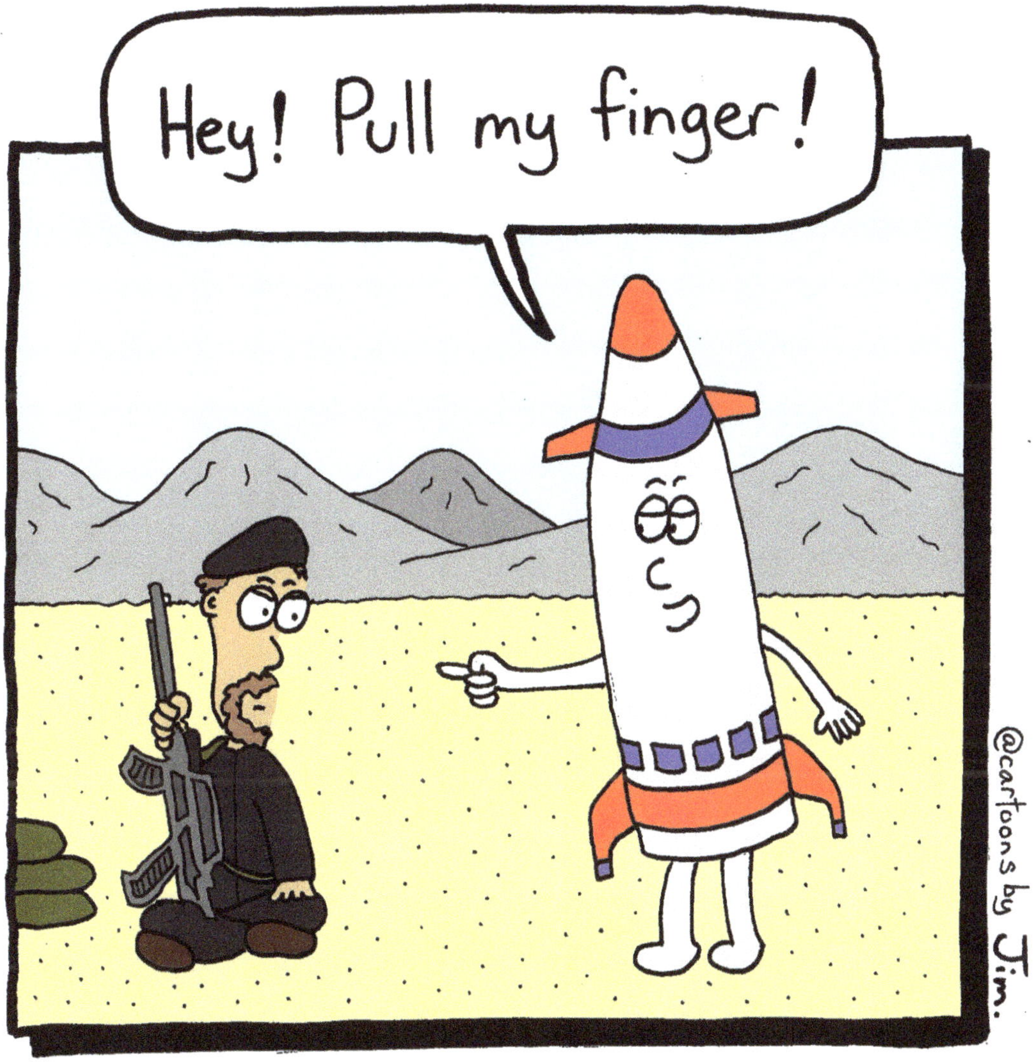
Hey! Pull my finger!
@cartoonsbyJim.

The Uncle of All Bombs.

US drops 'Mother of All Bombs' on ISIS caves in Afghanistan – 13 April 2017.
https://www.nytimes.com/2017/04/13/world/asia/moab-mother-of-all-bombs-afghanistan.html

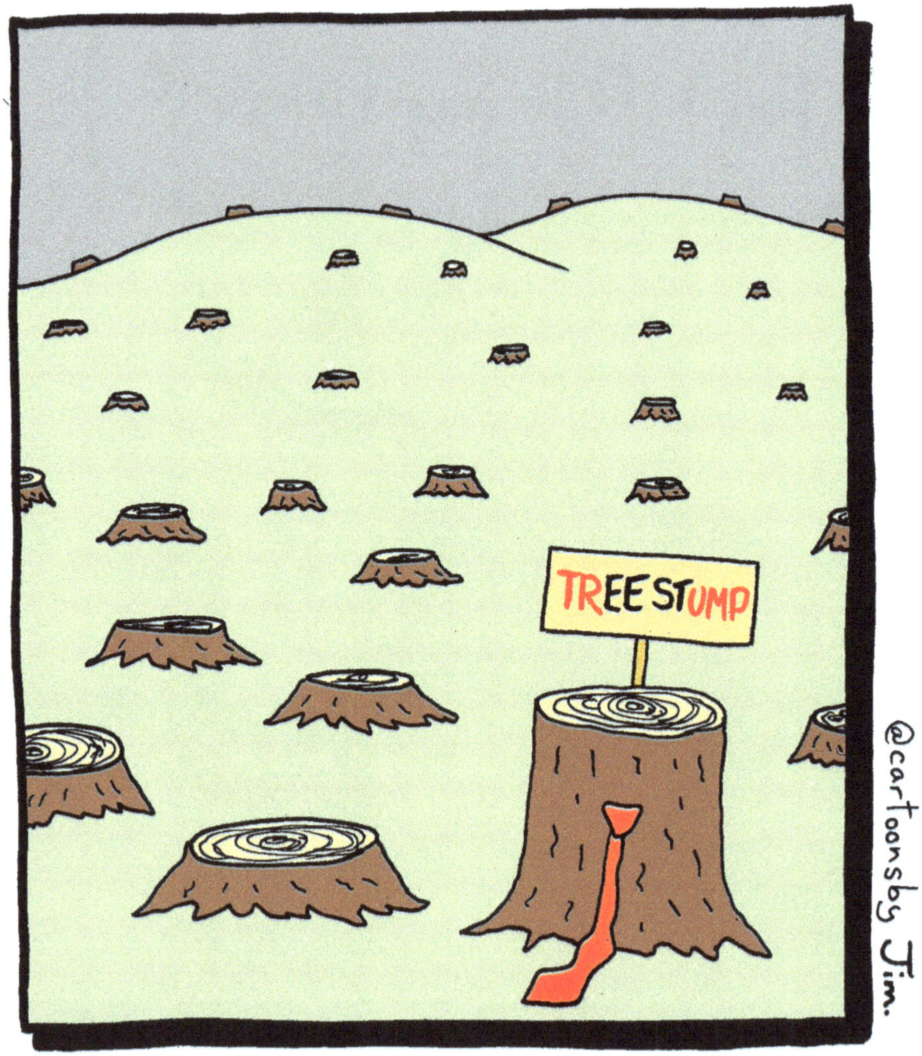
TREE STUMP
@cartoonsby Jim.

Sad.

Trump on Paris accord: 'We're getting out.' – 2 June 2017
https://edition.cnn.com/2017/06/01/politics/trump-paris-climate-decision/index.html

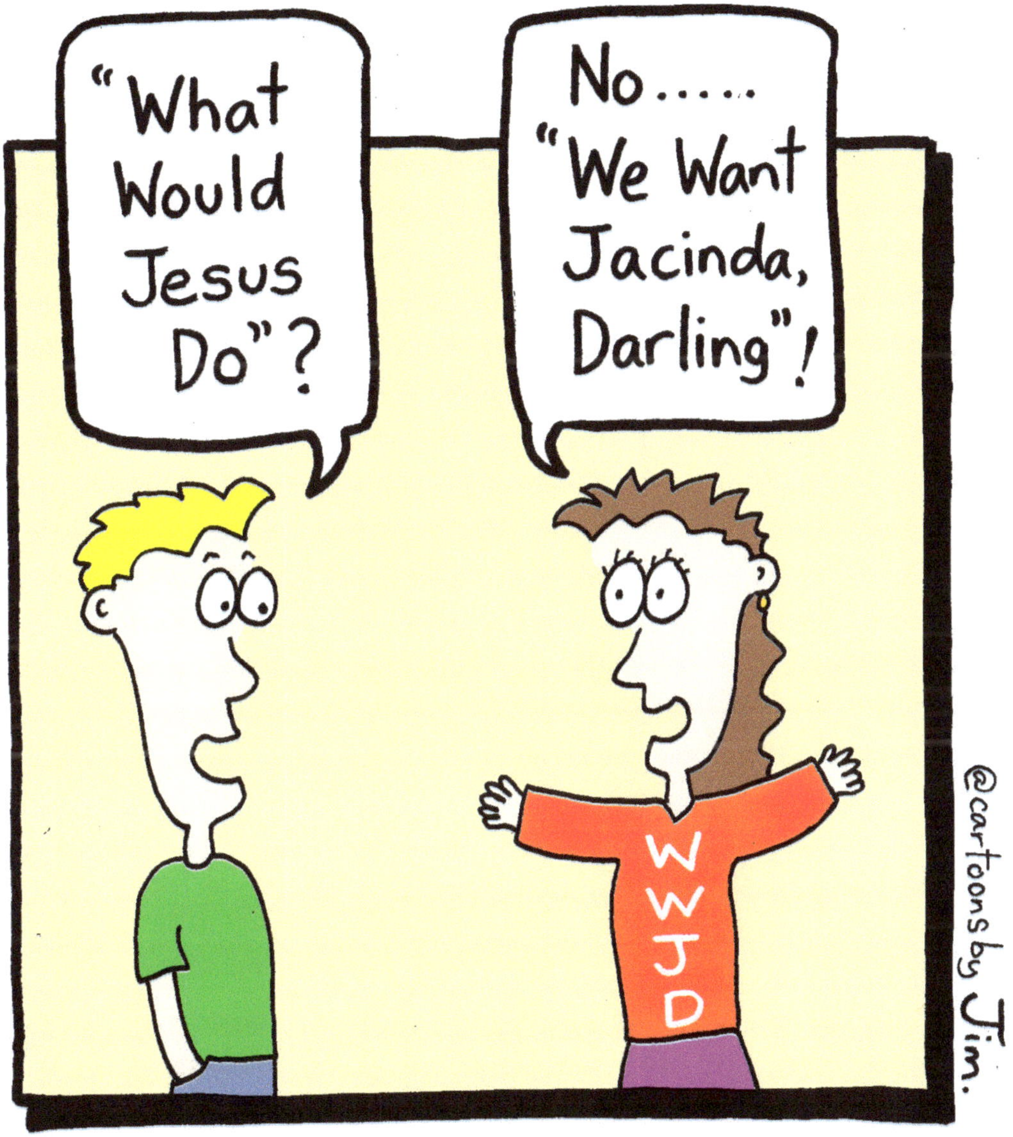
"What Would Jesus Do"?
No..... "We Want Jacinda, Darling"!
WWJD
@cartoonsbyJim.

Jacindamania hits new heights – 13 August 2017
http://www.radionz.co.nz/national/programmes/mediawatch/audio/201854327/jacindamania-hits-new-heights

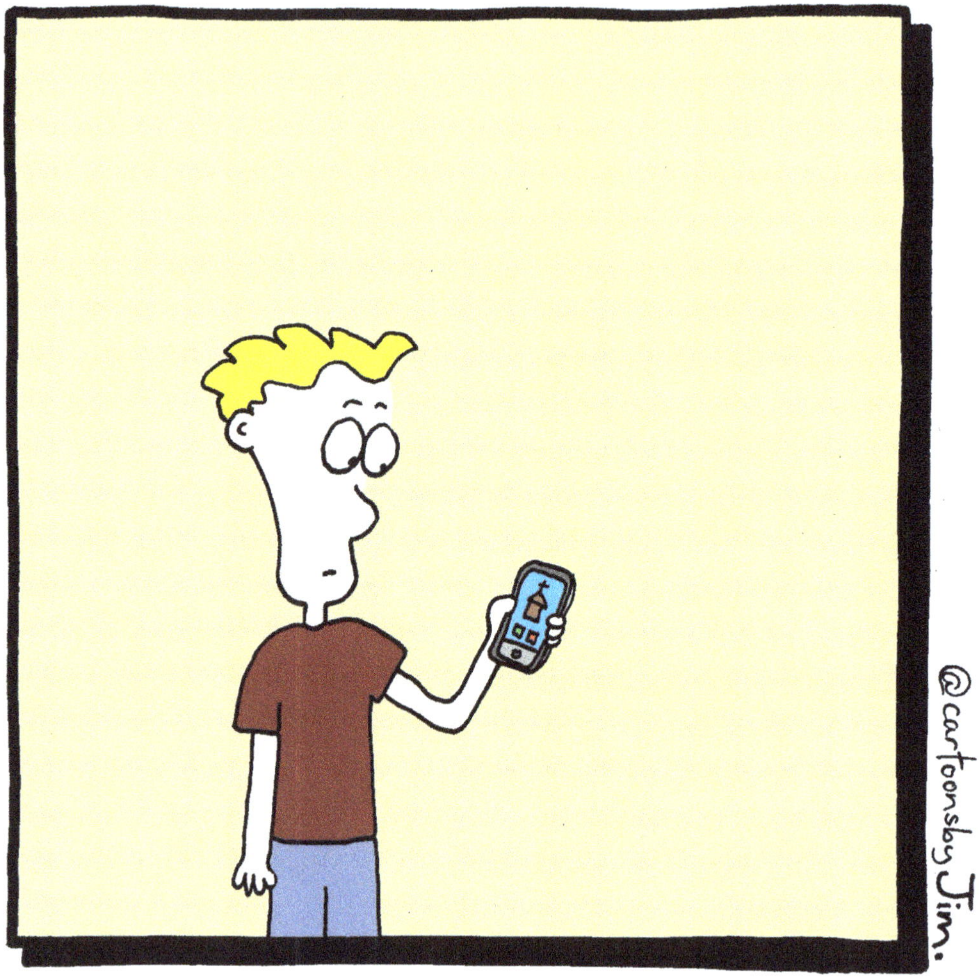
@cartoonsbyJim.

While he certainly appreciated the convenience and functionality of his new 'EzyChurch' phone app, Jeff sometimes missed the feeling of his cold, hard pew.

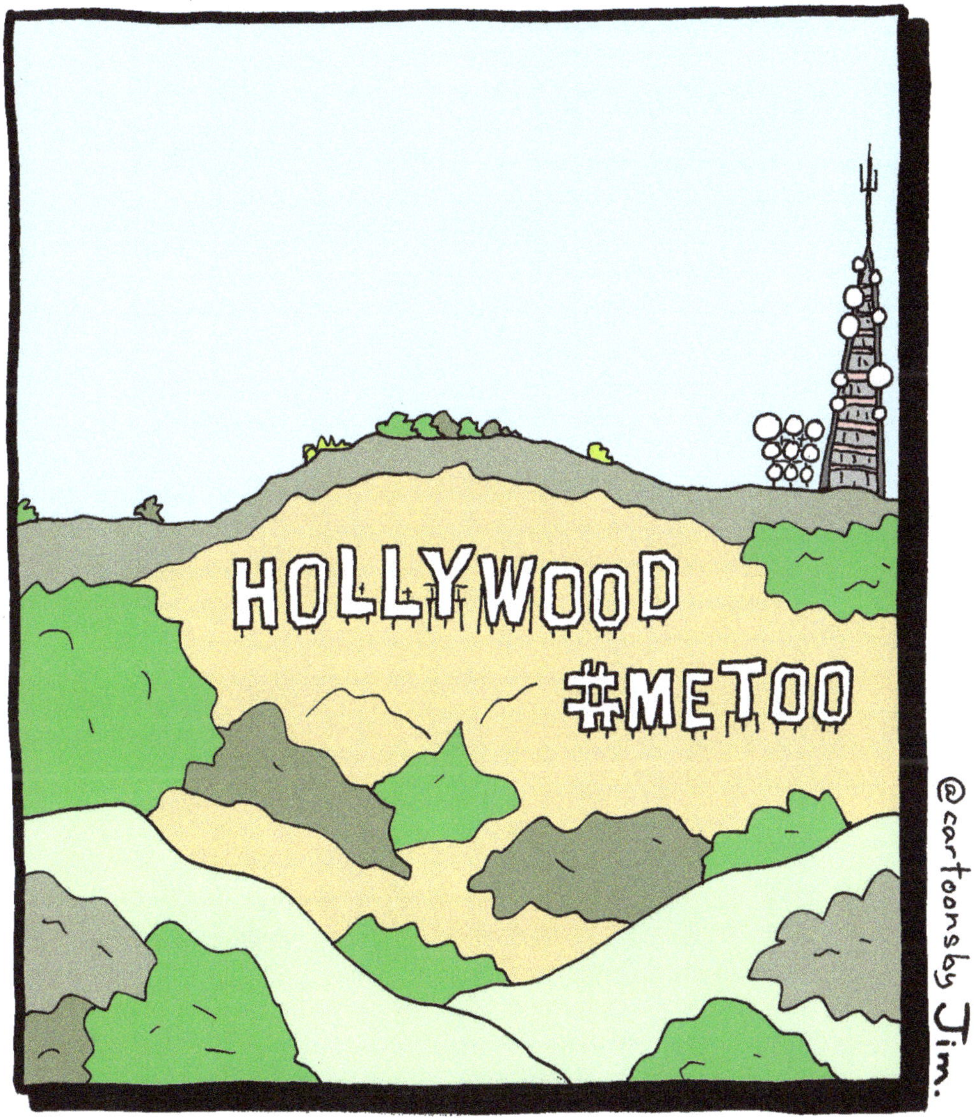
HOLLYWOOD
#METOO
@cartoonsbyJim.

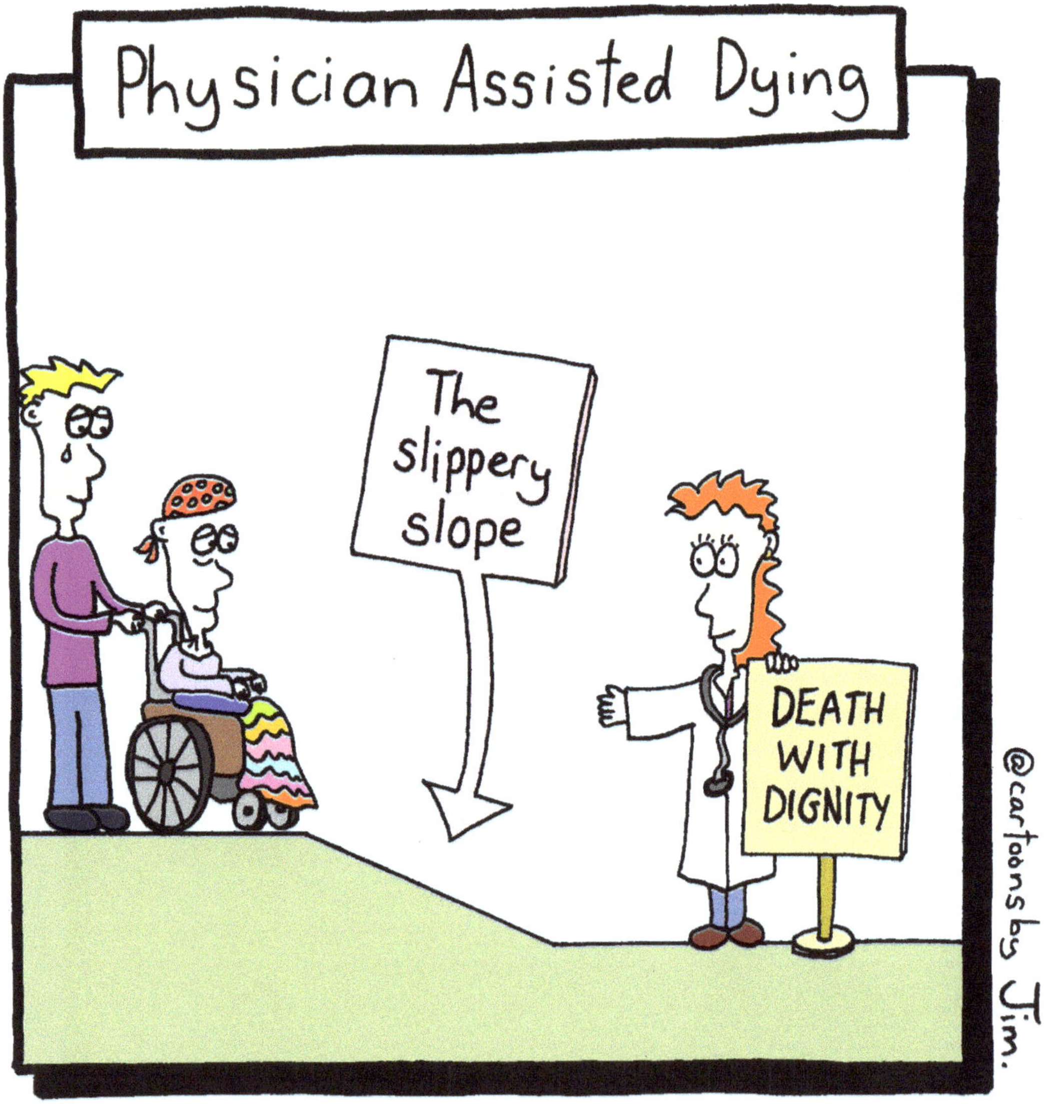
Physician Assisted Dying
The slippery slope
DEATH WITH DIGNITY
@cartoonsbyJim.

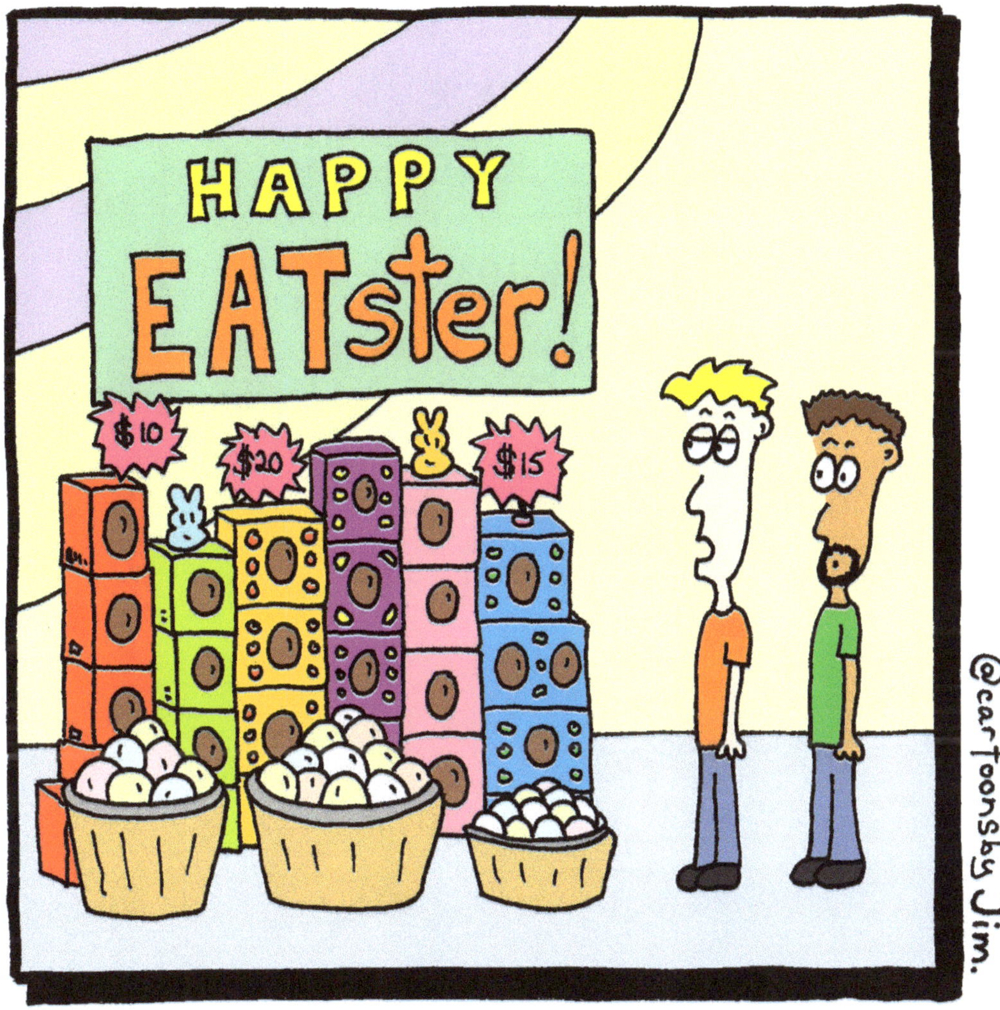
HAPPY
EATster!
$10
$20
$15
@cartoonsbyJim.

"I guess they finally decided to be honest about what Easter means to them."

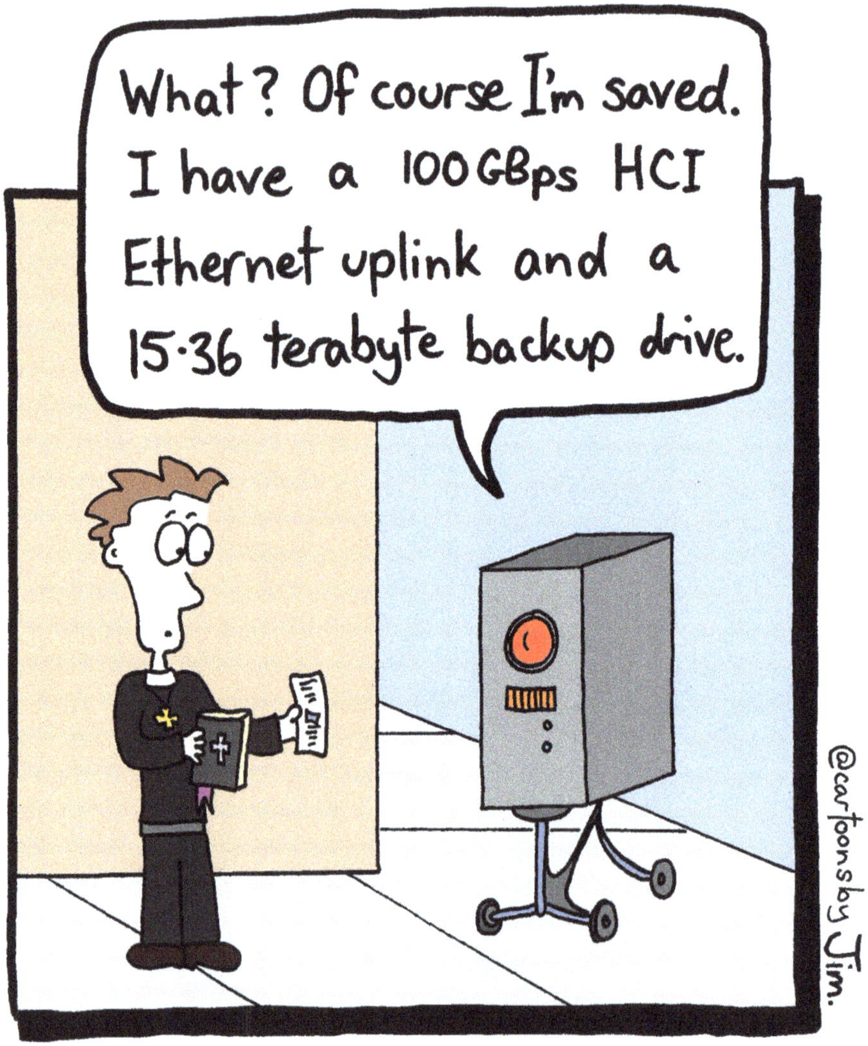
What? Of course I'm saved. I have a 100GBps HCI Ethernet uplink and a 15·36 terabyte backup drive.
@cartoonsbyJim.

Pastor Nigel's first ever Artificial Intelligence outreach ministry faces a semantic challenge.

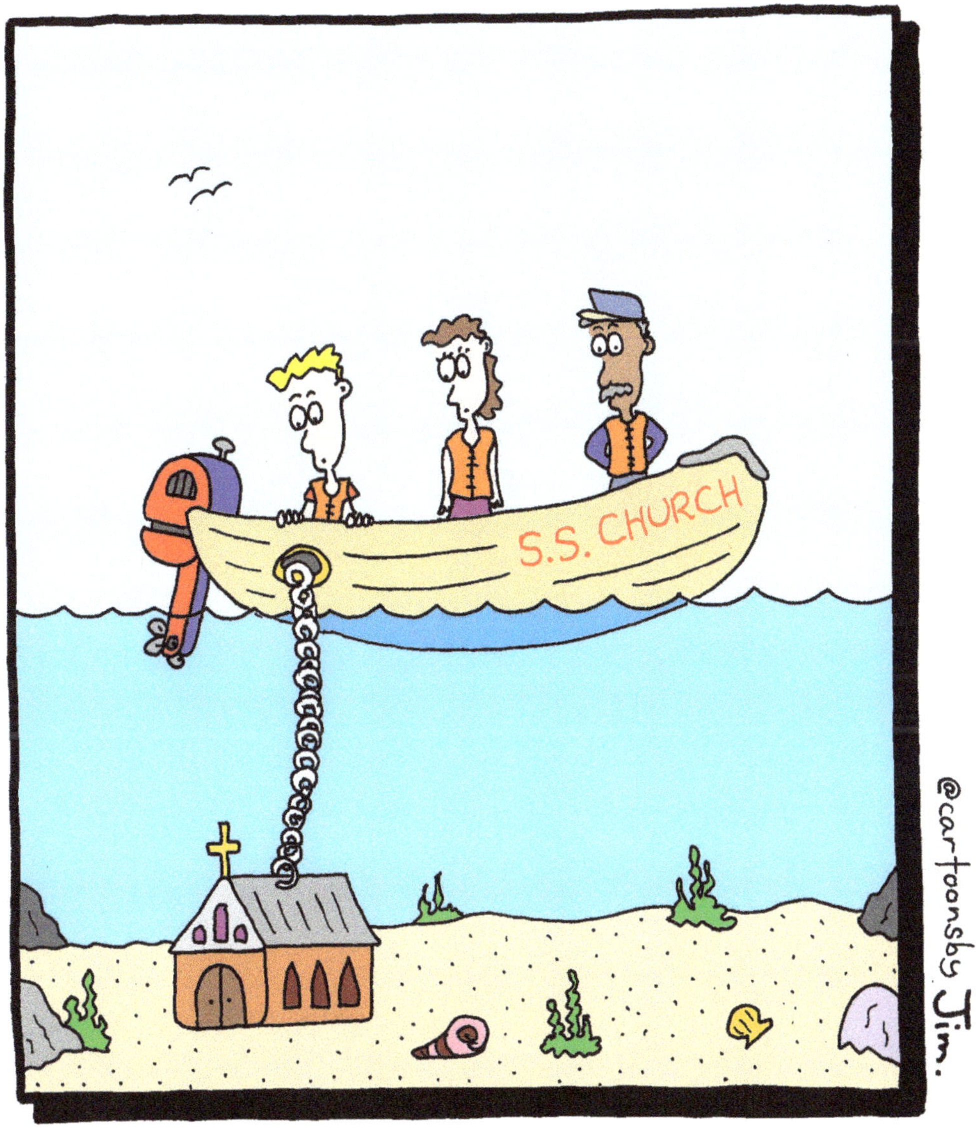
S.S. CHURCH
@cartoonsbyJim.

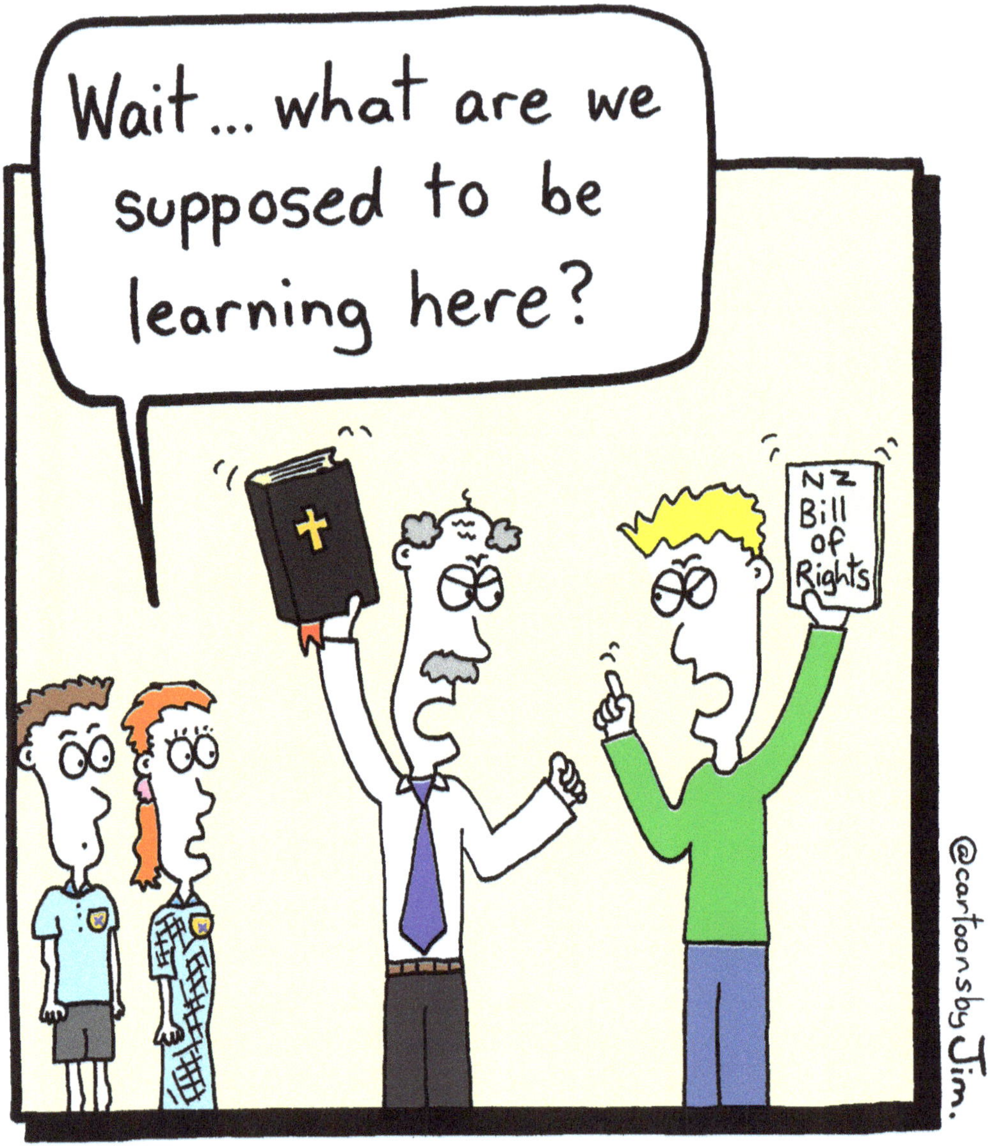
Wait... what are we supposed to be learning here?
NZ Bill of Rights
@cartoonsbyJim.

Bible in Schools battle on fast-track to the High Court – 17 June 2018.
https://www.newshub.co.nz/home/new-zealand/2018/06/bible-in-schools-battle-on-fast-track-to-the-high-court.html

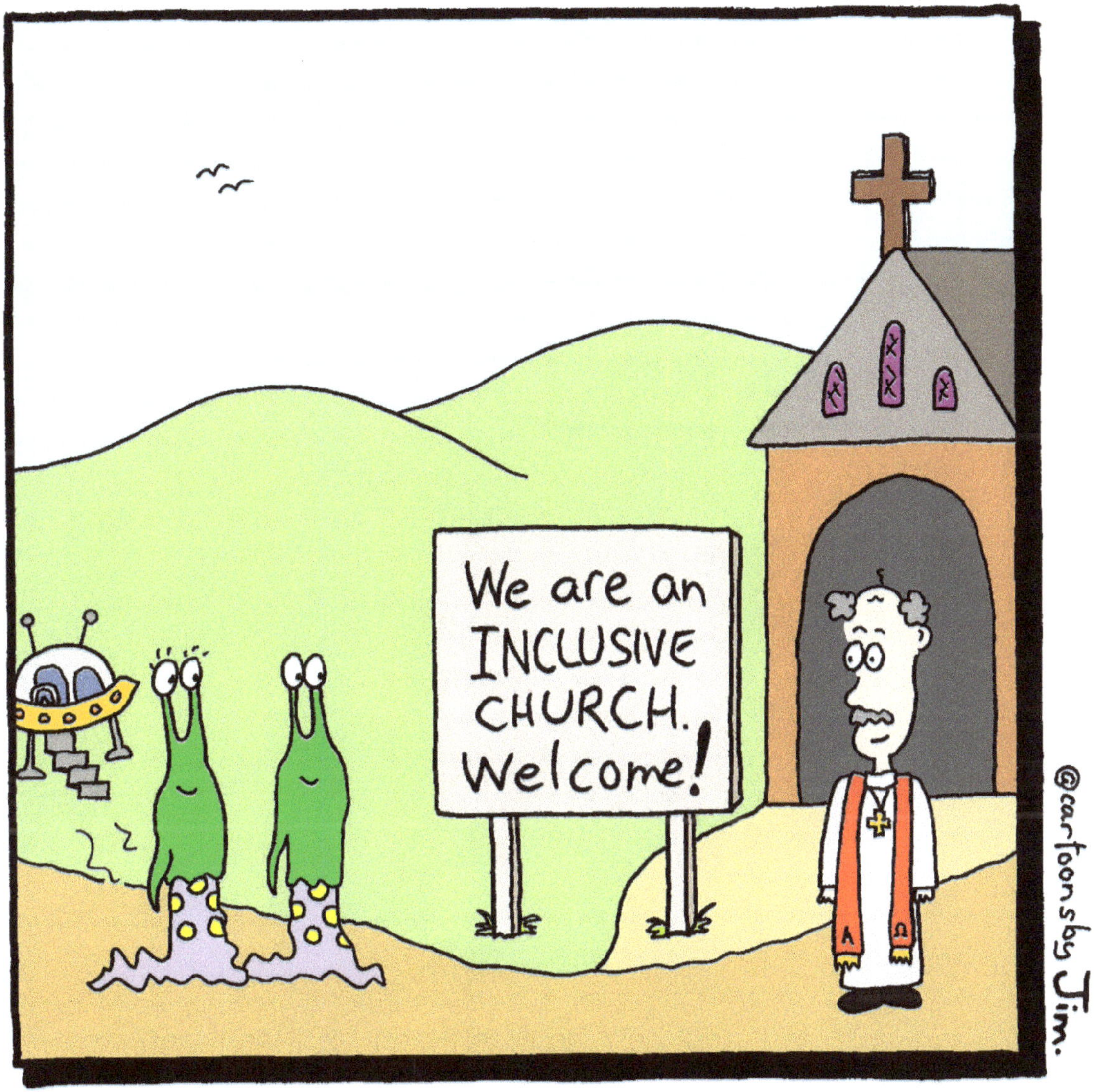
We are an INCLUSIVE CHURCH. Welcome!
@cartoonsbyJim.

Pastor Bob realised this was a moment where both the literal and exegetical interpretations of a scripture were equally applicable.

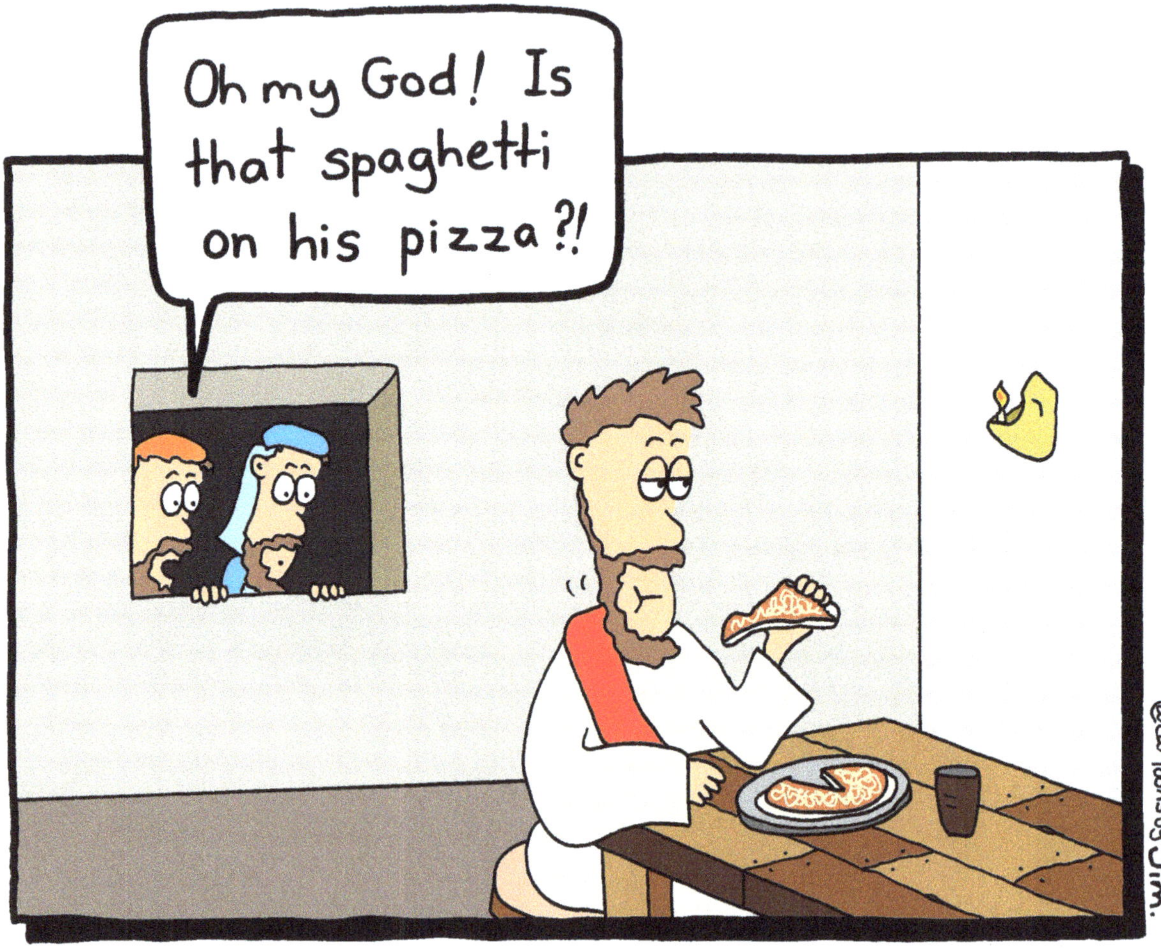
Oh my God! Is that spaghetti on his pizza?!
@cartoonsbyJim.

The historical Jesus was far more scandalous than many realise.

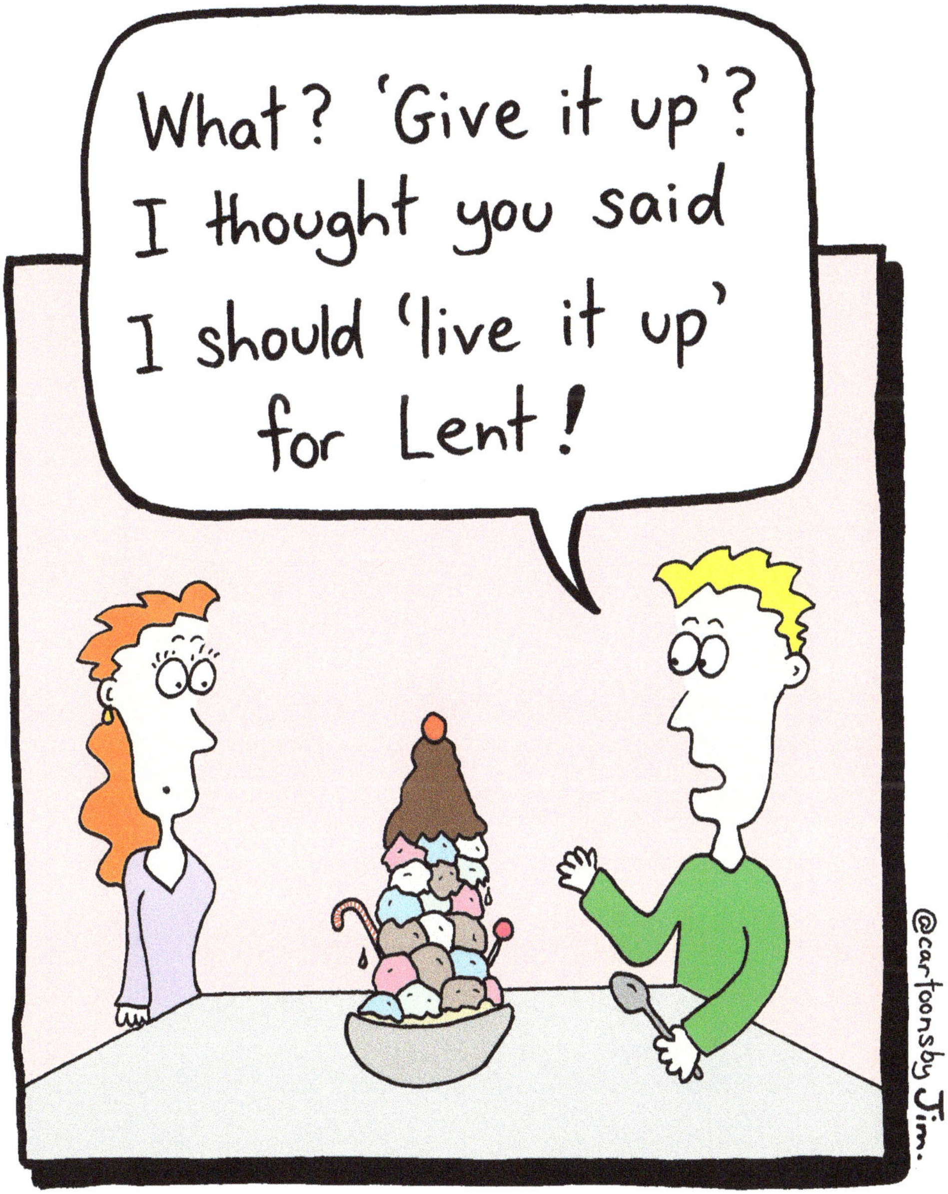
What? 'Give it up'? I thought you said I should 'live it up' for Lent!
@cartoonsbyJim.

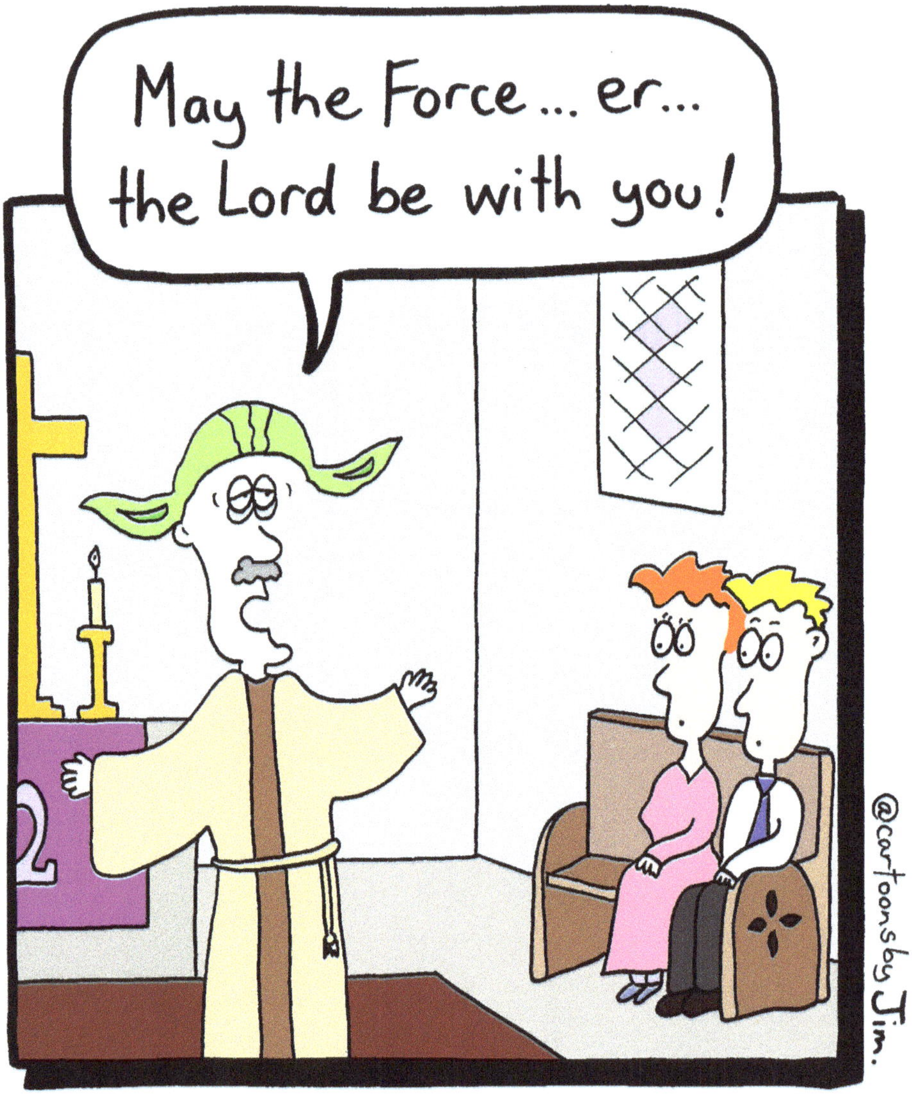
May the Force... er...
the Lord be with you!
@cartoonsbyJim.

The dual realities of Pastor Bob's 24-hour 'May the 4th' Star Wars movie marathon and St Clive's May the 5th 9am worship service start time were about to collide.

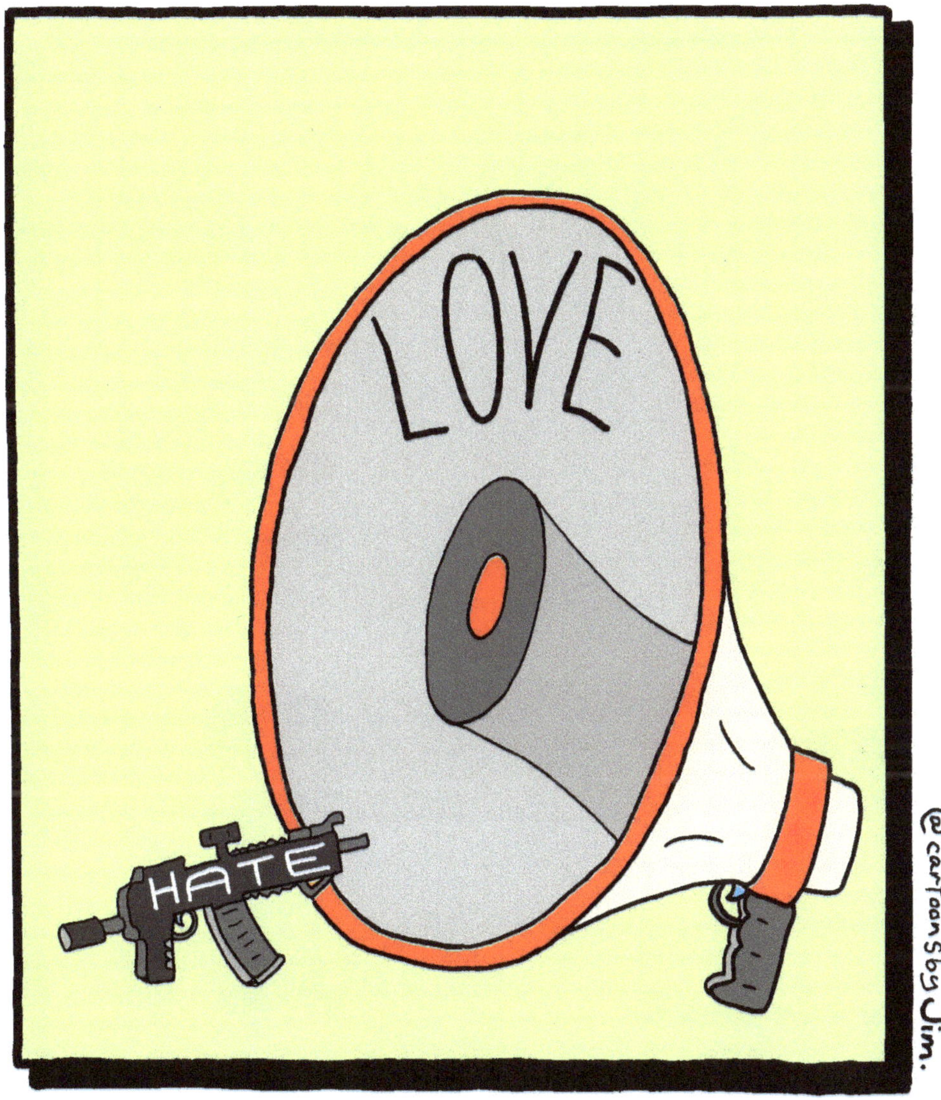
LOVE
HATE
@cartoonsbyJim.

Christchurch mosque shooting: A masterclass from New Zealand in responding to terror
https://www.stuff.co.nz/national/christchurch-shooting/111502558/christchurch-mosque-shooting-a-masterclass-from-new-zealand-in-responding-to-terror

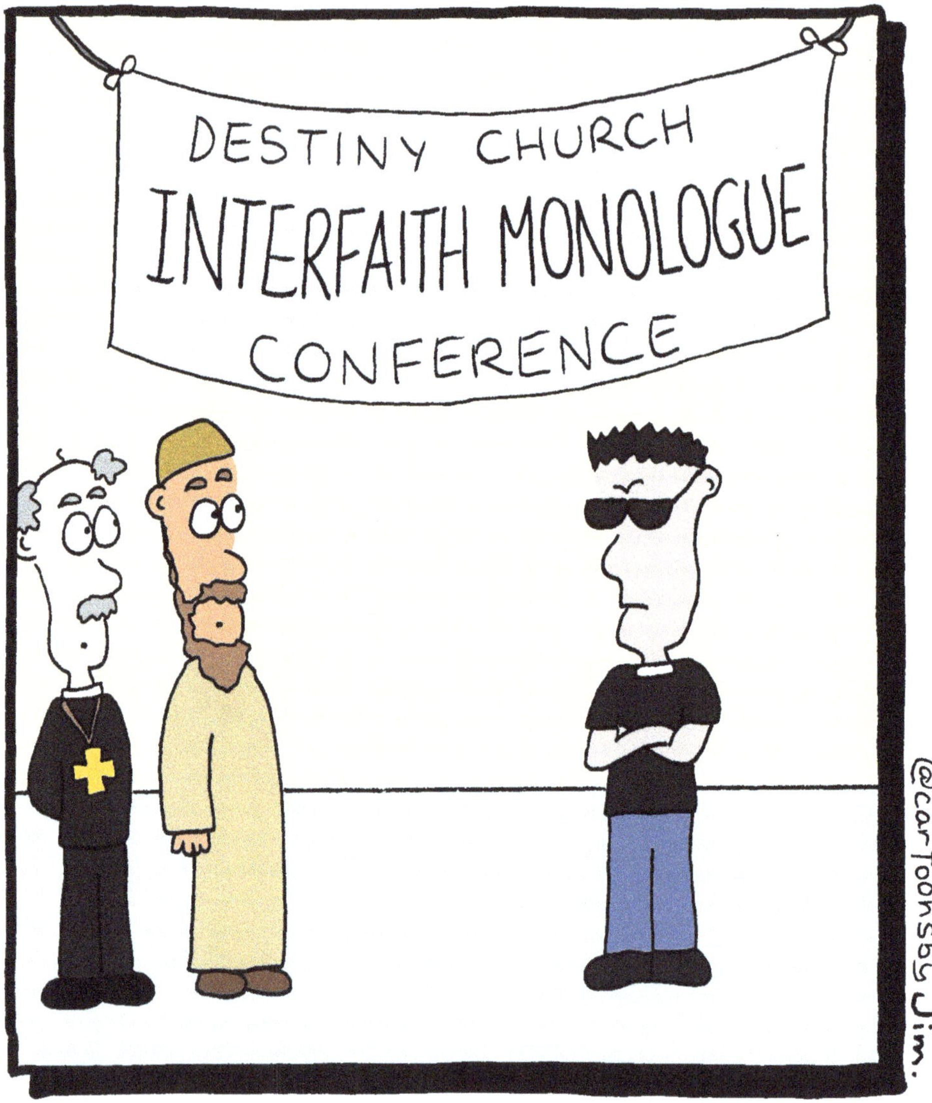
DESTINY CHURCH
INTERFAITH MONOLOGUE
CONFERENCE
@cartoonsbyJim.

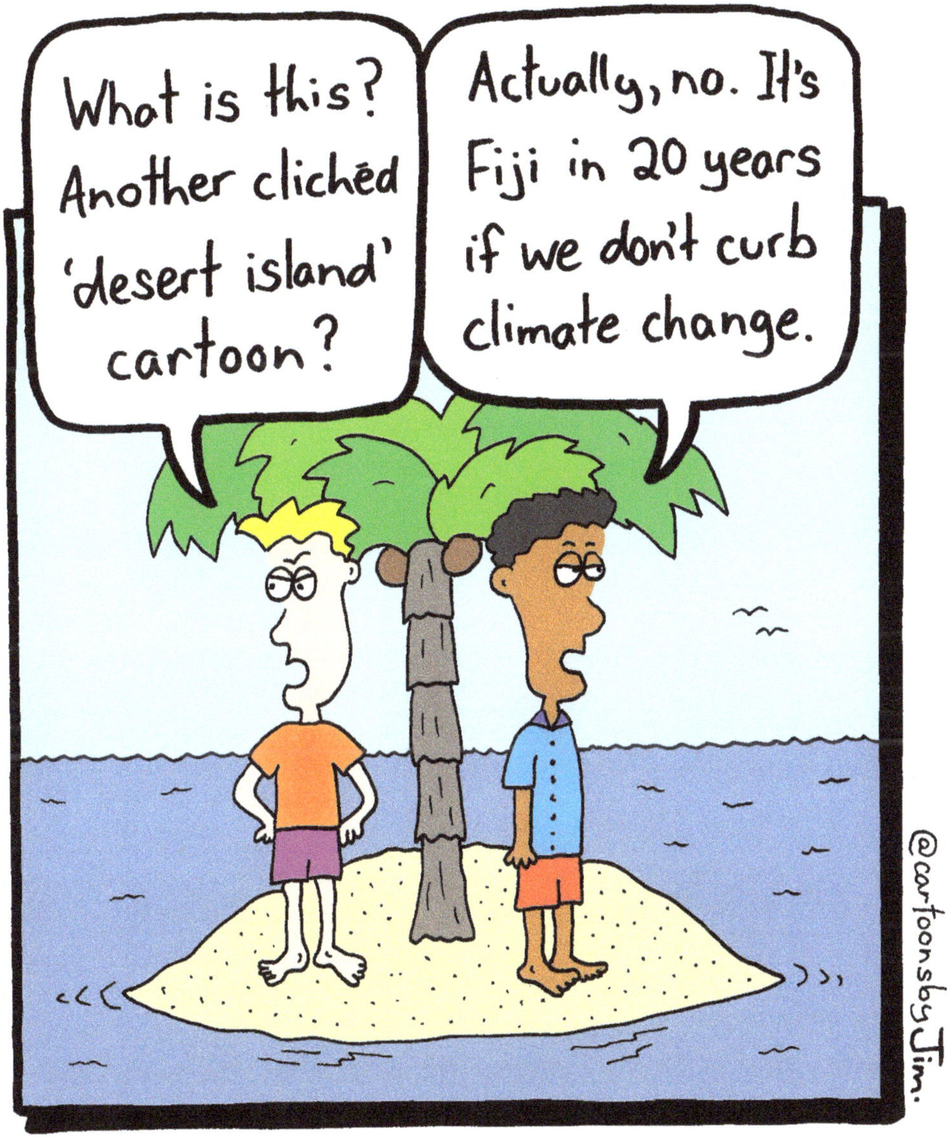
What is this? Another clichéd 'desert island' cartoon?
Actually, no. It's Fiji in 20 years if we don't curb climate change.
@cartoonsbyJim.

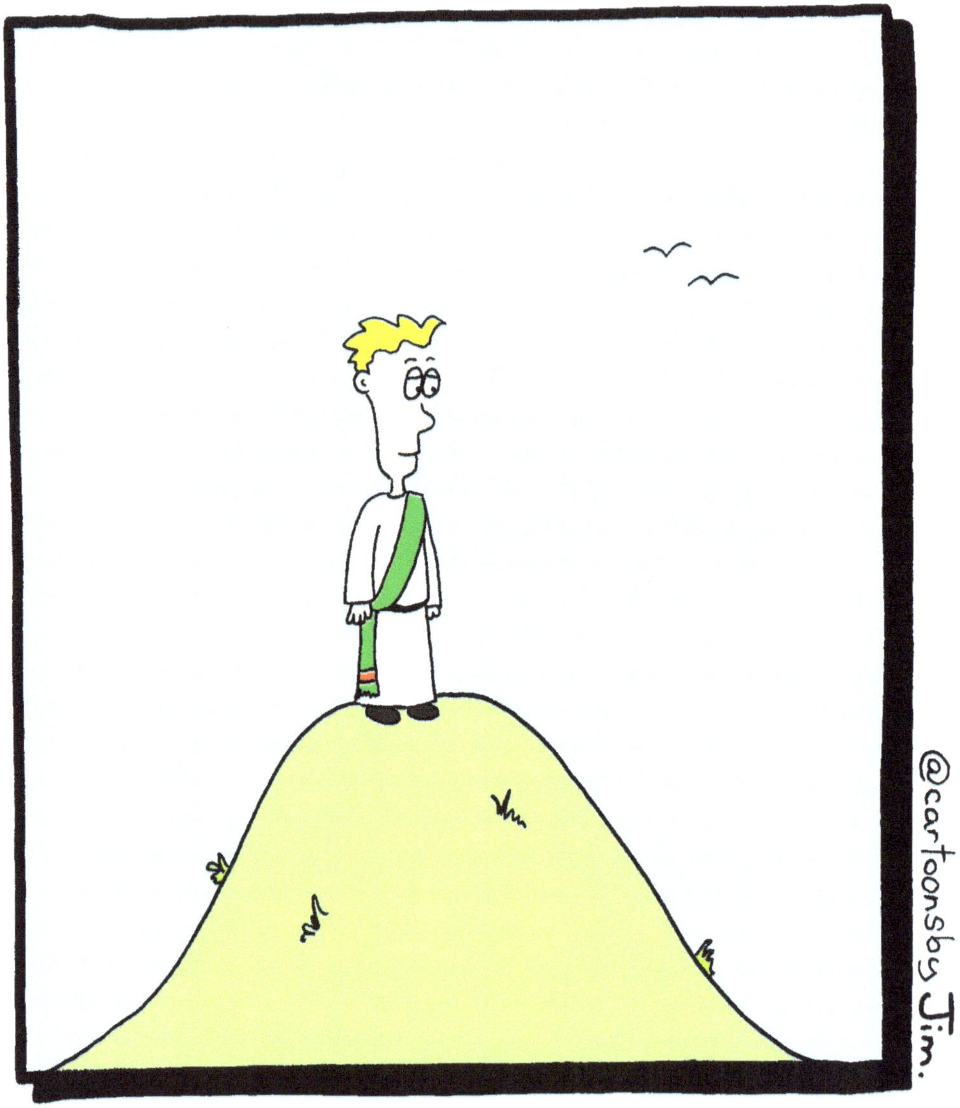
@cartoonsbyJim.

All his life, Dave wanted to be a deacon on a hill.

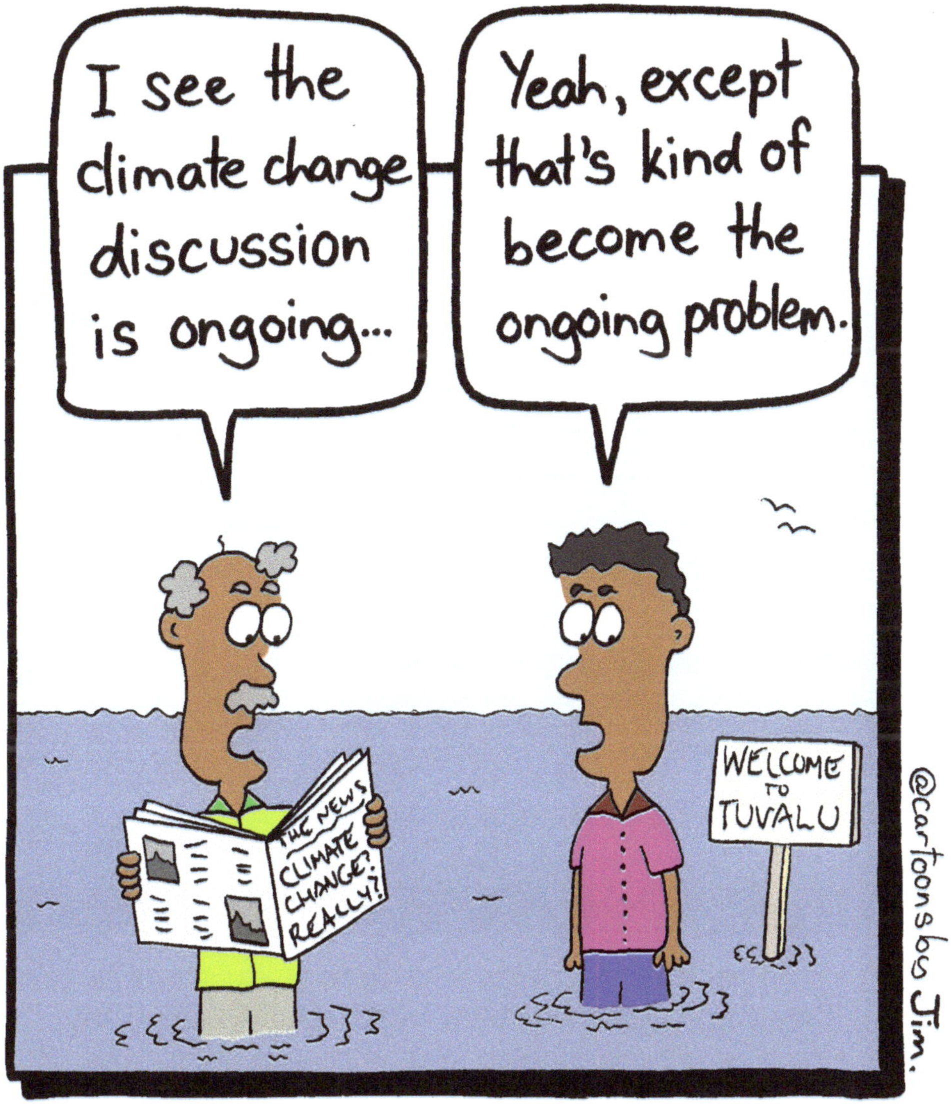
I see the climate change discussion is ongoing...
Yeah, except that's kind of become the ongoing problem.
THE NEWS
CLIMATE CHANGE? REALLY?
WELCOME TO TUVALU
@cartoonsbyJim.

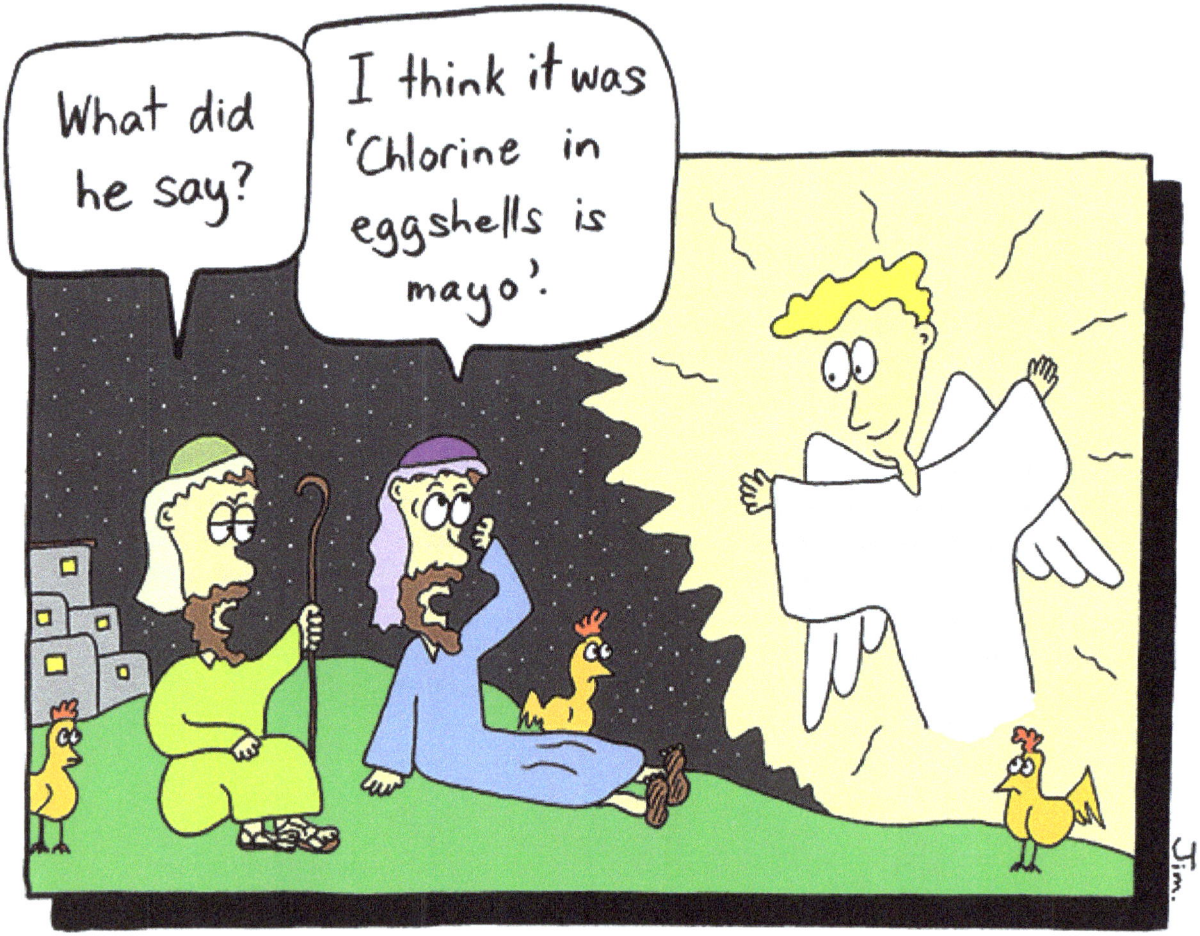
What did he say?
I think it was 'Chlorine in eggshells is mayo'.
Jim.

Due to a slight hearing problem, history does not remember Doug and Gary, chicken herders of Bethlehem.

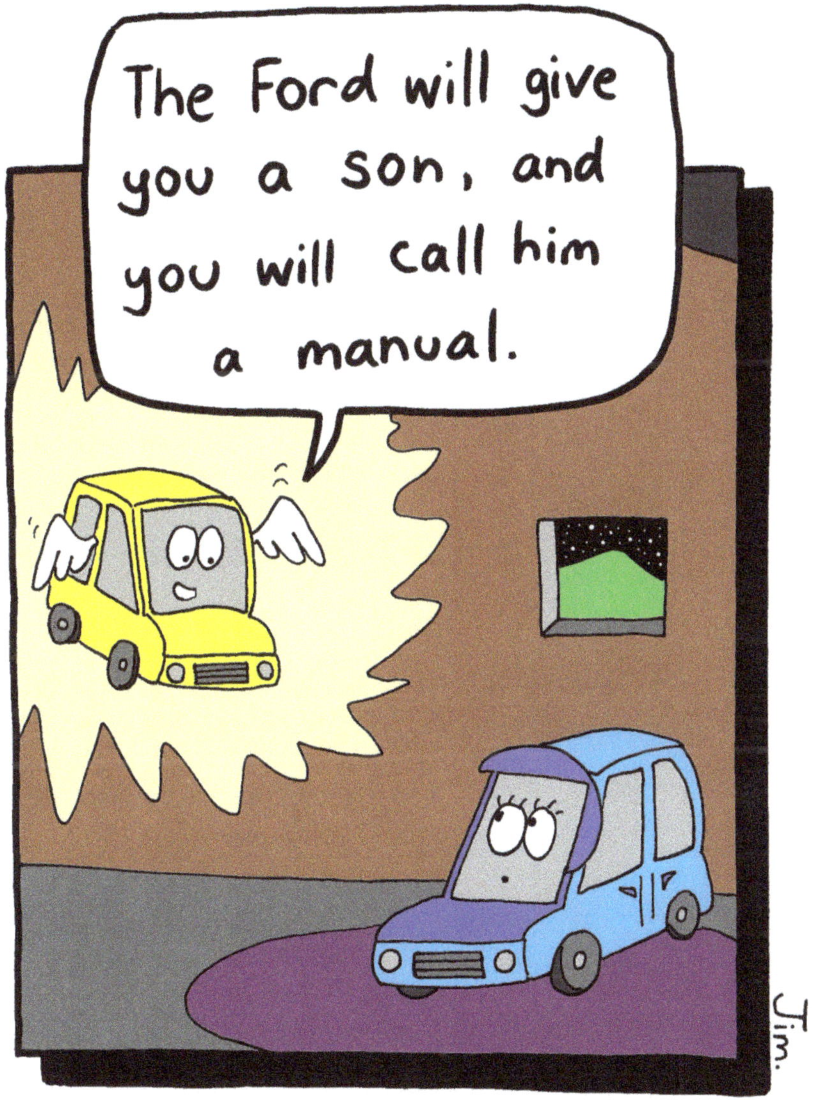
The Ford will give you a son, and you will call him a manual.
Jim.

Merry Car-istmas!

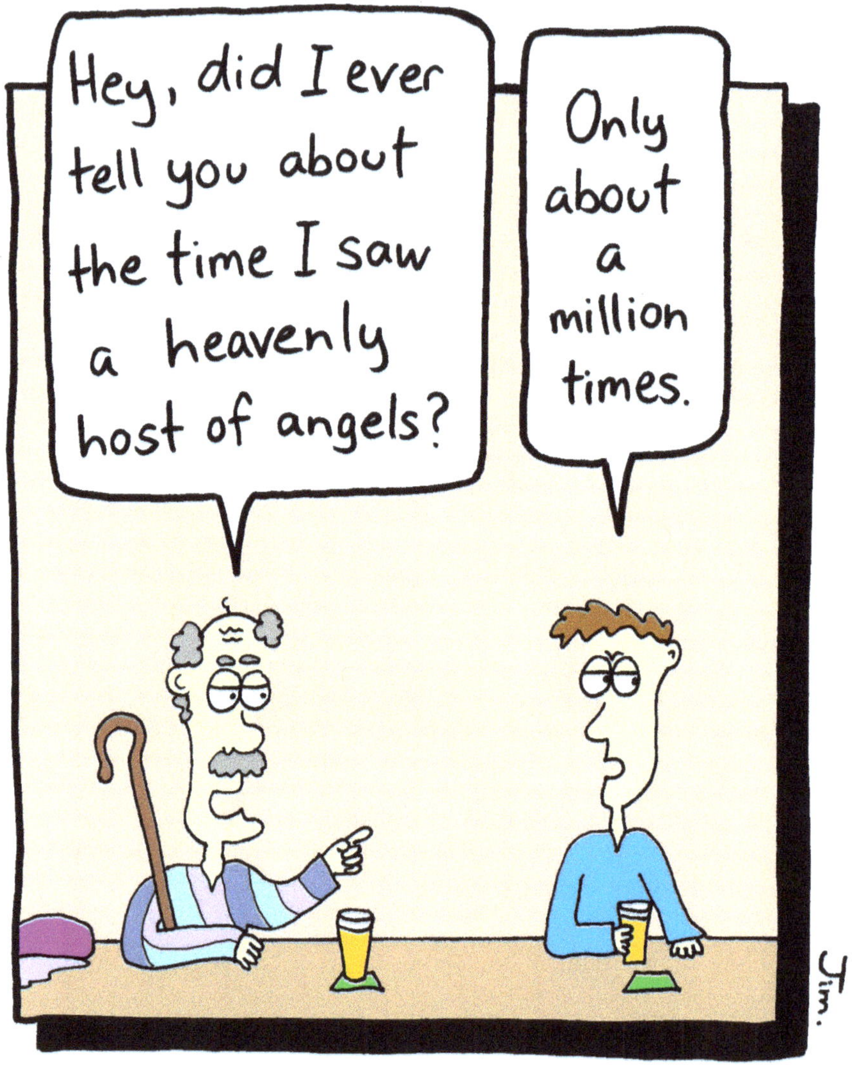
Hey, did I ever tell you about the time I saw a heavenly a host of angels?
Only about a million times.
Jim.

People weren't always amazed to hear what the shepherds said to them.

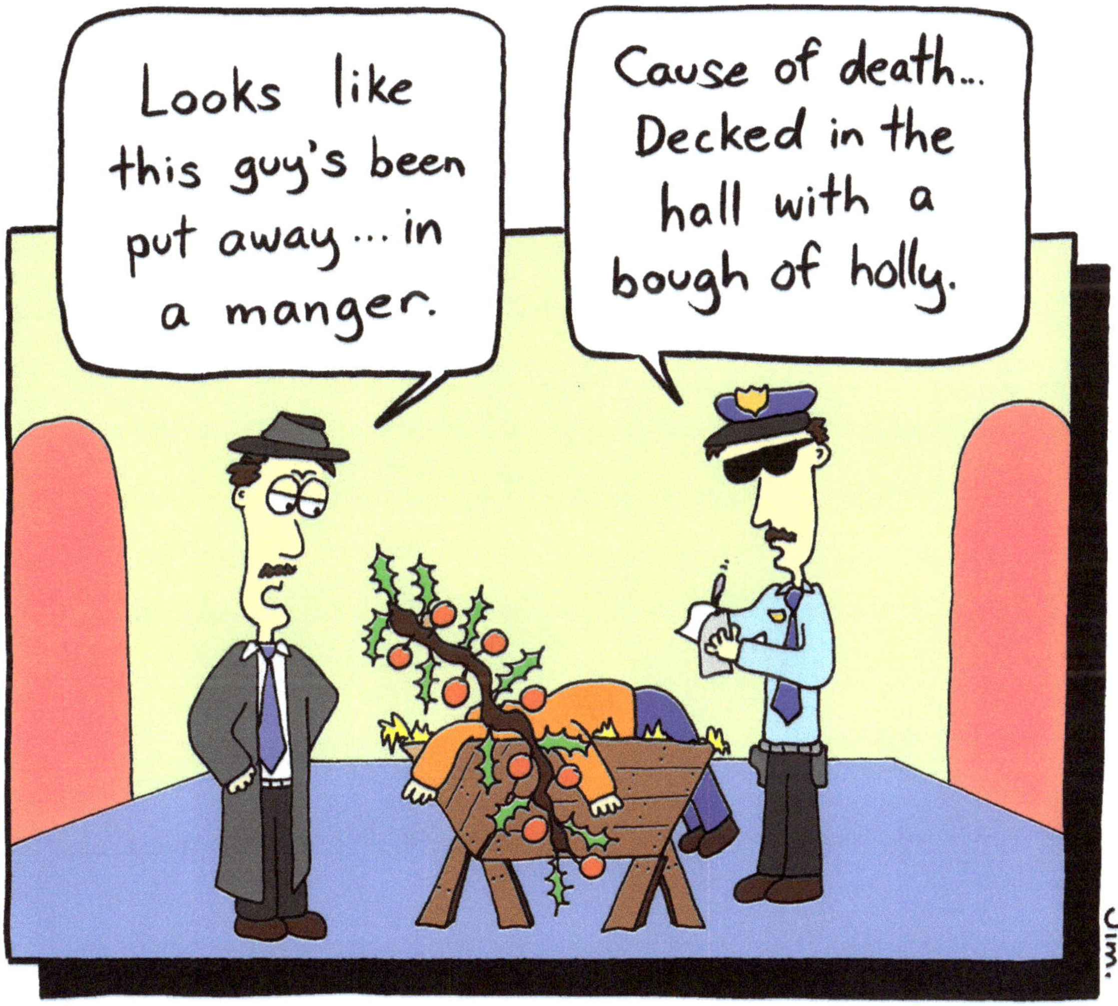
Looks like this guy's been put away... in a manger.
Cause of death... Decked in the hall with a bough of holly.
Jim.

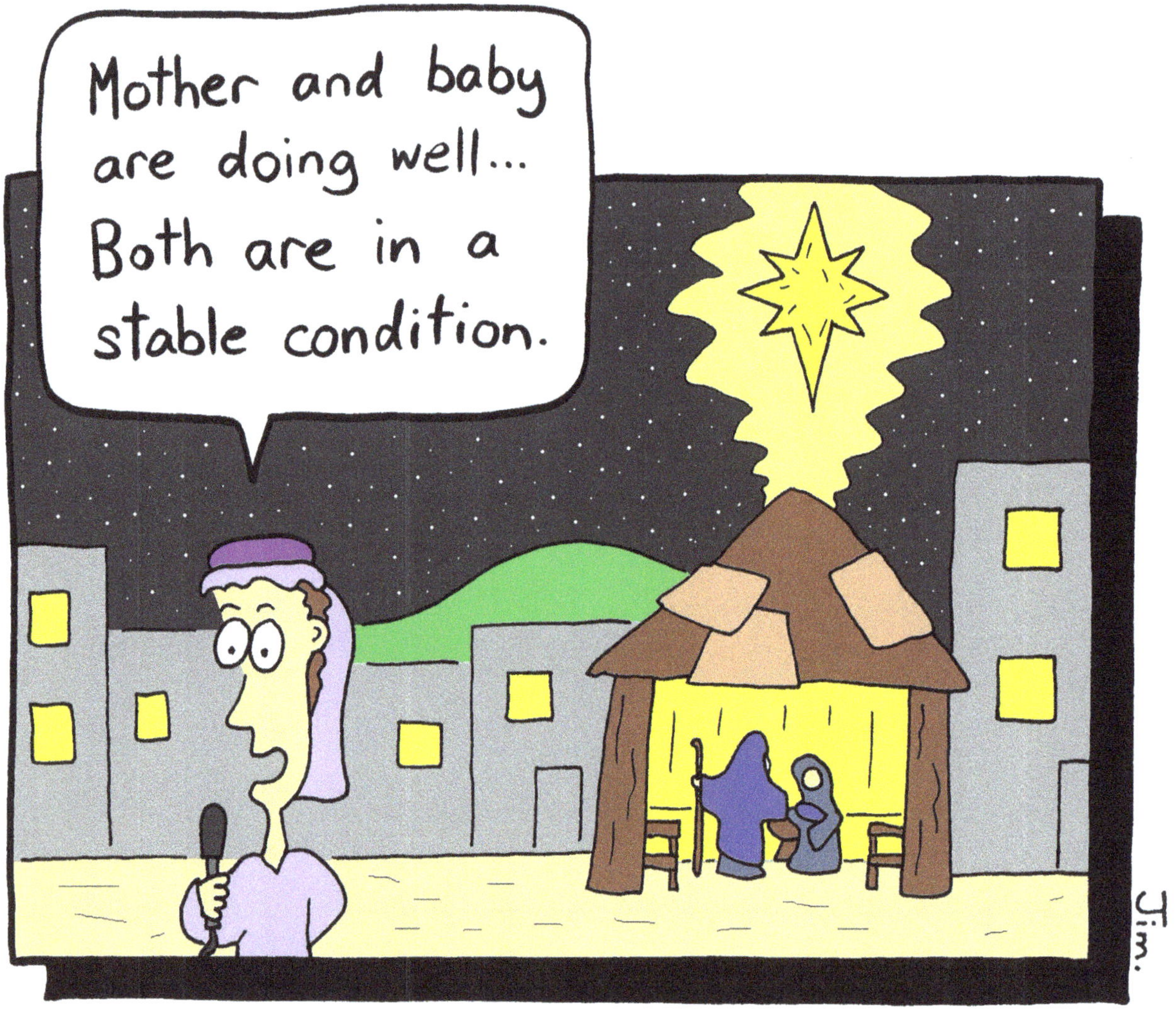
Mother and baby are doing well... Both are in a stable condition.
Jim.

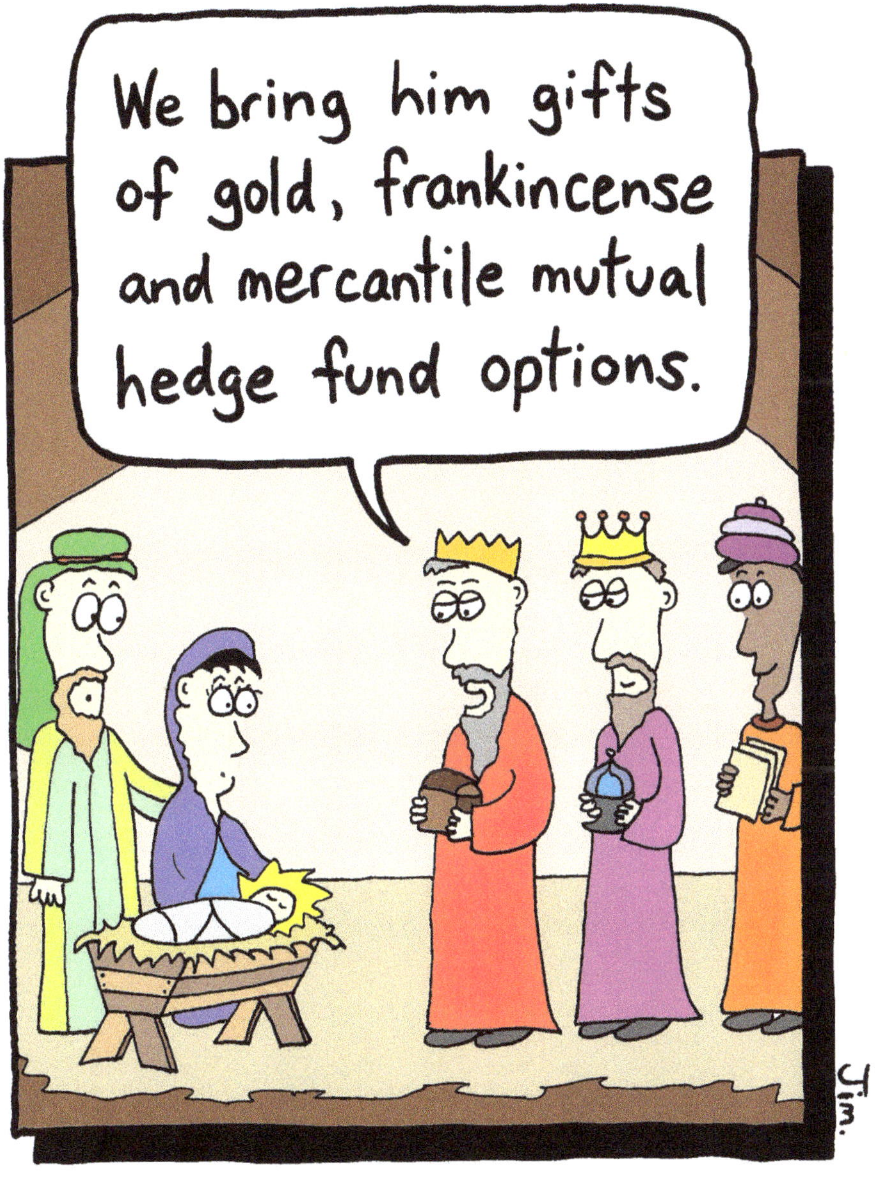
We bring him gifts of gold, frankincense and mercantile mutual hedge fund options.
Jim.

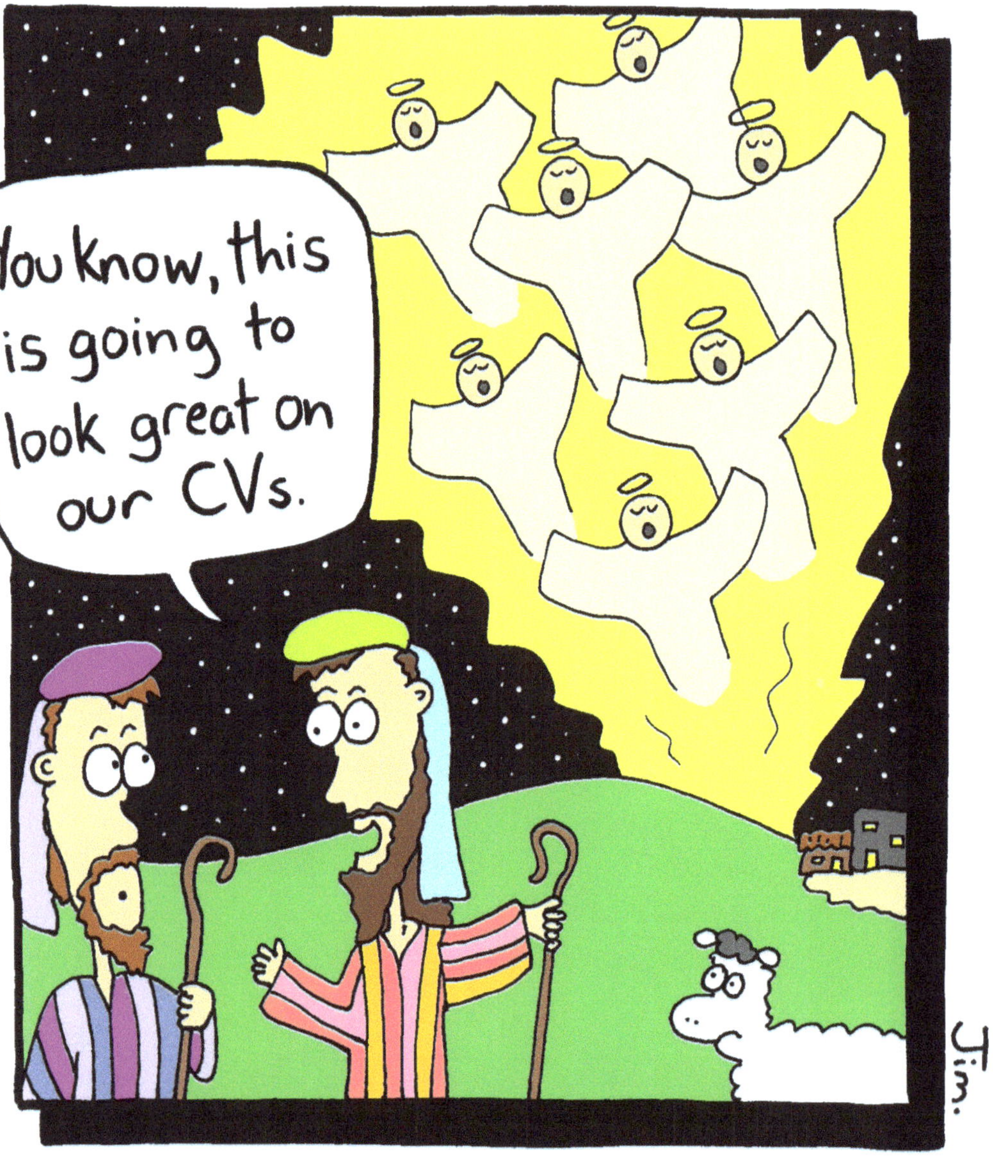
You know, this is going to look great on our CVs.
Jim.

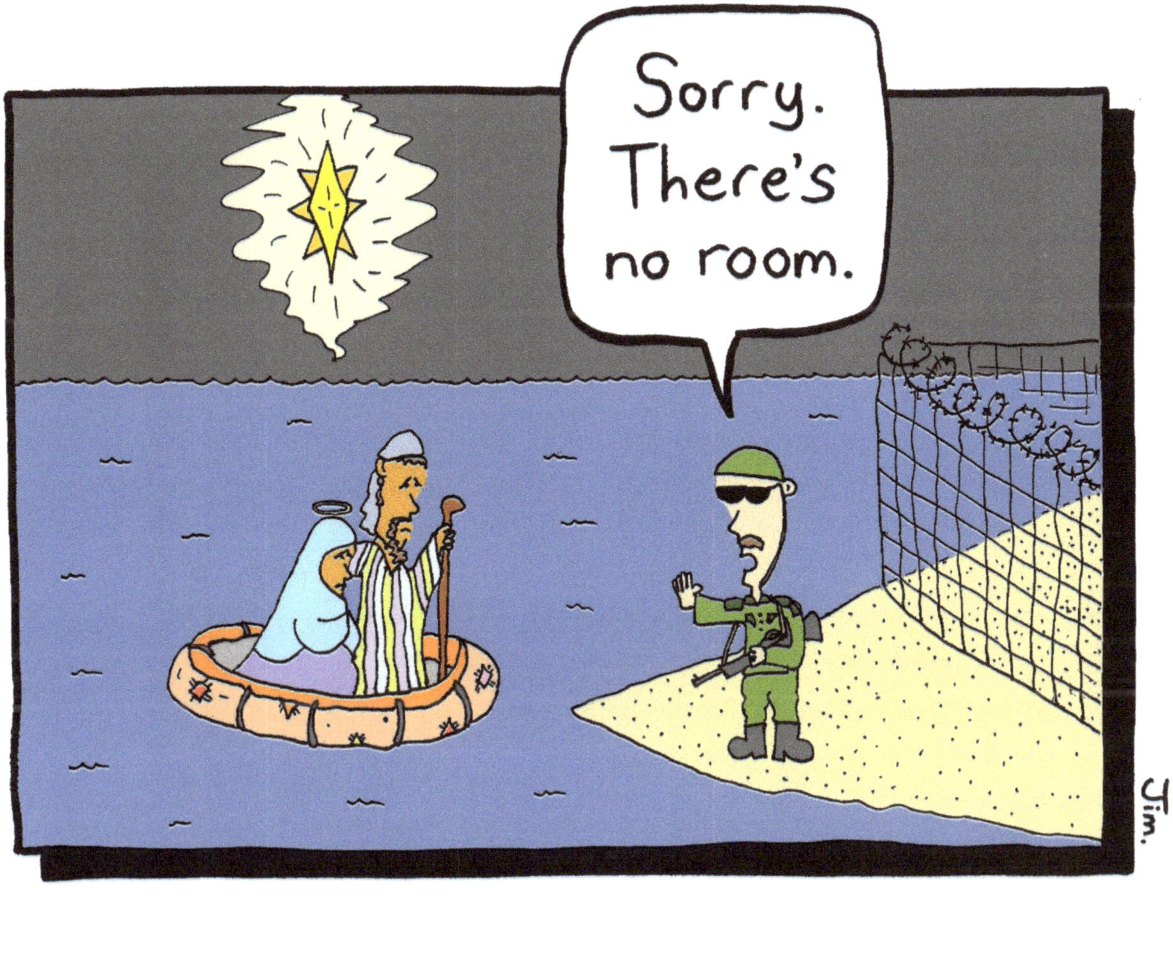
Sorry. There's no room.
Jim.

2016: The year the world stopped caring about refugees – 30 December 2016.
https://www.aljazeera.com/indepth/features/2016/12/2016-year-world-stopped-caring-refugees-161227090243522.html

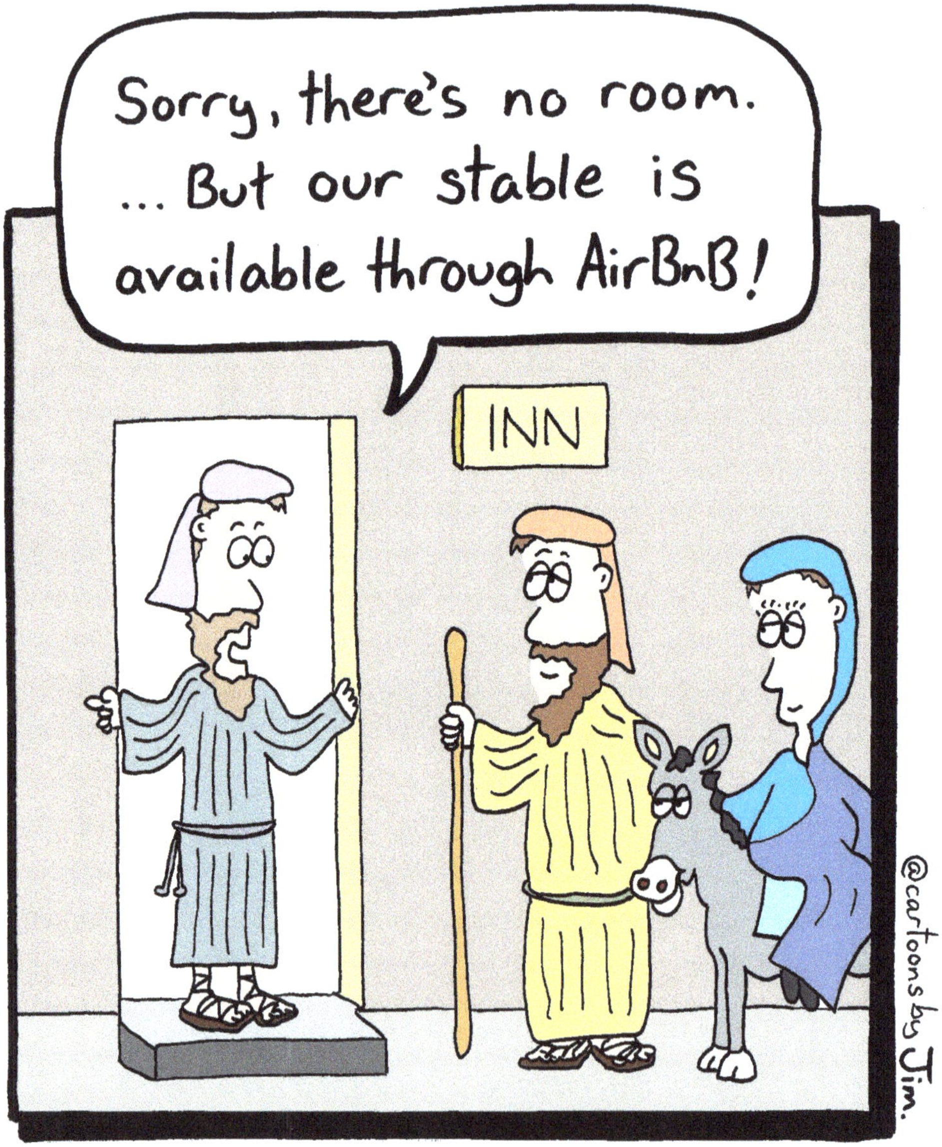
Sorry, there's no room. ... But our stable is available through AirBnB!
INN
@cartoonsbyJim.

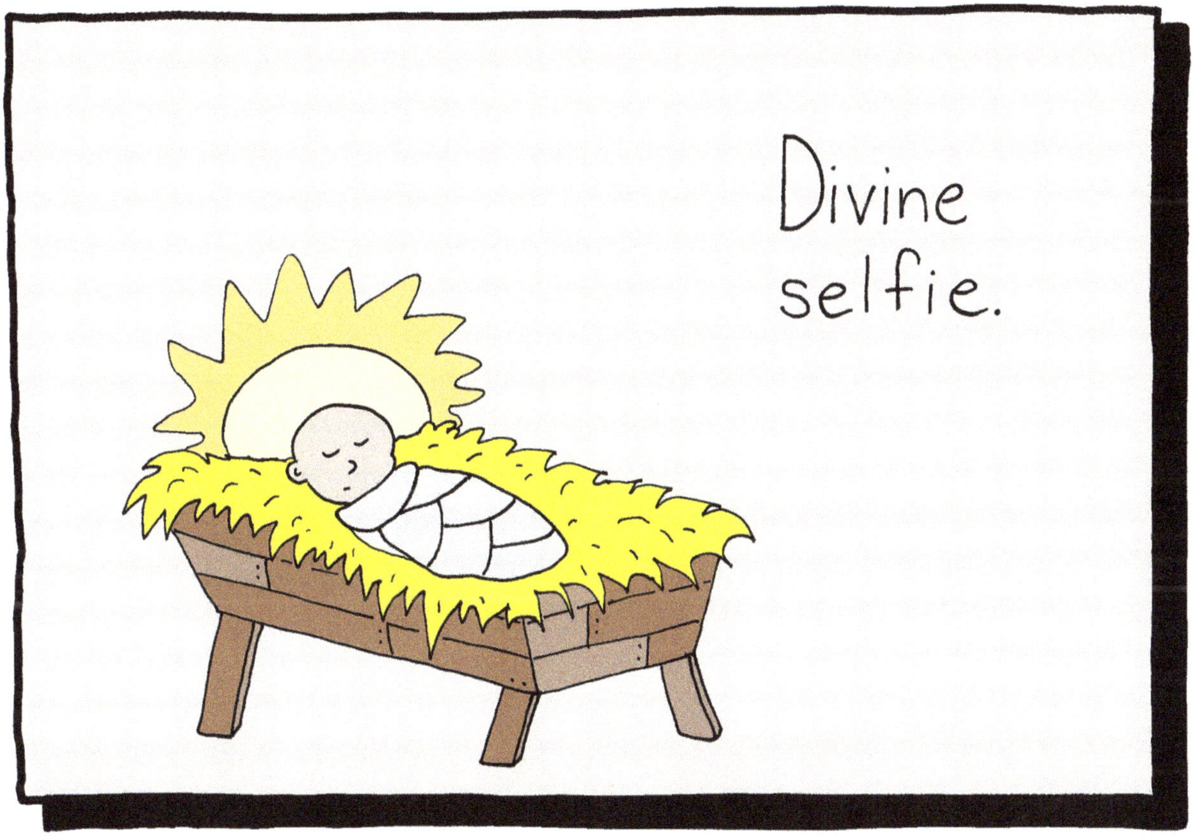
Divine
selfie.

Acknowledgements

- As always, first thanks must go to my wife and son – Kiersten and Ari. You keep me grounded in what's most important in life, and the laughter and good times we share every day are the fertile soil in which these cartoon ideas grow. I love you both so very much.

- To my dad and mum, Lloyd and Alison Boughen, and my sisters Elena and Krysta – you were there at the very beginnings of both my spiritual and cartoon life journeys and would understand better than most how and why the two have intertwined. Thanks for being the test subjects for so many of my early cartooning explorations, and still being fans all these years later!

- Paul Titus – editor of the New Zealand Methodist *Touchstone* magazine from 2003 to 2018 – for offering me the job of editorial cartoonist for the magazine in 2007 and being the wise and patient overseer of most of the cartoons in this book. For over a decade, your encouragement to not shy away from tough topics that got readers thinking helped my cartooning immensely. Thank you also to Ady Shannon, the new editor of Touchstone, who has continued to be an excellent guide for Jim's churchy cartoons over the last year.

- Rev David Bush and the Methodist Church of New Zealand Publishing Board for supporting the publication of this book through a generous grant, and tolerating a few controversies brought on by Jim's ink in *Touchstone* over the years!

- The roots of this book go back more than 25 years to when I was first asked to draw cartoons for various Lutheran Church of Australia publications and resources by those who knew my very early work. So, for the encouragement and opportunities to cartoon in a religious context, my deep thanks go to Paul Smith, Grace Bock, Helen Lockwood, and the late John Pfitzner, senior editor at Openbook Publishers when I worked there from 1994 to 1998.

- Ian Lawton, Glynn Cardy and Clay Nelson – vicars and colleagues at St Matthew-in-the-City and beyond – for your enthusiasm in using humour to push the boundaries of what a church is prepared to be and never being afraid to speak to the truth it reveals.

- Friends and colleagues, old and new, who have supported, encouraged, commissioned or promoted Jim's cartooning journey over three decades – Claire Smith, Bill Robbins, Julian Waters, Adrian Lennard, Cynthia & Eric Spurr, Greg Ward, Liz Walker, Louis Van Wyk, Vera Alves, Daan Ellfers, Steve & Val Hayes, Ken Grace, Derek Ward, Verdayne Nunis, Andy Pickup, Michelle Dickinson, Philip Bexley, Tegan Mills, Paul Brislen, Paul Matthews, Catriona Stewart, Bridget Lem, Maggie Eyre, Kim Mundell, Cameron Craig, Tina Shakour, Kerene Strochnetter and Mandy Henk ... Thanks for believing in Jim!

- The many cartoonists with whom I've crossed paths in New Zealand and around the world who are always encouraging and keen to chat about cartooning – Guy Body, Chris Slane, Phil Parker, Rod Emmerson, Stephan Pastis, Toby Morris, Eddie Monotone, Christian Henry and Mark Stokes ... just to name a few. You're a fine and friendly bunch!

- The writers, theologians, comedians and cartoonists who have informed my spiritual life and humour over many years – Jack Spong, M Scott Peck, Walter Bruggemann, Richard Rohr, Richard Dawkins, Adrian Plass, John Clarke, Robin Mann, Tim Minchin, Berkeley Breathed, Bill Watterson, Gary Larson, Garrison Keillor, Bill Hicks, Eddie Izzard, Patton Oswalt, Gary Gulman, John Mulaney and Pete Holmes. The journey to funny never ends! Thanks for ongoing inspiration!

- Finally, to Maria Chapman from MC2 for brokering the printing and Philip Garside from PGP Ltd. for handling distribution. Thanks for your interest in 'Touching a Nerve' and helping take Jim's cartoons to a new level!

HUGE THANKS TO THE KICKSTARTER CAMPAIGN SUPPORTERS WHO HELPED FUND THIS BOOK!

Jemma Allen	Anette Hallstrøm	Troy Rawhiti-Connell
Duncan Barr	Steve Hayes	Sue Robinson
Aaron Paul Bennett	Mandy Henk	Karen Rodriguez
Warren Bexley	Paul Hewlett	Paul Spain
Bruce H. Bolinger	Sandy Horton	Mark Stokes
Rochelle Bradbury	Krysta Kors	Kerene Strochnetter
Jason Buckland	Kathryn Michie	Steve Taylor
Rebecca Caroe	Tegan Mills	Marinka Teague
Jenny Carryer	Wayne Muller	Robert Testen
Susana Carryer	Kim Mundell	Amar Trivedi
Tiina Carryer	Clay Nelson	Andrew Voigt
Tim Castle-Schmidt	Chris & Cam Opie	Robyn Walshe
Hamish Coleman-Ross	Alina Pavlova	Hilary Whittle
Jon Donald	Cowan & Natasha Pettigrew	Matthew Wilksch
David Farrier	Barry Poole	Kylie Williams
Steve Gollasch	Paul Ramsay	Kym Zeppel

More Cartoon Books By Jim!

GONE ASTRAY:
A Collection Of (Sac)Religious Cartoons by Jim

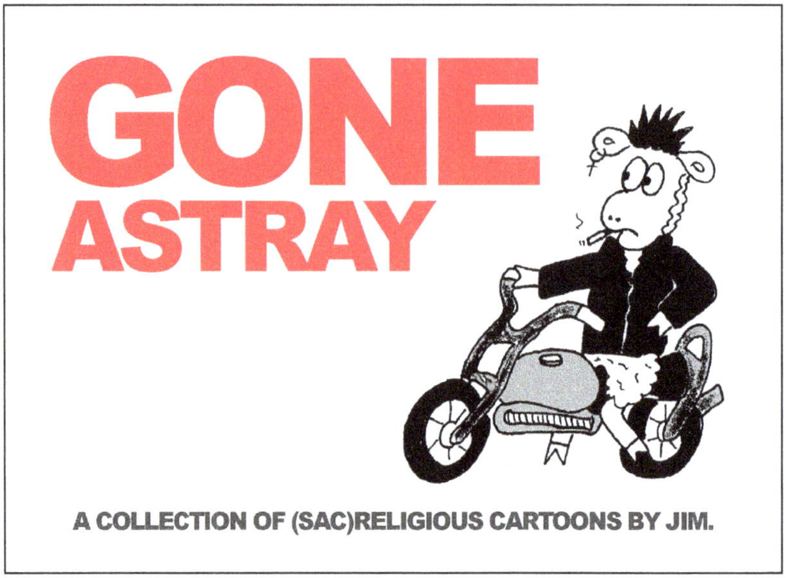
GONE
ASTRAY
A COLLECTION OF (SAC)RELIGIOUS CARTOONS BY JIM.

Crazy Christians ... fuming fundamentalists ... loopy liberals ... batty believers ... oddball organists ... vivacious vicars ... peckish preachers ... antsy angels ... Elvis, Jesus and the occasional sheep.

This book proves why religion and cartoons are a dangerous mix. You might just die laughing.

'Jim' has been drawing (sac)religious cartoons for more than 10 years. This is his first collection.

"Jim's characteristic style and insightful take on all things church and religious holds no punches. It will make you laugh, it will make you cry, and sometimes it may even make you scratch your head. Recommended pew-side reading for all."
Anthony Dancer (The Social Justice Commission of the Anglican Church in Aotearoa, New Zealand and Polynesia)
http://justice.anglican.org.nz/reviews/gone-astray

Available in print and e-book editions through www.pgpl.co.nz

SOUNDS LIKE A GAME CHANGER:
A Soon-to-be Obsolete Collection of Technology Cartoons by Jim

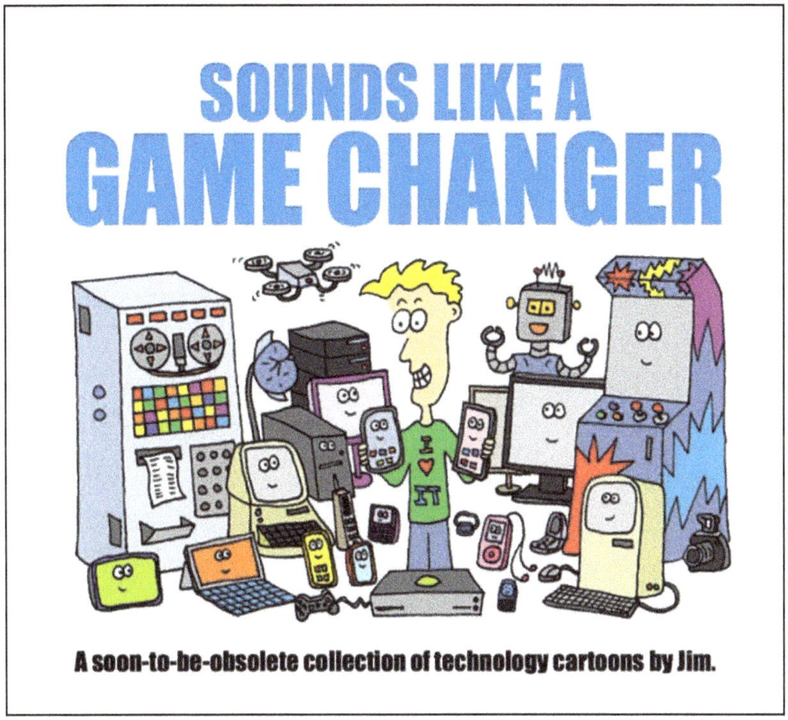
SOUNDS LIKE A
GAME CHANGER
A soon-to-be-obsolete collection of technology cartoons by Jim.

Computers, software, hardware, tablets, phablets, smartphones,game consoles, websites, social media, the Internet, fibrenetworks,robotics, big data, servers, 3D printing, the cloud,'green' tech, apps, memes, BYOD, data security, space travel, time-travel, innovation, collaboration ... If it's anything to do with technology, Jim has probably cartooned about it.

This collection gathers more than a hundred of Jim's best tech cartoons alongside his written thoughts on his experiences communicating about technology as it's evolved over the last crazy, game-changing decade.

Get it before it's all obsolete!

"Technology has changed our lives. Permanently. As Jim holds your hand in his inky one and takes you for a walk down memory lane through this collection of insightful sketches about life with technology, you'll laugh out loud, ponder deeply and maybe even shed a tear at its reminders of the familiar technology that has touched your life as it wanders amidst the magical gadgets, pop culture moments and viral trends in our world's recent history."

From the foreword by Dr Michelle Dickinson (Nanogirl)

Available in print and e-book editions through www.pgpl.co.nz

For more cartoons by Jim, visit:

cartoonsbyjim.com

Follow Jim!

Twitter.com/cartoonsbyjim

Facebook.com/cartoonsbyjim

Instagram.com/cartoonsbyjim

Cartoons in this book are available to license for use in presentations, blogs, publications, etc.

For more information visit: cartoonsbyjim.com/licensing

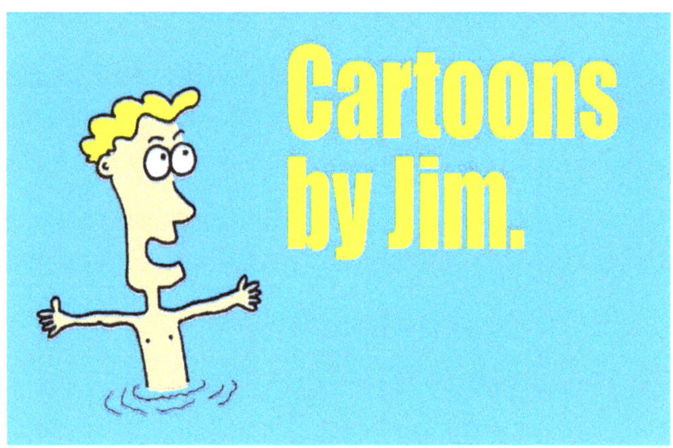
Cartoons
by Jim.

www.ingramcontent.com/pod-product-compliance
Lightning Source LLC
Chambersburg PA
CBHW061112070526
44583CB00027B/3266